GAUNTLET Exploring The Limits Of Free Expression

Published by *Gauntlet*, Inc.
Barry Hoffman, President

Founder/Editor-in-Chief
Barry Hoffman

Assistant to the Editor
David Reed

Circulation Manager
Cheryl Meyer

Research Assistants
Dara Lise, D. Kingsley Hahn,
Barbara McDonald

Columnists
Richard G. Carter, Richard R.
Becker

Investigative Reporters
Richard Cusick

Layout and Design
Kara Tipton

Cover Illustration
Mark Bode

Front Cover Layout
Mark Michaelson

Editorial Cartoons
Andy Wahl, George Gehlert,
John Bergstrom, Paul Wardle,
Joe Lee

Address all letters/queries/orders
to: *Gauntlet*, Dept. B94, 309 Powell
Rd., Springfield, Pa. 19064

Advertising Rates: Full page — $400;
Half Page — $250; Quarter Page —
$175; Inside Covers — $500

Subscriptions: *Gauntlet* is published
twice a year in November and May.
One year (2 issues) subscription is
$20 plus $2 p&h. Canadian Orders
add $4 postage per issue; Foreign
Orders add $7 postage per issue.
Checks made payable to *Gauntlet*,
Inc. sent to the above address. **U.S.
Funds Only**.

Back Issues: Issues #2-7 are available
in limited quantities. Send $14.95 for
issue #2, $12.95 for issue #3, and
$9.95 for issues #4, #5 & 6, and #&
plus $2 p&h for **each** issue, payable
to *Gauntlet*, Inc. to the above address.
A limited quantity of the hardcover

GAUNTLET CORRESPONDENTS:
Gauntlet seeks journalists/investiga-
tive reporters from around the country willing to track down and
investigate stories dealing with censorship and free expression issues.
Query with SASE.

ARTISTS/CARTOONISTS: *Gauntlet* seeks artists and cartoonists. Send
samples of your work to be kept on
file to Cheryl Meyer, at the above
address. Enclose SASE for response.

ADVERTISING EXECUTIVE:
Gauntlet seeks an advertising executive, to be paid with a generous commission. Work from your home.
Query with resume and SASE.

EDITORIAL MEANDERINGS

In the wake of Waco, an issue on cults seemed natural. David Koresh and the Branch Davidians captured the attention of the country, much the same way the saga of O.J. Simpson has during this summer. (Okay, *nothing* — for some perverse reason — has captured people's attention like O.J., but Waco *did* galvanize the media.) With the passage of time, however, I wondered just how fresh such a topic would be. Were the Davidians an isolated group or were so-called cults widespread? I began my search, naturally enough, by contacting anti-cult groups (one *Gauntlet* journalist calls them "anti-cult cultists" — and for good reason; many are former-cult members and currently make a good living off of cult activity) and entered a world of paranoia that all but engulfed me.

Cults were more pervasive than I had thought — that is a fact. But, I found that while these anti-cultists were more than willing to bend my ear over the phone, they "didn't have the time" to commit themselves to paper. Then came a phone call from an expert I'd queried. "You don't really want to get deeply into this," was her message. What I could expect, if I followed through with an issue on cults, she said, was harassment and lawsuits which could drive *Gauntlet* out of business. *That* was why she and so many of her colleagues were reluctant to write about

cult activity. Lawsuits had become a way of life, and was draining the resources of groups and individuals who were trying to combat these organizations.

I had no desire to see *Gauntlet* derailed by lawsuits, but by the same token, if I didn't print anything libelous, I didn't feel the publication had anything to worry about. "It doesn't matter," she said. "You'll be hit with nuisance suits, with the sole purpose to incur legal expenses." Even if not successful these would tie me up in court and deplete our meager financial resources. A scary thought. Groups with unlimited financial resources siccing their lawyers on you solely to intimidate.

It just so happened at this time that I met Richard Cusick, who was intrigued by the concept of litigation to keep the public from being informed. With Richard's dogged determination, new light was shed on how the media, in many cases, has caved in to alternative religions, that were often mislabeled as cults. I liken it to the aura that surrounds Disney. It is *known* — though not necessarily true — that to parody Disney means to incur a lawsuit . . . and possible ruin. This, even though, Disney had made *threats* (cease-and-desist letters from their legal staff), but had not been particularly litigious. The same is the case with alternative religions that have been labeled cults. Few lawsuits against the media have been filed, but there was *one* huge, well-publicized suit that seems to have just about everyone in the media running scared.

This, then, became the focus of our look at cults. Has the media been intimidated by alternative religious groups the same way many artists *feel* intimidated by Disney? And, to a certain extent, do these groups have a point. Has the media unfairly labeled religious groups, who operate outside the mainstream, cults when in fact they are not?

Our lead story answers many of these questions. As for the rest of our section on cults — and yes, *cults* do exist — we try to define what a cult is, look at various cults in our midst, as well as groups that are as armed-to-the-teeth as the Branch Davidians which the government has left alone. We have journalistic accounts (for, in the end, they provide the most balanced view), as well as personal accounts by some who have been most affected by cult activity. We've even given some room to "professional" anti-cult groups and individuals when they help clarify or define the debate.

As always, the final judgment is yours. What constitutes a cult? Just when, if ever, should the government step in to curb alleged abuses? And are some alternative religions getting a bad rap because they operate outside the mainstream of what *we* consider normal?

Finally, we are actively seeking material for our next issue dealing with *"Myths of Sexual Harassment."* Have government laws, political correctness on college campuses, and corporate regulations gone too far to protect women to the point where an innocent remark or *look* is grounds for dismissal or a lawsuit? Are some women using sexual harassment for their own personal agenda? And are these recent laws and regulations actually anti-feminist in nature? — telling women they don't have the power (under existing laws) to fight for themselves so big-brother will protect them. We are interested in personal accounts of sexual harassment gone awry. Query us. We *will* get back to you. A number of our readers have provided material for this issue. We're not necessarily going after "big names" to write small articles. As you'll see from this issue, some of the most poignant stories are those from people who have dealt with cults, are regular *Gauntlet* subscribers and asked for a forum to speak their mind. Our deadline for our next issue is December 15, so let's hear from you if you have something to say.

Enough already. This issue is jam-packed, so read.

— *Barry Hoffman*
August 1994

Dictionary of Cautionary Words and Phrases

Project: As in public housing project, has come to denote race. Use public housing development or subsidized housing.

OPENERS

In *Gauntlet #7*, we told you the story about A Little Off the Top, a hair salon in Las Vegas that features girls who cut hair in lingerie. We also told you how fifty residents and the Clark County Commission's Sex and Tease Task Force tried to shut them down. Ultimately, they did have to move their location as co-owner Davy-O Thompson promised the commissioners.

Still, things have taken a turn for the better. *The Las Vegas Review-Journal*, Southern Nevada's largest paper, voted A Little Off the Top the #1 hair cut in Las Vegas during their annual reader's poll — when readers and journalists state their favorites. Meanwhile, Davy-O Thompson may be able to prevent further First Amendment abuses on his establishment in a new way. He's running for a seat on the Clark County Commission. As the old saying goes: Only in Las Vegas.

CONS

This Fall the Judiciary Committee of the Pennsylvania General Assembly will debate H.B. 2982, which if passed could have far-ranging implica-

tions well beyond the state of Pennsylvania. Representative T.J. Rooney's bill would make *all* recordings bearing the "Parental Advisory" sticker illegal to anyone under 18. Fines to stores found in violation range from $25 per album for a first offense to $100 per album for subsequent violations. Anyone under 18 caught attempting to buy a "stickered" album would be required to perform between 25 and 100 hours of community service at a domestic violence or rape crisis center.

Actual rapists get off easier (see

story below). Aside from other states following Pennsylvania's lead if the bill is passed and found Constitutional, there is concern how record stores will respond. It is feared many outlets will decide not to stock "stickered" material to escape harassment and persecution. [courtesy of Rock Out Censorship (R.O.C.), P.O. Box 147, Jewett, OH 43986. Phone: 814-946-6535.

CONS

The old expression, "It's not over until the fat lady sings," took on a new sinister meaning recently at a San Diego art gallery. In March, the Rita Dean Gallery was visited by vice squad police and told to remove or cover a photographic silkscreen by artist Charles Gatewood (see photo). Gallery owner, J.D. Healy was told to "cover the nipples, remove the artwork or you will be arrested." His response — the altered photo. In this case, to avert arrest the fat lady sang.

CONS

Talk about punishment fitting the crime: The USA Today ran two blurbs the same day dealing with the

sentencing of nefarious criminals. Earl Grant of Philadelphia was given three months federal *probation* for his part in a plot by Islamic fundamentalists to bomb New York landmarks. He had transported gunpowder across state lines.

Jeremiah Johnson did not get off so easily in Lakeland, Florida. He was sentenced to the maximum 179 days in jail for the way he appeared in court on a charge of driving without a license. Seems when told he couldn't appear in shorts, Johnson "made a statement" by returning to the courtroom naked.

The message is clear: taking part in a plot that could have caused wanton death and destruction warrants a slap on the wrist (actually less), but piss off a judge and you get the book thrown at you.

Justice, American style . . . *NOT*.

PROS

We applaud Disney's reaction to those who label megahit *The Lion King* sexist, racist and homophobic. After seeing psychologists and critics dissect the film with its subliminal messages that will forever scar the millions of youngsters flocking to the flick, Disney spokeswoman Terry Press suggested critics "Get a life. It's a story. It's fiction."

PROS

To Regina Elizabeth Guy for taking a stand against political correctness. Guy appeared at a hearing held so she could explain why her license shouldn't be revoked because she was a bit, uh, . . . portly. After demonstrating her weight (a svelte 336 pounds) did not hinder her ability to drive, Guy launched an attack at those sensitive souls who referred to her as weight-challenged or overweight. "Fat! The word is fat. Not overweight. Over whose weight? Over what weight? Being called overweight is not acceptable and 'fat' is not a four letter word!"

PROS

If it weren't our money paying for it, we could fully appreciate the Drug Enforcement Administration's embarrassment when charges were dropped against two drug suspects, and they received $190,000 because translators made mistakes transcribing wiretaps. According to the *New York Post*, the DEA had targeted a narcotics ring operating out of an auto repair center the two men worked. On one occasion the wife of one of the men asked him to bring home "tuna." The transcripts refer to "tuna" as a code word for drugs.

The other man received a call from a man saying he would "bring the papers" to him; "papers" translated as "money for drugs." The papers turned out to be Bibles the man's minister was going to bring him to distribute in the community.

The problem is not that Big Brother is listening (bad enough), but they don't understand what we're saying.

CONS

Another wacky sentence: In a plea bargaining arrangement in Houston a man pleading no contest to molesting two girls — ages nine and ten — escaped a prison sentence by agreeing to stay away from his piano for 20-years. According to the AP, the judge wanted to punish the piano teacher for molesting the children in a way that affected him most; hence the *harsh* punishment. They don't call them judges in Texas hanging judges for nothing, now do they?

PROS

Cudos to *New York Daily News* critic Eric Mink for taking "self-styled media and morality monitors" to task for objections to a segment of *seaQuest DSV*. Drawing complaints was an episode that revealed aliens (no, *not* illegal immigrants — ET-phone-home-kind-of-guys) naked bodies — front and rear, though not recognizable as male or female. Mink used the following analogy to show the absurdity of the protestors: "Jam a couple of sticks close together into a potato, and you have a crotch. Does that make Mr. Potato Head pornographic? HE'S A POTATO, for crying out loud."

PROS

A Grand Haven, MI video store owner cleared of obscenity charges is billing police about $8000 in late fees, the *USA Today* reports, for two X-rated videos they used as evidence against him. "Business is business," he says of the $2 per-day late charge on tapes rented by undercover police in 1991. Officials say they'll return the tapes, but call the bill "totally ridiculous." We say the owner should call the police . . . Whoops.

PROS

To Dennis Hopper who refused to back down to criticism of the "scary, sneaker-sniffing" referee he plays on Nike commercials. "I get all these people talking about how I'm making fun of the mentally ill," he said. I think of Jerry Lewis and Red Skelton — they weren't attacked for the characters they played."

PROS

Two thumbs up for Donald Wildmon's decision to spend the AFA's *entire* $3 million media budget to "dissuade" advertisers from buying into ABC's *NYPD Blue* this season, as reported in *Advertising Age*. Why the cudos? From a station in a major market that carries the show, we've learned advertisers were indeed slow buying into the show its first season. However, it received critical acclaim, appeals to key demographics advertisers crave, was a ratings winner and grabbed 28 Emmy nominations. The bottom line is the *bottom line* and that is why advertisers will purchase time on the program regardless of Wildmon's harangues. Meanwhile, he'll have spent his entire media wad and won't have the funds to attack other shows he feels offend our tastes. [D.K.H.]

PROS

To the Supreme Court for affirming Margaret Gilleo's right to display a sign from her window in 1991 calling for "Peace in the Gulf;" her protest against the Persian Gulf War. Her St. Louis suburb had called for her to remove the sign to avoid visual blight and protect real estate values. Judge John Paul Stevens countered: "A special respect for individual liberty in the home has long been part of our culture and our law." [B.M]

CONS

Kinkos refuses to print Andrew Rollers "erotic" 'zine as being offensive. After Rollers complained at the arbitrary censorship, the Kinkos manager responded: "Kinkos does not censor written material and we make no judgment on the merits of any item brought into one of our stores. Kinkos co-workers reserve the right not to handle copy . . . he or she finds personally offensive."

Rollers shot back: "Does this mean a pro-life Kinkos employee may refuse to copy pro-choice literature?"

No response from Kinkos. [B.M.]

PARTING SHOT

An IRS employee (a *Gauntlet* mole), who for obvious reasons wishes to remain anonymous, sent us a Dictionary of Cautionary Words and Phrases that emanated from Cindy W. Patterson of the Equal Employment Office to be used as guidelines in preparing official documents. Out, for instance, is "deaf and dumb," with the explanation, "Deaf people are not dumb. Preferred terms are deaf or hearing impaired or speech impaired." Another gem — forget about using the term "Dutch Treat To share the cost, as in a date. Implies that Dutch people are cheap." Other choice morsels from the dictionary appear in boxes throughout this issues.

*Thanks to D. Kingsley Hahn, Barbara McDonald, our government mole and others who have sent us tidbits for our Openers Section. We wish we could use more; there are so many to choose from. Keep them coming. We **do** read them, and use as many as possible.*

IN THE NAME OF GOD: Part 1

Richard Cusick

Religious Litigation in the Media

"The question is," said Alice, "whether you can make words mean so many different things."
"The question is," said Humpty Dumpty, "who is to be master. That is all."

— *Lewis Carrol*

"Those who can define are the masters."

— *Stokley Carmichael*

"Cult" is a dangerous word. It is imprecise and overused, two qualities which render any word a coinage of no great currency. It is pejorative, a sharp word, given offensively and taken as such. The same word accurately applied to the burning horrors at Waco in the winter of 1992 is used to describe the flaky New Age doctrines of the Maharishi Mahesh Yogi. "Cult" is a provocative word, a sensational word, misused by dubious professionals with vested interests and dutifully reported, without question, by an unmindful media with a penchant for simplification and an aversion to complexity.

Conversely, this loose-fitting language is used as camouflage by a phalanx of hucksters and snowflakes and even by the sincere to conceal excess and deter critical

analysis. They point to the sizzle and claim that this proves that there is no steak, as if the presence of the superficial precludes the presence of the substantial. Not surprisingly, a lot of this stuff winds up in court.

In 1991, when *Time* ran a controversial cover story called "Scientology: The Cult of Greed" The Church of Scientology was quick to demand a retraction and spent an estimated $5.4 million in advertising to discredit the piece. *Time* stuck by its story and its writer Richard Behar, calling the article a "Well-researched piece of journalism." Scientology, in turn, sued *Time* for $412 million one week before the deadline for litigation ran out. Additionally, The Church sued five of Behar's sources and, prior, to those actions, sought injunctions in five separate countries seeking to bar the *Reader's Digest* from reprinting an excerpt of the work.

In 1991 the *Journal of The American Medical Association* (JAMA) ran an article by New Age medical maven Dr. Depak Chopra and two others supposedly on the benefits of an ancient Indian folk medicine called Ayru-Veda. In the past decade the practice of Ayru-Veda has been very successfully marketed in the west as Maharishi Ayru-Veda by the Maharishi Mahesh Yogi along with his trademark, Transcendental Meditation. Upon learning that the authors had undisclosed interests in the marketing scheme, JAMA ran the longest disclosure correction in its 111 year history. Five months later JAMA published a long and scathing article by Associate Editor Andrew Skolnick detailing a bevy of excessive claims by Chopra, the Maharishi and the TM movement. Chopra and the American Association of Ayru-Vedic Medicine, in their turn, sued JAMA and Skolnick for $194.4 million.

In its January, 1994 issue, *Wired* magazine, a journal of computer culture, ran a expose on the teaching of Rama, a supposedly 1000 year old enlightened being currently incarnate as Frederick K. Lenz of La Jolla, California. *Wired* said that Rama encouraged his followers to misrepresent themselves in the computer industry in an attempt to tap into the big bucks available on-line. The Wired article detailed not only professional excess but also sexual abuse and other impropriety. A Chicago computer consultant named in the article, Christine Comoford, filed a $30 million lawsuit, claiming that Lenz was a consultant in her firm.

No doubt about it there is something in the air which is being translated in the courts. As interesting as all of this is, just as intriguing is the reaction of the media to all the threats and litigation. An action doesn't have to have substance in order to be extremely costly to defend and any prudent editor or writer would be less than human not to wonder if it is worth it. The result is a de facto suppression of the press and some of the most important stories are not reported because the threat of litigation insures a very real intimidation.

In a world filled with vague acronyms and stretched combinations, S.L.A.P.P. suit stands particularly clear and trenchant. S.L.A.P.P. stands for Strategic Lawsuit Against Public Participation and it has it's pedigree in the U.S. labor movement. Any such noble connections have long ago given way to a gambol of frivolous court actions and nuisance suits that are designed not to win but to intimidate. Often without merit these actions take years to resolve, make lawyers rich and publishers miserable. There is no limit to the number of times a slapp-happy litigant can sue and the financial burden is on the defendant. Marsha Rudin of the American Family Foundation (AFF) is surprisingly charitable in her assessment of the motivations of these litigants. "These are not frivolous lawsuits," she told *Gauntlet*, "These people are suing for what they feel are valid reasons." But Herb Rosedale, president of the AFF is less sympathetic. "It doesn't matter if the suit is successful or not. It leaves a journalist with the choice of eviscerating a story or deciding not to publish. And sometimes" he said portentously, "they don't want to eviscerate the story."

Gauntlet spent ten weeks and interviewed over fifty people in preparation of this article. What follows is overview of the litigations certainly but, more significantly, it is also a documentation of the threats and intimidations that are more prevalent. It will be the purview of this article to discuss not the religions in question but the journalists who are asking the questions and providing the answers. Some overview of their subject matter is unavoidable but mostly it is the story of the media with a few real heros and too many cowards.

"One man's inconsequential story is another man's important story."

— Don Hewitt
replying to criticism of 60 Minutes
from Walter Cronkite, circa 1983

In 1983 the National Council of Churches (NCC) was the target of an investigative story produced by the top-rated CBS broadcast news magazine, *60 Minutes*. It was the first story produced by Marti Galovic, a former assistant to Morley Safer. At that time, the assistant general secretary for information at the NCC was a gentleman named Warren Day, and he told *Gauntlet* a story that would be a nightmare for any public relations man: "We were in Nashville for a meeting and I was called out of the meeting and Marti Galovic was on the phone and she said 'We have been criticized so much by the right wing religious groups we feel we must do a really critical piece on the left wing so we'd like to do a piece on you'. That was the opening sentence." Mr. Day recalled, "It never got better than that."

The highly questionable premise of the piece was that collection plate monies were being diverted to left-wing and Marxist programs in Nicaragua. "It was unbelievably stacked" said Mr. Day. "If you look at the opening of it you'll see how unbelievably stacked it is. The images — The image of Karl Marx and the image of us . . . The image of Castro and the image of us. No connection." "The Gospel According To Whom?" gave strong implications but offered little proof. Morley Safer told viewers that church money was supporting a Nicaraguan literacy campaign and that that campaign was rife with revolutionary rhetoric, but Safer failed to mention that the U.S. government was also supporting the program with substantially more money. The NCC was incensed and went on as much an offensive as their relatively lilliputian budget allowed. Mr. Day said, "We had everybody from Coretta Scott King to . . . We had news conferences in five different cities the next day. We had no trouble doing it because people looked at the piece and said, 'My God, this is just god-awful.'" *60 Minutes* received more letters for that segment than for any other story they ever broadcast. Day said, "We also got the Columbia Journalism Review to run a piece criticizing it. We got three or four commentaries written. We could have never gotten that if people didn't look at it and say, 'Hey, this is really hack-journalism.' It was the worst kind of guilt-by-association . . . Before the thing even aired I wrote — and it was sent to them — a letter outlining concerns, a list of things they refused to do, people they (didn't) talk to or a list of issues they refused to look at. The kind of information, the kind of questions they had asked and so forth. They went to their lawyers and said that this letter is, in effect, a notice, you know, that (the NCC) may sue. What we were concerned with at that point was accuracy. I didn't mind them being critical."

You sent a letter and they in turn went to their lawyers because they considered that a prelude to a lawsuit?

"That's what I was told by someone from the inside of *60 Minutes*. One of the on-air people later told me that . . . Seemingly that was taken extremely serious inside.

"What I actually thought also I was doing — This may sound very naive — I actually thought in light of *60 Minutes* record, they would like to know the following . . . When I was working in management in news at ABC I would have loved to have known if a reporter had done the following things and so I sent them the letter to

explain 'I think you would like to know the following things have happened.' Seemingly though, the letter was not received as 'This person is trying to help us to make sure we don't make a big mistake.' Instead it was received as 'Ah-ha! This letter is a warning to us that they are going to sue.'"

The legal option was further considered; the NCC wanted to sue. "We went as far as getting an estimation from our lawyers about what it would take to do this" said Mr. Day.

Was the lawsuit filed?

"No." He said, his voice still tinged with disappointment after eleven years. "It's just that we could not use the money for that purpose."

In fact, the NCC had determined that it would have cost them $2.5 million to sue, an option that was patently out of the question. The decision not to file a lawsuit "was already decided and announced" Day recalled, "and then Don Hewitt called just to confirm." Hewitt was then — and remains now — the Executive Producer of *60 Minutes* and is an Olympian figure in broadcast investigative journalism. "My one and only conversation with him," Day thinks back. "And I picked up the phone and it was Don Hewitt, no secretary or anything — Don Hewitt — and he said 'I understand you're not going to do a lawsuit.' And I said, 'No, we cannot afford to do one.' (He said) 'I just wanted to know' and that was about the whole conversation.

"You know what was scary to me? It was scary to me how scared they were of us . . . I feel very strongly about the First Amendment. I think the First Amendment means that (a news organization) shouldn't be scared of other people threatening lawsuits. I sort of lost respect for them on both sides: I lost respect for how bad the piece was done and then I lost respect because how much we scared them. I mean if the piece was done correctly you ought to stand by it then. My letter obviously scared them very much."

The NCC asked that *60 Minutes* join in an arbitration but the television news magazine refused. Two months later it came out that, despite the fact that Galovic said it was her idea, the story was spoon-fed to *60 Minutes* by an arch-conservative group, the Institute on Religion & Democracy. The FCC demanded that CBS answer complaints about "The Gospel According

SUNUNU: Headed for a Fall?

TIME

SCIENTOLOGY

THE CULT OF GREED

HOW THE GROWING
DIANETICS EMPIRE
SQUEEZES MILLIONS FROM
BELIEVERS WORLDWIDE

To Whom?" but then the FCC mitigated those complaints when they decided that the NCC could not invoke the personal attack rule because the story did not address a "controversial issue of public importance."

"Before this I was a big fan of *60 Minutes*" said Warren Day. "I was really disillusioned after."

60 Minutes is now in its 27th season. At the end of last year it was the number one news magazine on the air and the number two broadcast show in all of prime time television. It has occupied the number one slot four times in its history, and, based on the most recent numbers, reaches thirty million viewers on average.

When *Gauntlet* began its investigation of religious litigation and the media, *60 Minutes* seemed to be an obvious place to start. It had defined the standard of broadcast investigative journalism for a generation and had garnered more than its share of awards and lawsuits.

A data base containing all of the programs that *60 Minutes* has produced kicked out the word 'Scientology' four times. There were two broadcasts in 1980: an original airing and a summer rerun of a story called "Scientology: The Clearwater Conspiracy". Three days before Christmas in 1985 the same producer, Allan Maraynes, aired a segment simply titled "Scientology", and, in 1991, producer Kathy Olian

essayed "Scientology Wants To Ban Prozac". A call to the CBS contracted transcript service revealed that a transcript of the 1991 piece by Kathy Olian was available but that the first two reports were put on a "legal hold" and could not be obtained. The young lady at the transcription service could not elaborate.

Roy Brunett, spokesman for *60 Minutes*, promptly returned our first phone call. While he couldn't explain the legal hold off the top of his head, he did provide the name of the producer of the segments in question. He explained that Allan Maraynes now worked for the competitor, that he was a producer for *20/20* at ABC. Asked if he knew of any litigation surrounding these two shows Brunett said "I think some letters went back and forth."

Allan Maraynes, now the Senior Investigative Producer at *20/20* was polite but also of little help. "This was ten years ago," he pleaded. "I've done hundreds of stories since then." He didn't remember any litigation specifically, and when informed of the legal hold on the broadcasts, Maraynes said thoughtfully, "Hmmm . . . I wonder why?" We sent him a copy of *Gauntlet*.

Another phone call to Burrelle's Transcripts seemed to be in order. Perhaps the legal hold was generated from within the transcript service. But the very same, very pleasant young lady said that only CBS could implement a legal hold on transcript materials. She suggested that we speak with her boss, Art Wynn III, and Mr. Wynn explained the particulars of the transcription business. He said he had a quarterly memo from CBS dated Feb 18, 1994: an updated and ongoing list of all CBS shows on legal hold. This list included these two programs (with a total of three air dates) The entire program was on hold; not just the segments on Scientology. Mr. Wynn does not keep the previous lists, only the most current update, so these legal holds could have been put in place at any time prior to February 18. There are four categories to the legal list which include 'Do Not Distribute Tapes', 'Do Not Distribute Transcripts' 'Do Not Rebroadcast' and 'No Need To Hold Materials' Mr. Wynn interprets The final category as 'This material will never be released' and the two shows referring to Scientology were indeed subject to this final category.

Do you have 60 Minutes from the begin-

ning, Mr. Wynn?

"Yes."

Are there a great amount of CBS transcripts on legal hold?

"No."

How long is his list?

"I couldn't even begin to guess."

Around this time we spoke with Kathy Olian, the producer of the singular segment which is available to the public, "Scientology Wants To Ban Prozac". We had obtained this transcript from Burrell's and found it to be a well-balanced piece on the Prozac controversy. Dennis Clark from the Citizens Commission On Human Rights was on hand as well a whole crew of witnesses, pro and con. The report was mild by *60 Minutes* usual standards, but it did take Scientology to task for 'waging war' on Prozac. The strongest language that Scientologists could have objected to was delivered by *60 Minutes* reporter Leslie Stahl:

STAHL: Instead of going to psychiatrists, Scientologists get counseling sessions with a device called an E-meter, which is supposed to monitor negative thoughts. The money Scientology gets from E-meter sales — the devices cost thousands of dollars — and from counseling sessions is a major source of income for the church. But psychiatrists call the E-meter quackery, and helps make psychiatry public enemy number one for the Citizens Commission . . .

The report did not challenge Scientology otherwise; nor should it have. It was, after all, primarily a story about Prozac. I spoke with producer Kathy Olian:

Did you get any flak from Scientology when you approached them with this story idea?

"Not in any way," she said. "I think that the fact that we were doing a story on Prozac and not Scientology had something to do with it . . . When I was working on the story I was aware that Time magazine was doing a big cover story.

The lawsuit hadn't come down yet, had it?

"The lawsuit hadn't but the story was being done and (allegedly) the people who did it were being harassed. We were waiting for the other shoe to drop but it never did."

Asked if she was aware of the legal hold on the first two stories she said, "No, I wasn't. I became aware of (the earlier shows) when I was doing my research . . . Were we sued on them?"

I told her we couldn't find any lawsuit.

Wouldn't the legal hold come up in her research too?

"Not necessarily because it's in-house. We all work independently of each other," she said. "This was my third season with *60 Minutes* . . . I've been with CBS since 1978, and no one's ever asked me not to do a story because of legal problems."

What could be happening here? At first, I thought perhaps CBS Legal was intimidated by the situation at *Time* magazine. That thesis flew in the face of *60 Minutes* bulldog reputation for courage and aggression, but reputations can be wrong. *Why take chances?* the logic seemed to go. *If Scientology is feeling SLAPP happy these days, why take chances?* For some reason, it seemed less likely that *60 Minutes* was hiding something, and if there had been a legitimate lawsuit certainly it would have been reported elsewhere before this. At this point, the date on which the legal hold was applied became paramount. If the legal hold was applied in 1992, then a case for intimidation could be made. Anything earlier would almost certainly point to some extraordinary legal circumstance. We asked ourselves again: What could be happening here?

Mr. Brunett, how long have you been with Media Relations for 60 Minutes?

"About nine years."

Why does any show have a legal hold?

"As a matter of policy once an action has been taken."

So you're saying that an action was taken, and as a matter of policy it was placed on legal hold?

"Yes, until such time as the matter is resolved."

What was the date that the legal hold on these two transcripts went in place?

"Once an action has been taken and we've been received." That was an evasion of the question.

Who made the decision to put these two shows on hold?

"I don't know. Someone in legal."

But who? There must be a party responsible for the quarterly list. I need to get the date, Roy.

"You'd have to contact the attorneys. John Sternburg. He's an attorney who works for CBS."

Over the next six working days I called Sternburg's office eight times. I stressed to his secretary that I didn't want the transcript, just the date and circumstances of the legal hold. It seemed like a simple direct question but Sternburg never returned my calls. His secretary assured us that she had given my messages to him and seemed surprised that we hadn't heard from him. On the eighth try I lucked out when Sternburg picked up the phone while his secretary was out to lunch.

Mr. Sternburg, this is my eighth call to your office. Did you get any of my messages?

"I'm not sure."

We would like to find out the dates that the legal holds were applied and the circumstances surrounding those decisions.

"I don't know" said Sternburg, "And quite frankly I'm not going to do the research to find out." He said that he was very busy with important matters and didn't have the time to do this. "I don't remember" the circumstances, he said. "This is done as a matter of routine in an action," and "It was done a long time ago."

If it's is typical in an action, what action? I told him that a third show concerning Scientology is not on legal hold, and I would also be interested in knowing why two shows are on hold and one is not. I suggested that perhaps an aide could be consigned to answer my questions and he said, "Give me your number and I'll see what's readily available." He did not ask for show specifics. He did not give me the impression that he would get back to me and indeed, he didn't.

This was beginning of a very frustrating month. What began as a casual inquiry was devolving into a full-blown search. *60 Minutes* and its legal counsel were clearly not cooperating with a legitimate journalistic inquiry. Could this be mere arrogance? Are Don Hewitt and his colleagues the only professionals capable of defining an "important" question? Is it possible that they can dish it out, but that they can't take it?

On the afternoon of June 23 I spoke with Roy Brunett again. He obviously had talked with someone as he had some new information. He said, "If they bring a suit it is routine to put it on legal hold."

What suit? Who's the plaintiff? Who's the defendant? In what court is it placed?

"The only thing I could tell you is what I have in front of me . . . *New Era vs. CBS.*

When a matter is brought against *60 Minutes* or CBS it goes to the legal department."

Referring to the legal hold and the unwillingness of CBS Legal to provide further he said: "That's their call. I don't know the reason. There may be a legal reason. There may be a company reason. I don't know. It has nothing to do with *60 Minutes*. *60 Minutes* is the broadcaster and takes the advice of counsel who in this case is CBS Legal."

Are you saying that there was a legal action against CBS from Scientology?

"All I know is what I gave you. It could have been a threat or it could be an action. I don't know. You could ask Scientology."

What I'd like to know is when was the legal hold placed on the material? I think that's relevant to my story.

"Then you have to go back to Sternberg."

I'm not looking to sensationalize this. I'm just looking for the answers to those two questions.

"Yeah, I know that."

I mean if our positions were reversed and 60 Minutes were on this end of the phone, you'd be curious too, wouldn't you?

Well, sure.

I mean, is there a lawsuit against CBS?

"Well, I'm sure you could find that out. The court records must be a matter of public record."

Yeah, I could find out. I could do a Lexis search. And I can probably get a copy of the tapes on hold. I mean there's Scientology watchers out there who could provide them, I sure.

"There must be somewhere you can get them."

I'm sure there is.

During the next week I made over a dozen phone calls to cult awareness personnel, exit counselors, lawyers and former members of Scientology. Finding "Scientology: The Clearwater Conspiracy" and "Scientology" was not as easy as I thought it would be. To begin with, because of the duplicitous nature of adversarial litigation, everyone wanted to check me out and make sure I was who I said I was. I spoke with Gabe Cezares, the former mayor of Clearwater, Florida (where Scientology has a large presence and which was, presumably, the subject matter of the first broadcast). Mr. Cezares remembered the broadcast and thought that he could provide a copy of the tapes but after several days said that he couldn't find them. Everyone had a horror story but no one had a copy of the tapes. Finally on June 29, I received a call from exit counsellor David Clark. He was on the road calling from a Texas airport and he said that he had a copy of the material and would forward it to me as soon as he got back.

In the meantime I tried to track down "New Era." I knew I was going to speak with attorneys for Scientology before this was through, but I wanted to garner as much information on my own before that became necessary. I could not find out much at first. There was no "New Era" in L.A. or Helmut, California where Scientology is headquartered, and New Era Development of Clearwater, Florida turned out to be an unrelated company. Then a computer search produced a reference. In 1990, the United States Court of Appeals for the Second Circuit reversed a lower court ruling and held that a publisher was not required to delete published material written by L. Ron Hubbard from an upcoming biography. Conversely, the same Court held in another case that Henry Holt & Company had exceeded the permissible "fair use" of Hubbard's *unpublished* writings, holding that writers may make only "minimal" use of unpublished material. The complainant in both cases was the Danish corporation licensed to hold copyrights bequeathed to the Church of Scientology by L. Ron Hubbard. That corporation is New Era International.

Shortly thereafter I contacted Jonathan Lubell for the first time. Lubell has been Scientology's outside libel lawyer since 1977 and he wanted to cooperate with me not because he's a friend of the press but, more practically, because I had something he wanted. I had come into possession of a piece of information that could have been very useful to Lubell and, for very good reasons, I was willing to share it with him in exchange for his cooperation in this matter. Lubell had to go to Canada on the next working day but made sure his secretary called to confirm that I would be available if need be. No doubt about it, Jonathan Lubell wanted to help. I wanted an interview and a copy of whatever went to CBS to make them so skittish. "I will be back in touch with you," said Lubell. But a week later he had to admit failure. "It's just not possible" he said bleakly. "I spoke with

a few people and they can't— Whatever we had has been warehoused a long time ago." It should be pointed out that this is the same reason that *60 Minutes* was offering, but the point of departure is that I was asking Lubell for a private letter and I was asking *60 Minutes* for a segment made for public consumption (or at least an explanation why I couldn't have it).

Another week went by before the tapes arrived in the mail. Both the 1980 and 1985 broadcasts were provided by Clark. As one might expect, I popped in the tapes with a certain amount of anticipation.

"The Clearwater Conspiracy" (1980) and "Scientology" (1985) are both fine examples of hard hitting comprehensive investigative journalism. Both are admirable and in keeping with the standards of courage and intelligence that are usually associated with *60 Minutes*. There is original material in both segments. We are reduced to hypothesis: Since the complainant is the licensee of Hubbard's published and unpublished works, then perhaps the complaints are concerned with those areas also. Repeated viewings and a bit of deconstruction lead to few interesting facts: Hubbard's words are quoted in both segments. Different words but Hubbard's nonetheless.

In "Clearwater" Mike Wallace reports on Scientology's attempt to economically take over a Florida community and the fear and intimidation that the Church rained down upon its local adversaries. Gabe Cezares is on hand as is Paulette Cooper. Both were targets of Scientology in the heyday of church harassment when phony bomb threats and false accusations of sexual infidelity were on the agenda. Wallace reads from church memos documenting the bizarre plots as camera shots of the memos are shown on-screen. Later, and perhaps more to the point, Wallace confronts two church officials with the 1966 "Policy Letter", written by Hubbard and widely reported elsewhere. Sentences within the documents themselves are given close-ups for effect.

The stylistic tool is used even more frequently in 1985. "Scientology" shows some of the same footage as the previous segment and adds shots of pages of Hubbard's published work. At one point Mike Wallace reads a litany of claims that Hubbard had made over the years to biographer, Omar Garrison. Point by point, Garrison disavows each detail. Wallace later reports that Garrison (and others on the broadcast) were reportedly "purged from the church . . . According to church leaders they are all disgruntled and have personal gripes. And so the church says they are lying . . . " Garrison and others "have all been called as witnesses in court about their experience with Scientology . . . . In that case" says Wallace, "the (former) Scientologists did not testify to all they told us in this report."

These reports utilize the written work of L.R. Hubbard and one can glean the possible framework of a libel complaint. Perhaps not a *successful* complaint but it doesn't have to be successful to be debilitating. This may have something to do with the action at CBS; it may not.

On June 30 I spoke with Roy Brunett in the late afternoon. I told him earlier that day that Sternburg was not returning my calls and he asked me to call back in a few hours. He had a statement. What follows is an edited transcript:

BRUNETT: Alright, I spoke to the litigator . . . So here's what I can tell you. Well . . . I'm sorry this is the best I can tell you . . . Within months — this is the best we can do — closest we can tell you to these dates . . . a claim was received. And I guess Sternberg told you either it's a claim or a —

RC: No, he didn't tell me anything; you told me.

BRUNETT: All right. Either of two actions can take place. Either a claim or a lawsuit.

RC: Okay.

BRUNETT: Alright, a claim basically . . . is a letter. Without a lawsuit . . . . Alleging or claiming they have been wronged or what have you. It can threaten the lawsuit.

RC: Right.

BRUNETT: So within months of those two broadcasts the claim was received by . . . the two parties.

RC: New Era verses CBS.

BRUNETT: Right.

RC: So you're saying—

BRUNETT: Within months of the broadcasts.

RC: Well, they're five years apart.

BRUNETT: Right, within months of those two broadcasts. So, the first one was in nineteen eighty . . . and the second one was in eighty-five.

RC: And you got . . . two separate claims are involved?

BRUNETT: We got— we received letters.

RC: Right. Okay.

BRUNETT: Now, to the best of our record the merits of the claim(s) were never resolved . . . because the matter was dropped. Not by us— but by them.

RC: So, you're saying there was two separate letters?

BRUNETT: To the best of our recollection, based on those two broadcasts, claims were received . . . . Now to date . . . well it's not to date but, according to our legal department — the claim was dropped. Both claims were dropped. Now, why is it still on legal hold? As I mentioned the merits of the claim have never been resolved.

RC: Right.

BRUNETT: So the opinions of the legal department is simply because the news value . . . to rebroadcast at this time is questionable because of — of — of any news value today — could be outdated, could be stale. There's no reason to rebroadcast at this time.

RC: Well, rebroadcast it, sure, but what about transcripts and . . .

BRUNETT: Well, right. The transcripts, what have you. Because in [the legal departments] opinion it could resurrect the claims and [we'd] have to go through this process all over again . . . And it's their opinion that 'Why bother?' There's no reason since there is no news value . . .

RC: Hard question. Could that be construed as backing off of a story?

BRUNETT: I doubt it. Because the odds are because of it being no news value, in their opinion.

RC: We have the tapes. How do you feel about us putting this to fair use?

BRUNETT: I can't comment on that.

That's your own decision. You would have to take up with your own attorneys. So that's pretty much . . .

RC: *Other than that, what the claims were is not known to you?*

BRUNETT: That would require . . . having to go back into his files which [the legal department is] not too thrilled about having to do . . . It's not a . . . I — I don't know what the the the ah—

RC: *I'm probably going to pursue it; I'm going to send them a letter—*

BRUNETT: Yeah. You can send it to the attention of Doug Jacobs.

RC: *Doug Jacobs is in CBS Legal?*

BRUNETT: Yeah. I'll give you his title . . . General Counsel. But just don't hold your breath [that] you're gonna get any— It's just not . . .

RC: *Okay. . . . You do things as a matter of policy when you get an action. Whether it's a letter or whether it's an actual [lawsuit]. I'm trying to determine whether the rules are different for Scientology.*

BRUNETT: I doubt it. Not from this place . . . because [if 60 Minutes were intimidated by the first letter] why bother doing the follow-up story or why do . . . Yeah, I don't know much about it. I mean, I just don't think what we — what they did and what we have was anything to shake sticks at.

RC: *Right. Neither did we until people weren't answering my questions. Then I'm saying 'Geez that sure is strange' And the irony was incredible.*

BRUNETT: Yeah.

RC: *You know, 60 minutes not cooperating with the press on an investigative piece — I mean that — the irony was incredible.*

Mr. Brunett made perfect sense concerning the rebroadcasting of material. If there was additional news value Don Hewitt would simply assign a new segment, not rebroadcast an older one. But the concept of standing bravely behind a story that no one has access to is questionable. A week later, I called Brunett back to continue:

RC: *Roy, if this were a print medium, let's say the New York Times, I'd go to the library and get a copy of the New York Times. Now the correlation here is that I go to the transcription service, and they tell me there is a legal hold on these materials so I go to you guys and say I'd like to see these tapes and you say, "Well, there's a legal hold on that material. There is nothing we can do about that." It seems to me that that is a situation unique to broadcast journalism.*

BRUNETT: I guess in a sense it is, in a sense that because, it's only within recent years that videotapes of news broadcasts and/or transcripts have become available to the general public. So it is within that it's unique, in the sense that it's only been available within the last — oh, I don't know — so many years . . . and I only could guess that perhaps those questions and those issues just have not been addressed.

RC: *Don't you think that broadcast journalism should be held to the same standard of accessibility, of accountability, as print journalism and that by not making it accessible you're are, in fact, not standing behind a story?*

BRUNETT: Not at all.

RC: *Why not?*

BRUNETT: Well, we are accountable in that we put the piece on air . . . We should be judged as a broadcast medium. Print and broadcast, I mean there are journalists but there are print journalists and broadcast journalists. And we are — this is not — What we do or how we do do what we do in terms of our internal business perhaps differs from what NBC or ABC or what have you. Each will do it — will deal in it's own way and this is the procedure that CBS has established . . . and, you know, it's only unique to the individual organization. I don't know how ABC handles that.

I do. A call to JournalGraphics, the transcript service for ABC, reveals that transcripts that exist for the comparable ABC television show *20/20* are 99.85% available. *20/20* has been on the air for sixteen years and the transcript service has twelve of those years on file. *One* segment in 615 shows is on legal hold.

I spoke with Allan Maraynes, senior investigative producer for *20/20* (and the producer of both *60 Minutes* broadcasts) about the amount of threatened litigation at *20/20*:

RC: *There's a lot of lawyer letters?*

Maraynes: That's for sure.

RC: I mean you guys get lawyer letters, right?

AM: Yeah, that's right. Sure . . . Lots of lawyer letters.

I asked Beth Comstock, a spokesperson for NBC what was the policy on legal holds as concerns threatened litigation. Ms. Comstock got back quickly with an answer. "I checked with our legal department," she said, "and basically, as a matter of course, we do not put transcripts on legal hold, but we certainly reserve the right to should the need arise. It wouldn't be unusual if we did but as a matter of course, do not."

This policy was demonstrated as the Unification Church sent an "action" to NBC, stating in no uncertain terms its intention to sue over the *Today Show* broadcast of November 8, 1993. The comparison is strong. A large church with deep pockets who has been known to litigate. To date, that lawsuit has not been filed nor withdrawn but this reporter had no difficulty obtaining the transcripts of that material from the same transcription service that distributes *60 Minutes*. We return to Mr. Brunett:

RC: Roy, let's go back to the New York Times example – the New York Times is on record – this is what they said (just to pick out a date) on June 19, 1994. If I want the same accountability with CBS I've got to go to CBS.

BRUNETT: The delivery— It's the delivery system. I mean the *New York Times* goes in libraries and what have you. Because it's broadcast, our delivery system is different. It's just a means of doing — you know, how the message is delivered.

RC: Would it be fair to say then that the accountability is different?

BRUNETT: Well, the accountability, in terms of what you put on the air is it's out there, you know.

RC: Well what you put in the paper on a daily basis is out there after that it goes into the library.

BRUNETT: Yeah, but it's been delivered to your home, it's been delivered . . . You know, there was nothing stopping you from recording that broadcast.

RC: Right, which is how I got it ultimately.

BRUNETT: Right. There is nothing stopping anyone else from recording it so it's not as if you don't have the means. Giving a transcript is a service, it's not an obligation.

RC: That's true but on the other hand but if I went to the New York Times — Let's say that the Unification Church sued the New York Times over an article and I said to the Times 'Could you please provide me with this article on such and such a date?' They're not going to say, 'Oh, there's a legal hold on that article. You'll have to go elsewhere to find that article.'

BRUNETT: I don't know. Will they?

Roy got me there. I don't know if the *New York Times* would provide an issue in which an alleged libel occurred. I do know however that in the course of researching this story *Time* and *Premier* magazine as well as the *Journal of the American Medical Association* each provided this reporter with specific issues of their publications despite the fact that each issue contained an article that was the focus of a major unresolved litigation. Serious money.

BRUNETT: Well, then that's their internal policy. I don't know. As I've said, each company, each business, handles it's internal business differently.

RC: You don't see that there is any inherent contradiction there?

BRUNETT: No. No, I don't see it. We've gone on record. We put it— We've put it on air and the audience has seen it.

RC: And not making it available to a journalist at a later date when a question comes up, making it inaccessible—

BRUNETT: It's been available. It's been on air.

RC: It's been – past tense – but not making it available in the future is not backing off of the story in your view?

BRUNETT: No.

RC: Okay. Because that's certainly an interpretation.

BRUNETT: Well, it's a criticism. If you want to . . . Certainly, it's a valid criticism if you, as a writer or however you're doing this but, um . . . That's how CBS — The Legal

Department has set procedures and they might not be the best or they might not be the worst but it is what it is and until they . . . it's reviewed and amended, changed, what have you, that's the st— That's the policy that we have in place at this time.

A bit of summary is in order. In 1980 and 1985 CBS newsmagazine *60 Minutes* aired two distinct segments about the Church of Scientology and "within months" of each broadcast received two separate "actions" — defined by Mr. Brunett as "letters" — from a Church-related corporation threatening litigation of some kind. CBS Legal, "as a matter of policy," put each show on an indefinite legal hold at the time that each "action" was received. Both shows in their entirety have been on legal hold for all these years meaning that they will not be rebroadcast and neither tapes nor transcripts will be given to anyone who asks, be he broadcast consumer or fellow journalist. The reason that the shows have remained on hold all these years is because "the matter was dropped" by the claimant and, being unresolved, the material in question stays on legal hold. Sounds like a lot of trouble to go through for a couple of letters. Does that sound reasonable to you?

And what about the National Council of Churches? What about that unresolved "action"? That lawsuit that lay fallow because the litigants couldn't afford to bring it to court. But I was able to obtain the transcript from Burrell's unencumbered.

You say Don Hewitt called to confirm, right? That was probably the deciding call which saved "The Gospel According To Whom?" from having a legal lock applied to it forever and a day. Fair enough.

And, what about the Metropolitan Museum of Art? A transcript of that show is available; it is not on legal hold. But, if the CBS policy was consistent, maybe the story about the Met *should* be on hold.

On March 21, 1982, *60 Minutes* aired "Is It A Fake?", produced by John Tiffin, which cast doubt upon the authenticity of a painting called "one of the great treasures of the Metropolitan Museum of Art in New York." Executive Vice President of the Metropolitan Museum, Ashton Hawkins, said, "What they do with *60 Minutes* — they used to do anyway — was they circulate the script about a week in advance to broadcasters and other people who are on their list so

you could see what's coming. And we looked at it, called them up and we talked to Don Hewitt and said that we were going to sue them if they ran it that way because basically we felt that it was a libel to the painting, a libel to property, that it had been discredited and that they knew that."

In an interview with *Gauntlet* Mr. Hawkins recalled that the BBC was doing a segment on the same controversy and when *60 Minutes* found that out they responded by rushing through the piece.

"[Morley Safer] went ahead and did the program on a very quick basis written from the point of view from what we felt was a discredited art historian's allegation . . . It was malicious," Mr. Hawkins claimed, "because the [BBC] program that had aired was really very thorough — more or less answered the same questions."

On March 19, two days before airtime, the Museum put CBS on notice. "I wrote to Hewitt saying that if this was not changed we would consider all our options including bringing a suit," Hawkins recalled.

The next day the *New York Times* reported that a spokesman for the Met said, "The Museum views this proposed telecast as false in portraying the picture as a forgery. The broadcast is a disservice to the public as well as a terrible disservice to the picture itself. It needlessly maligns the Metropolitan Museum as well as a number of individuals. We have expressed this opinion to CBS and the matter is now in the hands of our lawyers, Lord, Day & Lord." The grounds were "defamation" of the museum and property.

Ashton Hawkins said that when the segment aired on Sunday, "They made a little change but it wasn't much . . . . I mean they tacked on a little ending in which he said, 'Well, the museum has objected and we still stand by our story.' It was that kind of ending."

CBS News in New York made a effort to appease and a paragraph that a ran in the *New York Times* three days later is particularly telling: "CBS," the *Times* reported, "already apprised that legal action was being considered by the Met on the grounds of 'Defamation' did mount a hasty 'interview' with Phillippe de Montebello, the Met's director, on its late night news program following *60 Minutes*. But Mr. Montebello, who appeared to hedge a little about the painting, says the brief interview was torn from the context of a 20 minute filming in which he had repeatedly affirmed it. *Asked to provide a transcript of the full interview, a CBS spokesman refused, but said that the network 'stands by its story.'" (Emphasis mine. Okay it's ironic but it's not the same thing. They didn't broadcast the full interview. They should not have given up the full interview. The unedited tape is the equivalent of the reporter's notebook. Not giving up the notebook is what reporter's draw contempt charges forand good reporters have been known to go to jail rather than give up the notebook)*

Ashton Hawkins said, "Morley did make a few changes but they were really — As I remember we found them typically unsatisfactory . It's like when you try to get a retraction from a newspaper. They'll put in something and then the author will say 'I stand by what I said.'"

Did you ever follow through with the lawsuit?

"No. We never filed any kind of suit. We simply had a letter, but we never actually followed through."

If you weren't satisfied, why did you let the matter drop?

"Because there didn't seem to be any point. We didn't seem to think we would get any better satisfaction."

Did you ever get in touch with 60 Minutes afterward and say you will not sue?

"We did not because we weren't satisfied. [The changes] were not that great.

You did not give an absolute (statement) to 60 Minutes (expressing), 'We are satisfied now. We will not sue.'

"Not at all. No, no . . . We dropped the matter. They did take a little bit of action in response, but we never said anything like we were satisfied with the result."

It appears that the policy of legal holds at CBS is selective at best. When I explained to Mr. Hawkins the purpose of my call he said, "It sounds as if they do have something of a double standard on what they don't let out and what they do let out. It's a business decision . . . They try to get it both ways."

The National Council of Churches had a willingness to litigate, but not enough money to carry through; the Metropolitan Museum of Art had the money but lacked the willingness. Scientology, as we shall see in a moment, had both.

On July 25, Douglas Jacobs, General Counsel for CBS sent me a letter which said in part, "While CBS continues to stand behind both of the above broadcasts, the decision to place a legal hold on these or any broadcasts may be made for many reasons. Those reasons are privileged and cannot be revealed to you."

End of story.

Not quite.

There is an Old Guard, as it were. Veterans of litigations past, victims of vintage campaigns so heavy-handed and unrelenting that they have left scars upon each of these soldiers in their war against Scientology. Like old army buddies, they know about each other. Some of them stay in touch. It's not an easy network to penetrate because they can be a paranoid bunch but once you're in it blossoms like a flower.

That's how I found Omar Garrison.

Omar Garrison is a journalist who was once contracted by New Era International to write a biography of L. Ron Hubbard. Despite what Mike Wallace had to report in 1985, Omar Garrison has never been a member of Scientology. "Scientology didn't mean a damn thing to me," Mr, Garrison told me, "but the encroachment of government into private lives did and that's why I wrote another book and it was on that basis that they came to me.

"For two years they had wanted me to do a biography of L. Ron Hubbard because Hubbard liked my writing. I never talked to him in person other than back in 1950 when Dianetics came out."

According to Garrison, negotiations for the biography were finalized and the book was more than half-finished when he had a falling out with New Era over money. "New Era is a Danish corporation, in fact a creature and alter ego of the Church of Scientology," he said. He claims to have come into possession of sensitive documentation in the course of his research and when that fact came up in negotiations Scientology accused Garrison of blackmail.

"When they said 'blackmail'," Garrison recalled, "They had to peel me off the walls. I said, 'Hereafter you will speak to me only through my attorney.'

"Eventually the lawyers agreed to make a settlement to compensate me for what had been done, and I was to return the material I had. Much of it very damaging; some of this stuff is still under steel. And of course I was to receive a certain amount of money for that which I did."

"And there it sat until *60 Minutes*," he said.

"In the agreement it's written that they are not to come near my neighbors, my wife, and at this time I had a very close friend they were harassing . . . but they came up here, came to one of my neighbors and were generally behaving the way they usually do. And I called them, I said, 'Goddamn it, You've breached the contract, the understanding we've had! To hell with you!' Just about that time *60 Minutes* called me and asked if I'd be on the show and I said, 'Hell, yes, I'd be on the show!' So it was on that basis that they brought the suit."

According to Garrison, New Era sued both CBS and himself for conspiring to break Garrison's contract.

"I was a co-defendant with CBS," he said. "They had brought a complaint because . . . on that show Mike ask me about Hubbard. So he said, 'Was he ever in Tibet?' and I said, 'No.'. 'Or India?' 'No.' All this . . . all these ridiculous claims. In the agreement — They put this in — I was not to speak about L. Ron Hubbard. On this basis, they said, it breached the contract."

What did they charge CBS with?

"Well, they said that, in effect, CBS had knowingly aided me in breaching the contract which, of course if you consider it a breach, they did because when I talked to the producer I said, 'You know what the situation is. You know about the agreement. Now there's going to be a suit.' I said, 'Now am I going to be protected by CBS?' They've got insurance goddammit! Because undoubtedly there'll be a lawsuit.'. . . And sure enough there was."

Garrison claims that a lawsuit was filed in Federal Court in Salt Lake City naming him and CBS as co-defendants.

The Federal District Court in Salt Lake City was able to confirm on the phone that on February 21, 1986 New Era Publications filed a lawsuit against Omar V. Garrison and his company, Faith Publications. The clerk office said that the case was dismissed by the court "with prejudice" on February 25, 1988 and that each party was to pay their own costs. I asked if CBS was named in the complaint and the clerk said that she only had the "hard docket" available, meaning that the case was not on her computer. "It's possible that there are other defendants listed in the case file," she said. A copy of the case file was ordered and will be forwarded to *Gauntlet* shortly.

Garrison faxed *Gauntlet* the complaint as we went to press and the title is listed as "New Era Publications vs. Omar, V. Garrison, Faith Publications, CBS Inc., Mike Wallace, Allan Maraynes and John Doe 1 through 10" (Civil Case 86-C-0144W). When told that the Federal Court was only able to confirm his name on the complaint Mr. Garrison said he thought that was "significant". Mr. Garrison claims that CBS made a separate settlement with New Era the terms of which he was not privy to.

"I never saw the agreement that CBS made with them," Garrison told *Gauntlet*, "but I understand that it was much to the Scientologists satisfaction.

"We were co-defendants for God's sake!"

I asked Mr. Garrison if he felt that CBS was intimidated by Scientology.

"Hell, yes!" he replied emphatically.

"I told [my lawyer] 'You can tell the bastards I don't care what CBS does; I'm going to take my case to the courthouse!' And that's when [New Era] settled with me a second time." Mr. Garrison claims that he received a cash settlement in this case also.

Former *60 Minutes* producer Allan Maraynes remembers Mr. Garrison, "They accused him of a breach of contract. They alleged that they made a deal with him to keep his mouth shut and he didn't."

Did you know that he had a deal with Scientology?

"No."

Do you know how it was resolved?

I don't think it went anywhere. It was resolved somehow.

Was there an agreement with CBS?

"I don't know what the agreement said."

You were named in it. Do you remember that?

"I do remember that."

Maraynes goes on to opine that there "wasn't a settlement with CBS, and I don't think it was a monetary settlement with Garrison." One moment later he admits, "The lawyers have their conversations, and they don't always tell us what they did."

Regarding the 1980 broadcast Maraynes said, "Allegations of conspiracy . . . The greatest thread that I can remember is that there were allegations that we were involved in a conspiracy with a Boston lawyer to do Scientology in. Nothing could have been further from the truth. He was a source in our story but there was no conspiracy. We didn't know the guy before we talked to him.

Mr. Maraynes was speaking about personal injury lawyer Michael Flynn. Flynn, who does not appear on either broadcast, has represented more than two dozen plaintiffs against the church and was sued by the church more than a dozen times in four jurisdictions. Presumably he was used as a source for background material. Michael Flynn declined to be interviewed by *Gauntlet* pursuant to the terms of a settlement he received from the church in 1986.

This story is far from over. There are several questions that need to be answered. What really happened between New Era and Omar Garrison and *60 Minutes* in 1985? What happened in 1980 between Michael Flynn and *60 Minutes*? These matters obviously relate to the legal locks applied to these transcripts but in what regard? Is this a mere case of successful intimidation or is there something deeper moving these events?

When Roy Brunett finally told me that *60 Minutes* received letters from New Era, and that that was the extent of it, I believed him. I thought that CBS Legal received the classic American lawyer letter from an notorious organization with both money and will, and I believed that CBS caved like a house of cards. I thought that was my story. It's a good story — but now I'm not sure that's all there is to it.

Certainly there is more to this than CBS receiving a few lawyer letters. That is what Roy Brunett, spokesman for *60 Minutes*, led me to believe and that is *not* true.

60 Minutes wishes I would go away. *60 Minutes* fulfilled its stated mandate: it produced a hard-hitting insightful piece of investigative journalism twice and broadcast it three times. *60 Minutes* knew this rough beast for what it was, and if Don Hewitt did not expect a lawsuit then Don Hewitt was naive (and nobody ever accused Don Hewitt of being naive). When the lawsuit came they settled in some manner to which we are not privy. That too is reasonable. Having broadcast the piece CBS is not obligated to charge hellbent and Quixote-like into a legal melee. And they are certainly not obligated to reveal private business transactions such as the terms of a court settlement.

But that settlement made them part of the story of Scientology. Years later when a journalist comes calling looking into the history of this rough beast called Scientology, a history which they themselves once saw fit to investigate and a history of which they are now a part; at that time *60 Minutes* is obligated to say what was broadcast on December 22, 1985. Any news organization should be required to state what that news organization entered into the Public Domain on any given date. That is nothing less than responsibility.

Let us not mince words. The concept of this responsibility applies to any newspaper or television show but in our example the implications are particularly ominous. *60 Minutes* is a powerful news organization with a vast audience. The information that *60 Minutes* decides to report goes out into the ether and is delivered and has effect. It can cause people to change their religion or to switch their job, it can cause people to lose faith and let the scales fall from their eyes. Such power to inform and affect should come only with a great sense of responsibility.

It is not acceptable that CBS refuse to inform a legitimate journalistic inquiry of what was said by its broadcaster, *60 Minutes*, on December 22, 1985. It is not acceptable because there has been no retraction. It is not acceptable because they have stated "We stand behind our story," but they refuse to produce it. It is not acceptable because *60 Minutes* defines itself as the very touchstone of journalistic integrity at the same time that they claim a privilege that no newspaper in the country would claim as its own. Roy Brunett was wrong: he said, "There's broadcast journalism and there's print journalism." *Wrong*. There's only journalism and if you claim to adhere to a strong standard then you cannot mitigate that standard for convenience.

And, finally, on a purely professional note, when a journalist comes calling on another news organization it is unacceptable that that organization lie ("We received letters." "The matter was dropped."), spin, stall, evade and otherwise interfere with a journalistic inquiry. Because if they do, at that point precisely, they cease to be part of the solution and begin to be part of the problem.

That is the most significant question left unanswered at this point. Does any broadcast organization have the right to arbitrarily put their broadcast materials on a legal hold whenever they see fit? If you have proffered information into the public domain on a certain date and time, is that the end of your responsibility concerning that information? How can a news organization possibly stand behind a story that they refuse to produce?

If the *New York Times* published an article on page two of the June 18th edition and two weeks later that article was subjected to a threat of litigation (the classic American Lawyer Letter), the idea that the attorneys for the *Times* would call up their the morgue and say 'Don't distribute any issues of the June 18th edition. We got a legal problem on page 2' is patently absurd.

This is a new dynamic born of technology. It is not a legal problem; it is an ethical one. Not a lack in law but a lack of cajones. NBC provided a transcript under almost the exact same circumstances. Certainly it is a debatable issue, but I'm not sure if it's ever been brought up outside of the Columbia School of Journalism. Should the policy standards for broadcast journalism be the same as the policy standards we've come to expect from print journalism? If those standards are to be different, why are they to be different? It is no use pleading that one medium is more immediate than the other because the comparison doesn't hold up.

When a paper is delivered to my house, I have the story in my hand. The broadcast equivalent of that statement is that when I tune to CBS on Sunday night at 7:00 pm I have *60 Minutes* in my living room.

After I read the paper I can either elect to save it in an ever growing stack out by the backdoor or I can throw it away. The broadcast equivalent there is, "I can pop a tape in and save all sixty of those minutes." Or I can stay in my easy chair and watch the show once, in effect, throwing it away as I would yesterdays news.

But if I read a story that said the mayor was a thief and I threw it away with the rest of the newspaper, and six months later when the election rolled around my wife said, I'm going to vote for the mayor." I have to say "Well, I'm not voting for the mayor. Don't you know? He's a thief."

"Where did you hear that?" she asks.

"I read it in the paper about six months ago."

"I don't believe it," she says. "Prove it!"

Well, any paper in the U.S. worth a damn, from the *Pacific Sun* to Long Island's *Newsday*, is going to sell me a back copy of that paper if they have one left in the morgue. They will sell me that paper even if the mayor's lawyer sent them a letter that said, 'We didn't like what you said about the mayor and we're going to sue your pants off.' They will sell me that paper even if the mayor sued them. They will sell me that newspaper not because it is a legal obligation but because it is the only conceivable way to stand behind your story. To do any less would be backing off from having said that the mayor is a thief. That is a journalistic standard that is recognized throughout the land by almost everyone except perhaps Roy Brunett, Don Hewitt and the CBS Legal Department.

60 Minutes wishes I would go away but I'm not going to. *Gauntlet* will continue its investigation into this matter.

The Church of Scientology versus Time

Scientology is, by some definition, the great American religion (emphasis: small "g"). It is a natural outgrowth of the standards and practices that have increasingly become the American way of life. It is capitalism carried to its natural philosophical extreme: corporation as credenda.

Modern mythology, according to the Gospels of Woodward and Bernstein, holds that "Dirty Tricks", in the Nixonian sense, had its genesis in "Ratfucking", a political dynamic first practiced by H.R. Haldeman and his cronies at University of Southern California and brought with them to the White House in 1968. Ratfucking began by sending too many pizzas to your opponent's headquarters and was expanded to include the litany of obscene political practices that history has quantified as Watergate. Haldeman and his boys didn't invent "Ratfucking"; they just brought it with them into the highest office in the land.

Conventional wisdom holds that the modern concept of "spin" — lending a desired twist to any given story — was first practiced in big-time politics by young David Gergen. Gergen later perfected the technique during the Reagan Administration and now seeks to "spin" for the current administration, a continuing tap dance so deft that it makes Fred Astaire look like a clod.

But, truly, Ratfucking, Dirty Tricks and Spin have long been the tools of the Church of Scientology and, more particularly, the philosophy of its founder, L.R. Hubbard.

Lafayette Ronald Hubbard, unquestionably a prolific writer, left behind millions and millions of words when he died in 1986. The words most quoted by an adversarial press were written in the 1950's and 1960's and refer to number of truculent statements concerning the fourth estate: "We do not want Scientology to be reported in the press, anywhere else than on the religious pages of newspapers . . . " wrote Hubbard. "Therefore, we should be very alert to sue for slander at the slightest chance so as to discourage the public presses from mentioning Scientology.

"Never agree to an investigation of the attacker . . . Start feeding lurid, blood, sex crime, actual evidence on the attack to the press. Don't ever tamely submit to an investigation of us. Make it rough, rough on attackers all the way . . . " Hubbard's theory of litigation was stated plainly: "The purpose of the [lawsuit] is to harass and discourage rather than win."

Then there is the doctrine of "Fair Game". As defined by Hubbard in the mid-sixties, the detractors of Scientology are "Fair game" he said and can "be deprived of property or injured by any means by any Scientologist without any discipline of the Scientologist. May be tricked, sued, lied to or destroyed." Scientologists have said that the doctrine of Fair Game was rescinded by Hubbard three years after its inception because its original meaning had been twisted, but detractors insist that the doctrine remains in place and is exemplified by a bevy of harassments and harangues, documented and otherwise.

Such pugnacious prose has been recounted in the press ad nauseum and gives any story on Scientology a sensationalistic and "sexy" spin. The question of continuing abuses by Scientology seems valid (even provable) but equally valid is the question of the repeated use by reporters of hyperbolic dogma almost thirty years old.

Reporters often point to the sensational conviction of eleven top Scientologists in the early eighties for breaking into the IRS headquarters and readily inform that all eleven, including Hubbard's wife, served time for the crime. They dutifully report that Scientology acknowledges those abuses and claims to have "cleaned house" shortly thereafter. The subsequent use of private detectives to investigate the investigators, rifling through garbage cans, the slashing of tires, the drowning of dogs, the hang-up phone calls, innuendo and unsubstantiated rumor is also reported. What is less reported is the pre-publication phone calls from Scientology press agents made in an effort to "spin" a story a certain way. The letters from lawyers go unreported. The conversation that every reporter who ever did a story on Scientology has had with his editor — including this reporter and his editor at *Gauntlet* — goes unreported. "Be careful" they say, "Scientology will sue a medium for slander at the drop of a hat." And that supposition informs every decision made in the writing, the editorial and the publication or broadcast process. And it is a supposition that is demonstrably incorrect.

There is no doubt that Scientology is litigious. It has had, until recently, as many as sixty ongoing lawsuits according to a (1993) article in the *National Law Journal*. Most of those lawsuits involve former members who have mounted virtual crusades against their former religion and so-called "anti-cult" organizations like the Cult Awareness Network (CAN) and the American Family Foundation (AFF) which are, by their own definition, cult-like in their zeal. Add to this list a large number of cases involving Scientology's thirty year war with the IRS and also the psychiatric profession, and the conclusion of its litigious nature is inescapable. (The IRS suits have recently been dismissed owing to a November, 1993 ruling by the Internal Revenue Service to grant the Church of Scientology International (CSI) a tax exempt status on the grounds that it is a charitable organization.)

"Most of those cases, not all but just about, are gone now with the IRS settlement," said Church attorney Jonathan Lubell.

"When you ask 'Are you tired of being

as litigious?', Lubell says, "that reminds me of the question 'Are you tired of beating your wife?'."

Jonathan Lubell, Scientology's outside libel counsel since 1977, challenged that litigious reputation in an interview with *Gauntlet*. His voice is soporific and fey, not unlike Truman Capote on valium.

"The myth about the church is that it's in the business of litigation and that's— I don't believe it to be true and my belief on this is based a great deal on personal knowledge."

But the fact remains that Scientology units spent $30 million in legal bills in 1987 and 1988 alone. This figure became available when Scientology entities filed documents with the IRS in compliance with their new tax exempt status.

"I have no idea of how much the church spent on lawyer's fees." Lubell said. "[Also] I have no idea how much of those lawyer's fees are related to litigation. Churches are charitable corporations. You always need lawyers performing to make sure it complies with the IRS and various other provisions so there's a lot of simple corporate work that's done around the church. Any major organization in the United States spends a pretty good amount of money.

"The other thing that I would say is that— Now this is my own; I don't know for a fact because I don't have a overview of church litigation, but I'm willing to surmise that the bulk of the church litigation until recently has been in two areas. One is with the IRS and the other is the Freedom Of Information Act."

But if one accepts the notion that Scientology is, in fact, litigious, it cannot be said that that litigious nature includes a willingness to sue the media for defamation. The fact is that, with one major exception, the Church of Scientology has not lodged a lawsuit for defamation against any news medium in the United States for over ten years.

"When was the last one?" Lubell asks rhetorically, "I think it was against ABC in the very early eighties. And then there was a media lawsuit against a book also in the early eighties . . . I know that to be a fact."

Why then is it presumed that the Church of Scientology targets the media for slander? Certainly L. Ron's own oft-reported and relatively ancient words have

something to do with it (something of a self-fulfilling prophecy on the part of the media). And the Church's combativeness in other legal arenas must also inform this discussion. And let's not forget that the Church has a history of extra-legal as well as outright illegal practices. But, more to the point, it is about money. A dead Davidian cannot sue and a live guru may have limited resources but the Church of Scientology has deep, deep pockets and should the Church of Scientology decide to hit you with a lawsuit, you may feel the painful sting of that slapp (sic) until you lose or until you give up. Just ask the IRS.

Despite Lubell's emphatic denial, it seems clear that Scientology has engineered a reputation for itself as something you don't want to mess with. To reiterate, with one exception, in United States, the Church hasn't sued a press or broadcast medium for libel in over ten years, but that is not to say they haven't threatened to sue. It is true that Scientology *threatens* to sue at the drop of a hat. And the press, with a predisposition that is in conflict with its stated doctrine of objectivity, confuses threats with actions and believes its own hype.

The careful reader will have noticed two qualifiers. Scientology has not sued a medium for libel *in the United States,* "The common rubric is that it is easier to win a libel case outside the United States," Lubell said to one reporter. Scientology has certainly lodged it's share of libel litigation outside the U.S., but it is difficult to categorize because of the variety of situations and the distances involved . . . .

And there has been one domestic exception, one instance of recent libel litigation by the Church of Scientology against the free press within the U.S. borders. It is, depending on your viewpoint, a vigorous defense of religious freedom, or it is the granddaddy of all SLAPP suits and a serious threat to the freedom of the American press. Whichever view you ascribe to, one point is certain: you cannot think about writing about the followers of L.R. Hubbard without considering the case of *The Church of Scientology, International vs. Time Warner, Inc.*.

The story of *Time* magazine's controversial cover story and the behemoth litigation which followed begins long before its publication on May 6, 1991. Its author, *Time* associate editor Richard Behar, had a history of not only writing about Scientology but wrote of at least one other non-traditional belief system as well. Behar had graduated from NYU in 1982 and went to work for *Forbes* magazine shortly thereafter. At *Forbes* Behar wrote about Warner Erhard and the est movement and was threatened with litigation for that story. "I was served a subpoena" Behar told *Gauntlet*, "But we got it squashed."

While at *Forbes* Behar wrote "The Prophet & Profits of Scientology," a highly critical piece which centered on the financial aspects of the organization. Behar referred to the word religion only in quotes and categorized the principles of Scientology as "psychotherapy by lie detector". Scrupulously researched, the article erred in only one aspect: it concluded that that Scientology was on the wane, ending on a note of diminishing returns and predicted the dwindling of Hubbard's enterprise. In comparison, the cover story he published in *Time* five years later was called "The Thriving Cult of Greed and Power."

Behar stayed with *Forbes* until 1989. Between the years 1987 and 1989 he wrote a series of articles on the IRS for both *Forbes* and *Time* which prompted a congressional investigation. By the time Behar came to *Time* in 1989 he was a seasoned financial reporter. He brought with him an expertise in the labyrinthine byways of Scientology although Scientolgists would say he brought an ax to grind. He convinced his editors of the value of a cover story about the Church and began a massive investigation. Church officials refused to be interviewed. Scientology's response was to set hardball litigator Earle Cooley to the task of convincing *Time* editors and the magazine's counsel that Behar had an agenda. But the powers at *Time* demurred.

Several days after the article appeared *Time*'s lawyers were approached by the more tactful Jonathan Lubell. Lubell is a heavy gun, sophisticated and accomplished: he is best known for the "state of mind" doctrine which he won in a libel case against *60 Minutes*. In that case Lubell represented Lieut. Col. Anthony Herbert who maintained that he was defamed by the CBS news magazine. In a related motion that went to the Supreme Court, Lubell established that it was permissible to inquire into the "state of mind" of reporters, editors, or producers at the time they were preparing an article or television show. The decision was considered "devastating" to the press.

Lubell pointed out what he believed were gross inaccuracies in Behar's story and threatened to sue if matters were not corrected. "The church has been most interested in the truth . . . and the way to do that if you've gotten an adverse article, is to get a correction or a positive article or something like that." he said.

Again, *Time* demurred.

Immediately thereafter the Church of Scientology mounted a massive campaign to discredit the *Time* piece. The Church took out a different four-color, full-page ad in *USA Today* for two weeks straight. The first ad compared the Behar cover article with a 1936 *Time* cover that pronounced Adolf Hitler the 'messiah' of the Germans. "What Magazine Gets It Wrong In 1991?" the headlined asked. "The same one that was wrong in 1936." Scientology president Heber Jentzsch said that the campaign would cost "a couple of million dollars" but more recent estimates have put the figure at close to $5.4 million. The magazine, in response, said "*Time*'s article on Scientology speaks for itself and *Time* stands behind the article in its entirety."

In the fall of 1991 Scientology sued five of *Time*'s sources for the Behar article including former adherent Steven Fishman and his Florida psychiatrist, Uwe Geertz. The complaint stated that Fishman and Geertz had falsely claimed in the *Time* article that church officials had ordered Fishman to kill Geertz and then perform an "EOC" or "End Of Cycle" which is church jargon for suicide. According to Fishman, the order was given to cover up the churches role in a financial scam for which Fishman was convicted in 1988. At that time FBI evidence of Fishman's attempt to shift blame to the church was so strong that he also pleaded guilty to obstruction of justice. Fishman is now serving time for those crimes.

Scientology sought a million dollars each from Fishman and Geertz for their participation in the *Time* article. The complaint stated that the group "had enjoyed a good reputation as an organization dedicated to the dissemination and promotion of the Scientology religion."

Geertz attorney, Graham Berry told

Gauntlet, "Both *Time* magazine and ourselves allege that Scientology is libel proof, that their reputation is so bad that they are incapable of being defamed."

Did you actually use that tactic in the Geertz case?

"We made a motion for summary judgement which was denied," he said. Along with the motion Berry filed "maybe four or five thousand articles.

"We have on our data base here over eight thousand negative Scientology articles. Scientology calls that 'entheta press', Berry explains. "'Entheta Press' is press that is negative or critical of Scientology. 'Theta Press' is good press. And they keep statistics on it. So we, to support our defense of 'libel-proof', have accumulated over 8000 articles that are negative in regard to the Scientology organization. And we are continuing to compile the data on that, keep feeding the data base."

Of that database of 8000, is there any breakdown for how many of them might have originated in the United States?

"It would be a pure estimate on my part" cautions Mr. Berry, "but I would think at least half if not more."

Reader's Digest bought an excerpt from the *Time* article and published it in its October, 1991 issue under the title "A Dangerous Cult Goes Mainstream." *Reader's Digest* is a much larger publication with a worldwide readership. The Church, through its international franchises, sought injunctions against publication in France, Germany, the Netherlands, Italy and Switzerland. In almost all cases the motions were either dismissed or scheduled so far in the future as to make the injunctions moot. But an injunction barring distribution of the October issue was obtained in Lausanne, Switzerland on September 18, 1991.

Kenneth Tomlinson, worldwide editor in chief of the *Reader's Digest* said, "A publisher cannot accept a court prohibiting distribution of a serious journalistic piece. The court order violates freedom of speech and freedom of the press." And with ultimate *chutzputh* the *Reader's Digest* defied the court order on October 1, and mailed the October issue to its 326,000 Swiss subscribers.

Scientology, in its turn, filed a criminal complaint charging a "blatant violation" of the law. Michael Rindler, assistant to the

president of the Church of Scientology said, "When the article was first published in *Time* we went to some lengths to document its falsehoods. This *Reader's Digest* article is a digestion of that *Time* article with some remaining falsehoods that we had in fact documented as false and sent to *Reader's Digest.*"

The injunction was lifted in Lausanne on November 26, 1991. Not to be stopped, *Egiise de Scientologie de Lausanne* sued *Editions Selection du Reader's Digest f*or libel seeking $14,000 in damages. The difference between the dollar amounts in a Swiss libel litigation relative to an American libel litigation is fascinating to note. According to Jonathan Lubell the Swiss litigation is still pending.

"I do know it exists and I don't think it has been resolved," he told *Gauntlet*. The only reason I don't think it's resolved is because I suspect that somebody would have told me."

Church leaders continued to try and resolve the conflict in the United States without litigation. Proposals included that *Time* run a paid "advertorial" by the Church or that *Time* run an article on the Church's well-known positive role in such areas as drug rehabilitation. *Time* declined any such options and on April 27, 1992, nine days before the statute of limitations on a libel action ran out, the Church of Scientology, International sued Time Warner, Inc., Time Inc. Magazine Company and writer Richard Behar. The Church claimed that *Time* had knowingly assigned a biased writer to the article, had published false and defamatory statements and then refused to publish any corrections. The Church asked for $416 million in damages.

As the saying goes, Time Warner Inc. got the best lawyer money could buy. Floyd Abrams was co-counsel on the *Pentagon Papers* case which was argued in the Supreme Court for the *New York Times* and which earned Abrams a footnote in the history books as a consequence. His other Supreme Court appearances include *Nebraska Press Association v. Stuart* which virtually barred prior restraints on reporting of criminal trials, *Landmark Communications v. Virginia* which barred criminal prosecution of truthful reportage and *Harper & Row v. The Nation* which examined fair use under the Copyright Act. In *Minnick v. Mississippi* he established that, under the Fifth Amendment, a criminal conviction could not be sustained after counsel had been assigned on the basis of statements made outside the presence of counsel.

Professor Abrams has taught at Yale and Columbia Law Schools and is the William J. Brennan, Jr. Visiting Professor of Law and Journalism at the Columbia Graduate School of Journalism. His most celebrated defeat was losing an argument before the Supreme court against none other than Jonathan Lubell in the infamous and aforementioned "state of mind" trial. Together again, the formidable Floyd Abrams for *Time* Warner against the formidable Jonathan Lubell for The Church of Scientology, International promises to be a legal battle of epic proportions with the First Amendment merits of Freedom of Religion being pitted against the First Amendment guarantees of Freedom of The Press.

"The Thriving Cult of Greed and Power" has a lot of attitude. Behar must have known that Scientology hadn't sued in the U.S. for libel in over a decade, but he must have also known that this might be the straw that breaks the camels back. It is written in a take-no-prisoners prose, combative and unrelenting. In its own way a masterpiece of reductionism, taking the well-heeled horror stories and a few new ones and assembling his argument with a steel trap syntax. of 6000 words. The lawsuit centered around six particularly offensive paragraphs, one for each count in the complaint. One of those paragraphs reporting on church's labyrinthine business profile stated, "the Church of Spiritual Technology — listed $503 million in income just for 1987," a figure that the church sharply denies. The real income, they say, was $4 million, a discrepancy of almost a half a billion dollars. According to lawyers for the church, the $503 million figure was taken from an accountant worksheet's and Behar, a reporter with "considerable experience investigating financial matters" overlooked other papers in the file which clearly stated a $4 million income. Floyd Abrams gave *Gauntlet* a few minutes of his time to explain his client's position. His voice is stentorian and full of conviction:

"First, it's not defamatory. In libel law the first question is 'Is something defamatory?" That's the question we ask before we ask is it true? Is it defamatory in meaning? Does it hold someone up to shame and ridicule, etc. And [stating] the fact that someone makes a lot of money is not defamatory."

Is that your position or is that a tenet of libel law?

"No, no. Let me state straight libel law first," said a distinctly professorial Abrams. "Libel law is as I've defined it to you: The first issue in libel law is 'Is the statement at issue something which holds the person about whom you're speaking up to shame or hatred or ridicule'. That's a fact. It is my view that saying that Scientology makes more rather than less money a year is not defamatory."

Mr. Abrams also said that Behar had a "good faith basis" for using that figure and I asked him to explain.

"Well, a good faith basis means that he certainly believed the figure to be true, which is a defense in itself, but a good faith basis means also that there was some documentation that led him to believe it. And there was such documentation. Someone made a lot of money? Absolutely not. He said that they were very prosperous and they are."

Gauntlet discovered the $503 million figure in a book by *Gauntlet* contributor Michael Newton (see "Season of The Witch" in this issue). In his 1993 Avon paperback *Raising Hell*, Newton includes a chapter on L. Ron Hubbard's brief affiliation with Aleister Crowley's mystical Ordo Templi Orientis (OTO) in the 1940s. In the final paragraph of that chapter on page 191, Newton writes, "Most cults of personality die with their leader, but Scientology has proved itself an exception, hanging tough with a reported income of $503 million dollars in 1987 alone."

"Anything I put in about Scientology there, if it didn't relate directly to Hubbard and the OTO, it all came from that issue on Scientology that *Time* magazine did . . . " Newton told *Gauntlet*.

Such information can be used to increase the damage claim in a libel case. According to Jonathan Lubell, "It is a indication of why these false statements become so damaging because not only do they appear in *Time* magazine for that week and are read by people then, but now it's in a book which is certainly much more of a historical record."

Floyd Abrams has a different view,

"Look, it doesn't hurt for a few reasons. If it were part of the case we certainly have a defense to it on the ground that it was not said with Actual Malice . . . and if it were part of the case, we would then take discovery of Scientology's very secret books to find out what their books reveal about it. But I think you have to be careful not to accept as given what Scientology says about itself."

But most importantly, Abrams concludes, is that it is "not part of this case because it's already been thrown out by the Judge."

Of the six original counts, two were recently dismissed by the court because they were not "of and concerning" the Church of Scientology International. The paragraph that refers to the $503 million figure was one of the two counts that were dismissed. That leaves four points of contention which Abrams must continue to argue.

"It's a busy case and it's going to get busier in the summer . . . " he said. "Discovery is underway, and there is a cutoff date of September 30. There will be an end to the pre-trial discovery with respect to Actual Malice. At that time we will ask for Summary Judgement."

You're going to ask for Summary Judgement on September 30?

"Sometime after that date. Within a month. If we win, the case will be over; if we lose . . . then we will begin very probing discovery on the nature of Scientology.

"The other side is aware that we are going to ask for Summary Judgement in the fall." Then Abrams reveals, "There is a counterclaim in this case. Richard Behar has a counter-claim against Scientology based on all the things that he's been put through."

Behar wrote that he was harassed during the preparation of the *Time* article. *Has the alleged harassment continued?*

"I can't comment on that," said Mr. Abrams. "That's the only thing I don't want to talk about."

Abrams said " . . . a very probing discovery on the nature of Scientology." The mind reels. A Summary Judgement is a very difficult thing to get which means that, in all probability, this case is likely to go to a jury. For the record, Abrams does not think this case will go that far, "I'm confident," he said but added slowly,

"Sometimes you win; sometimes you don't." If the case is held for jury, the discovery process will permit some very deep explorations into the finances and practices and beliefs of Scientology, a prospect that Scientology is probably not too thrilled about.

Recently the Church dropped its claims against Fishman and Geertz in lieu of having its celebrity members deposed. Six process servers infiltrated a Scientology Christmas Party at its Celebrity Headquarters in Los Angeles to deliver deposition subpoenas to celebrity Scientologists Julliette Lewis, Kelly Preston Travolta, Isaac Hayes and Maxine Nightingale. Also served with a subpoena was actor Charles Durning who is not a Scientologist but who appeared at the Christmas party dressed as Santa Claus. The creative legal mind that conceived of that crafty tactical turnaround was Graham Berry. Hypnotically well-spoken, Berry mixes a world class erudite vocabulary with a liquid smooth accent of his native New Zealand, sort of a cross between William Safire and Crockadile Dundee. He clearly enjoys his work.

"We had received a copy of [an] advertising flyer for that particular day and those people were listed on that flyer and so our process servers were armed with subpoenas for those persons and, indeed, for others who we thought might be on hand such as [reclusive Church leader] David Miscavaige, Tom Cruise . . .

"John Travolta was one we wished to subpoena. When Kelly Preston Travolta was served she actually screamed; she turned on her heels [and] ran into her dressing room and hid."

The *Time* article said that "High level defectors claim that Travolta has long feared that if he defected, details of his sexual life would be made public."

Graham Berry explains that, "John Travolta had, of course, been the subject of statements in the *Time* magazine article, and we wished to inquire as to the truth of those [statements] as well.

"This is an action of a defamation," he continues. "We wanted further testimony that the statements alleged to be defamatory were not 'of and concerning' the Church of Scientology, International and did not cause the Church of Scientology, International any damage. That when these celebrities thought of the Church of

Scientology they didn't think of the Church of Scientology, International, a management church entity, but they thought of the Scientology organization generally and generically, and that as a consequence of reading the *Time* magazine article, or those portions argued to be defamatory, they did not diminish their contributions to Scientology at all. And therefore," he concludes, "the Church of Scientology, International was not damaged.

Then he delivers the punch line: "We were also aware that Scientology celebrities had never been served before.

So it was an original idea on your part?

"Yes, as a result of my expert consultants teaching me to think more like a Scientologist and less like a lawyer. And," Mr. Berry understates, "we expected it to um . . . to cause some consternation on the part of the Scientology organization."

"We fully expected them to approach the court to prevent the depositions from taking place. Which they did and which they lost."

On the eve of trial, lawyers for Scientology made a motion to dismiss their own case.

Did Berry expect the tactic to work as successfully as it did?

"The dismissal of the suit," says Berry, "came as a complete surprise."

In a motion seeking sanctions against Berry, Jonathan Lubell claimed that the attorney's conduct "was a calculated and relentless resort to false accusations, frivolous arguments, defiance of court rules and orders, and tactics designed not to defend against a claim but to inflict needless expense and effort." These words are eerily familiar to anyone acquainted with Scientology's litigious narrative. This is language that is very similar in substance to claims usually made *against* the church.

I asked Berry if he saw a similar sense of irony.

"There is a phrase in Scientology called 'crim-mind'," he said dryly, "which could be loosely interpreted as 'The pot calling the kettle black.'"

Following the dismissal Berry filed a new motion for sanctions seeking attorneys fees for Geertz. "And in connection with the motion for sanctions we believed we had to establish that the lawsuit lacked any proper basis in law or in fact and was pursued for an improper purpose. And it

that connection some forty-one declarations have been filed, many of them referring to upper level materials. And Fishman had earlier filed what he believed were a full set of the upper level materials. The OT materials. CSI moved to seal these documents on the basis that they contained trade secrets of the church."

I asked Graham Berry to define "OT materials"

"Operating thetans one through eight," he said. "OT 3, for example, that is the material that deals with 'The Incident', as they put it."

The Incident?

"'The Incident' is the explanation of how the earth came to be populated [according to Scientology].

"CSI had appealed the district courts refusal to seal certain declarations that are on the court record — the so called upper level materials — and that appeal is to be heard and argued on the second of August," said Mr. Berry.

The Church of Scientology notoriously protects its "sacred doctrines." Indeed, this practice has been a central factor to the charge that Scientology is a "cult". A "cult" maintains a secret agenda, according to church detractors, and this information is available to very few people. Graham Berry's tactics ensured that if the Church of Scientology wished to press its defamation lawsuit against Fishman & Geertz, it would have to do so at the expense of its trade secrets and its treasured celebrity adherents. L. Ron Hubbard's words echo: "Don't ever tamely submit to an investigation of us." said Hubbard. "Make it rough, rough on attackers all the way . . . "

"He's engaged," said Floyd Abrams of his colleague, Graham Berry.

The dismissal of the Fishman and Geertz complaints may bode well for Abram's defense of *Time* magazine.

"The deposition testimony given by the Rev. Lynn Farney, secretary of Church of Scientology, International, and documents he provided demonstrated that because the so-called *USA Today* Remedial Advertising Campaign in the approximate amount of $5.4 million was paid by Church of Scientology, International from a non-recourse grant from the International Association of Scientologists, that it was not a loan and that it did not have to be repaid." Berry states. "A large portion of CSI claimed damages [against *Time*] were, in fact, monies that had been advanced by other individuals with no obligation to be repaid."

Berry acquired copies of all the various Scientology entities applications for tax exempt status. According to this combative litigator, review of the annual finance statements contained in those applications for the relevant years immediately prior to and after publication of the *Time* article indicated that Scientology was not financially hurt by the article. Berry married that information with statements made by David Miscavaige, in his rebuttal of the *Premiere* magazine article, that press attacks did not cause Scientology any damage.

"We pursued discovery in the form of documents and testimonies as to any lost income on the part of CSI as a result of *Time* magazine. Rather than provide us with such evidence, if it existed, CSI chose to stipulate that their claim for damages in the Geertz case, did not include any claim for lost income presumably because they couldn't prove it."

Floyd Abrams finds that action to be very revealing. "In the California case of Geertz and Fishman . . . Scientology said that it basically lost no money . . . and that means that this $416 million is entirely punitive damages. They're saying that this is how much *Time* should be *punished*"" (emphasis Abrams).

Referring to the extraordinary sum that Scientology is seeking from *Time*, Abrams avers, "The $416 million dollar figure? It's nonsense. It's always been nonsense."

Berry asserts that the conduct of the legal opposition and church officials was less than professional. "They were accusing me of being a homosexual," he said in a March 9, declaration filed with the court. He maintains that a male Scientology official "blew me a kiss, threw a doily at me and said I might be needing that weekend." Additionally, Berry said, Kendrick Moxon of Moxon & Bowles, Scientology's main legal counsel, "made further remarks accusing me of outrageous sexual activities . . . ."

And so the stage is set for a legal battle which pits the First Amendment against itself, a battle upon which careers and reputations will ride and fortunes will be won or lost.

I asked Floyd Abrams if there were any Constitutional issues which might mark this case for the Supreme Court. Certainly both litigants have the money to go to all the way.

"Yes," said Mr. Abrams, "and probably the inclination if it came to that. I am confident that if somehow we were to lose this case, we would appeal it and we would appeal it on First Amendment grounds but that doesn't mean that there's anything unique about the case. The First Amendment affords a lot of protection for journalistic organizations when they engage in criticism of public figures like Scientology. So yes this case is suffused with First Amendment interests in the sense that it's very important that publications be able to report about controversial organizations. On the other hand I can't think of anything at this moment which I think is likely to uh . . . likely to ah . . . Let me think a minute.

"Let me go back one step," he said thoughtfully. "There is a possibility that the issue of whether the article is "of and concerning" the Church of Scientology International might be an independent issue for some appeal some day. You remember the motion that we won on with respect to two passages? Now, those were dismissed on the grounds that while they were about Scientology, they were not about this particular entity, the Church of Scientology International. And that sort of issue is a significant Constitutional one because in my view there is broad First Amendment protection for criticism of any church or any entity that holds itself out to be a church. We don't allow what are called 'group libel' cases to be brought in this country. That is to say we don't allow all people of Polish descent or all Jews to bring an action or have someone sue on their behalf. And we certainly don't allow all people who believe in Scientology, or who believe in any other cult, to bring an action on their behalf. Now one of our arguments was 'That's what this is about. This is an article about Scientology, that is critical of Scientology and you just can't have a Scientology lawsuit.' Well the other side said, 'It isn't a Scientology [lawsuit]. This is [about] the Church of Scientology International'. And the Judge said at this time in the case I going to throw out these two portions and we're going to leave the other four portions for a jury to decide. And my only point to you now is that sort of issue is one which might be of special interest on appeal at some later time. Right now I'm very comfortable and confident that we won't be the ones appealing in this case.

_____

Richard Cusick is a freelance journalist and *writer. He co-publishes and writes the alternative comic,* **Something Different.**

[The writer would like to thank Delaynie Cusick, Robert Carson, Dan Roos and Mike Mangan for their help in preparing this article.]

SCIENTOLOGY UPDATE

(The following excerpt is from a bootlegged version of the 1985 60 Minutes broadcast called "Scientology Update". We have no way of verifying its authenticity. Parts of this transcript is corroborated by portions of the documents provided by the Utah Federal Court. The section contained herein includes some of the language that New Era claimed violated the settlement agreement with Omar Garrison.)

WALLACE: In the course of reporting this story it became apparent to us that the Rev. Jentzsch is persuaded that *60 Minutes* itself is somehow involved with others in a plot to destroy Scientology.

REV. JENTZSCH: You may not like our religion. You may try to castigate it. You may try to denegrate it. You may try to bring down the image of Mr. Hubbard but you cannot change what has happened in the hearts and minds of every single Scientologist who has had benefit from this man and what he's done.

WALLACE: And ...

REV. JENTZSCH: We're here. We're here for all the centuries to come. All the centuries to come. After *60 Minutes* disappears and the electrons disappear off of the tapes we'll still be here.

(CUT TO GARRISON)

GARRISON: Everyone who has taken these courses come out with a super-ego and with a - with a truculent, if you will, a truculent view of anyone who dares disagree. Because the person who disagrees is perceived as what they call a 'suppresive person'.

WALLACE: An enemy.

GARRISON: And must be dealt with as such.

WALLACE: That's the gospel according to L. Ron Hubbard.

GARRISON: That's the dark side of Scientology.

WALLACE: Omar Garrison set out to write the Hubbard biography. According to church legend Hubbard is a man of extrodinary accomplishment. But Garrison says that he has learned that there is less to Hubbard than has painted over the years in church literature.

WALLACE: He fought in five theatres in World War II?

GARRISON: Not True

WALLACE: He commanded a squadron of corvettes?

GARRISON: Not True.

WALLACE: He was crippled and blinded in war?

GARRISON: Not true.

WALLACE: He was the first casualty of the war?

GARRISON: Not true.

WALLACE: Flown home in the Secratary of the Navy's private plane?

GARRISON (chuckles): Not true.

As we go to press *Gauntlet* has received over 180 pages from the Federal Court in Utah regarding Civil Complaint No. 86-C-0144W which is *"New Era Publications vs. Omar V. Garrison, CBS Inc., Mike Wallace, Allan Maraynes and John Does one through ten"*. Far from the casual complaint that CBS would have us believe, a brief review of the file shows a claim for damages in excess of ten million dollars in a court case that dragged on for two years. New Era Publications strongly asserted, in part, that Omar Garrison violated the terms of his settlement agreement by speaking about L. Ron Hubbard and that Allan Maraynes and Mike Wallace "were informed by Garrison both prior to and during the interview of Garrison that he was bound by provisions of confidentiality pursuant to the Settlement Agreement." CBS, Wallace and Maraynes just as vehemently "deny each and every allegation" of wrongdoing.

This was not a libel action. New Era did not accuse *60 Minutes* of being wrong in its report; it accused CBS and its agents of conspiring to break Omar Garrison's contract. Whatever complaint New Era had was resolved in a settlement conference in 1988. Perhaps as part of that settlement CBS agreed not to the distribute tape nor transcript of the offending segment in the future, a segment wherein no statement is questioned as libelious, a segment which CBS claims to stand behind one hundred percent. That is pure speculation on my part.

No retraction is proferred and apparently none is needed. If *60 Minutes* retracted the story then a legal hold might be understandable: "We were wrong. We can't distribute that tape." Unlike the response *Gauntlet* received from Roy Brunett, that is reasonable and lucid.

Suppose we were told "We can't distribute that tape as part of a settlement agreement with New Era. The case had nothing to do with libel and we stand behind the story." That too is lucid but particularly spineless. All of that valuable information is no longer available to the public because the offended party slapped CBS around in court.

Or perhaps the entire show is on hold for reasons we don't know. We do know that, short of a retraction, there is no good reason to mitigate the standards of serious journalism.

Mr. Yambrusic, an attorney for the U.S. Copyright Office explained that under Section 107 of the Copyright Act the doctrine of "Fair Use" allows brief excerpts of published news reporting to be reproduced for the purposes of commentary or review. In that circumstance the copyright holder might be obligated to produce the published materials for review. But, Mr. Yambrusic is quick to point out, "performance is not publishing". If all CBS did was broadcast the material to 30 million viewers then that material is essentially "unpublished".

If, on the other hand, CBS distributed a tape or a transcript of this material then perhaps the material can be considered published and perhaps the doctrine of Fair Use applies.

So as we go to press the question recurs: What was the date that the legal hold was put in place? Did CBS distribute tapes and transcripts through its contracted transcription service before the material was placed on hold? If they did then that material must be kept available for review and excerpt. And if CBS didn't distribute any materials then it is possible that *60 Minutes* (and other broadcast news medium) can "stand behind the story" without having to produce the broadcast material for review. No accountability. In defiance of common sense.

Gauntlet would like to explore all its options in this story including the legal option. *Gauntlet* contacted an attorney who was well-versed in broadcast law and who also had specific experience in going to court against *60 Minutes*. Discounting the David and Goliath aspect inherent in the phrase *"Gauntlet Publications vs. CBS, Inc.,"*, the attorney felt that this was a "significant First Amendment issue" and was anxious to explore the legal possibilities with us.

These matters will be comprehensively covered in the next issue of *Gauntlet*.

The ReLiGiOuS SYMPoSiUM on CULTS
by Joe Lee

THEY HAVE GATHERED, THE BLESSED, THE REVERAND FATHERS, RABBIS, MINISTERS OF THEIR RESPECTIVE MAINSTREAM FAITHS TO DEFINE AND, IF NEED BE, CASTIGATE THE RISE OF THE FRINGE CULTS THAT HAVE SEEMED TO APPEAL TO MANY IN OUR BELEAGURED AND FRACTURED COMMUNITIES.

YEP, THESE ARE THE BOYS OF THE OLD SCHOOL (SOME OLDER THAN OTHERS, OF COURSE) AND OFTEN THEIR ONLY HOPE OF A CONCENSUS IS ON WHO DOESN'T BELONG. SO, WHAT'S THE POOP ON THESE NEW BOYS, THE CULTS?

THEY ARE TERRIBLY DOGMATIC, ADHERING TO THE SCRIPTURAL INTERPRETATIONS OF OF ONE SUPPOSED 'INFALLIBLE' SOURCE.

THEY PURSUE THEIR EXCLUSIONARY AIMS BY BLAMING OTHER GROUPS FOR THEIR PERSONAL FAILURES, OFTEN TERMING THOSE GROUPS 'DEVILS'!

THEY FOLLOW A CHARISMATIC LEADER WITH SELF-PROCLAIMED MESSIANIC TENDENCIES.

MIND-MANIPULATING GROUPS:

ARE YOU, A FRIEND, OR FAMILY MEMBER A VICTIM?

Deception lies at the core of mind-manipulating groups. Therefore, many victims of such groups are not fully aware of the extent to which they have been abused and exploited. These victims may be members of religious cults, or certain large group awareness trainings. The following statements often characterize such groups. Comparing these statements to the group with which you, a friend, or a family member is involved may help you determine if this involvement is cause for concern. If you check any of these items as characterizing the group in question, and particularly if you check most of them, it may be advisable for you to begin to ask questions about the group and its relationship to you or your loved one.

[ ] The group is focused on a living charismatic leader to whom members seem to display excessively zealous, unquestioning commitment.

[ ] The group is preoccupied with bringing in new members.

[ ] The group is preoccupied with making money.

[ ] Questioning, doubt, and dissent are discouraged or even punished.

[ ] Mind-numbing techniques (for example: meditation, chanting, speaking in tongues, debilitating work routines) are used to suppress doubts about the group or its leader(s).

[ ] The group's leadership dictates — sometimes in great detail— how members should think, act and feel (for example: members must get permission from leaders to date, to change jobs, to get married; leaders may prescribe what types of clothes to wear, how much and what type of makeup to put on, when and if to have children; how to discipline children, etc.).

[ ] The group is elitist, claiming a special, exalted status for itself, its leader(s) and members (for example: the leader is considered the Messiah or an avatar; the group and/or the leader has a special mission to save humanity).

[ ] The group has a polarized, "we-they" mentality that causes conflict with the wider society.

[ ] The group's leader is not accountable to any authorities (as are, for example, military commanders and ministers, priests, monks, and rabbis of mainstream denominations).

[ ] The group teaches or implies that its supposedly exalted ends justify means (for example: collecting money for bogus charities) that members would have considered unethical before joining the group.

[ ] The group's leadership induces guilt feelings in members in order to control them.

[ ] Members' subservience to the group causes them to cut ties with family, friends, and personal pre-group goals and interests.

[ ] Members are expected to devote inordinate amounts of time to the group.

[ ] Members are encouraged or required to live and/or socialize only with other group members.

Reprinted from Cults and Psychological Abuse available from the American Family Foundation (P.O. Box 2265 Bonita Springs, FL 33959).

The Ant Hill Kids

Paul Kaihla and Ross Laver with Ann McLaughlin and Barry Came

Roch Theriault saw himself as God's emissary.
But to his victims, he was a beast from hell.

One psychiatrist recently described him as "a Renaissance man" with a "bright, inquisitive and sensitive" nature. Another said that he possesses "an intelligence that is much higher than average." But on Sept. 28, 1988, Roch Theriault displayed none of those admirable qualities. A self-styled prophet who lived with eight "wives" and two male disciples on an isolated commune 100 km northeast of Toronto, Theriault, 41, had spent the morning drinking and picking fights with his worshipful followers. Suddenly, he assumed an eerie calm — and, as he had many times in the past, asked whether any of his disciples required "medical treatment." Within minutes, 32-year-old Solange Boilard, who complained of stomach problems, lay naked on a wooden table in one of the commune's log cabins. Wearing red velour robes and a gold-covered crown — the symbols of his proclaimed role as "King of the Israelites" — Theriault punched Boilard in the stomach, jammed a plastic tube up her rectum and performed a crude enema with molasses and olive oil. Then, as she lay silent, he sliced open her abdomen with a freshly sharpened knife and ripped off a piece of her intestines with his bare hands. The "operation" completed, Theriault ordered another follower,

Gabrielle Lavallee, to stitch up the gaping wound with a needle and thread. A day later, Boilard died in almost unimaginable agony — a hapless victim of what police in Ontario and Quebec describe as the most bizarre and violent cult in the history of Canadian crime.

In mid-January, in a small Kingston, Ont., courtroom, some of the gruesome details of the cult's shadowy life finally came to light when Theriault, now 45, pleaded guilty to a charge of second-degree murder in connection with Boilard's death. And since then, in a wide-ranging investigation, *Maclean's* has pieced together the sordid story of Theriault's twisted cult — a shocking 11-year saga that claimed the lives of at least two people, left several others permanently maimed, and inflicted severe emotional scars on many of the 25 children Theriault fathered with eight of his concubines.

Since his conviction in October, 1989, for hacking off Lavallee's right arm with a dull meat cleaver — an act he committed nine months after she helped him dispose of Boilard's body — Theriault has been imprisoned in Kingston's maximum-security Millhaven Institution. Only after his arrest on four assault charges involving Lavallee did another cult member step forward and tell police about

Boilard's death — which had remained secret for more than a year. Now serving a life sentence for Boilard's murder, with no possibility of parole until the year 2000, Theriault was placed in protective custody last week because of death threats by other inmates. During his court appearance on Jan. 18, he expressed remorse for "traumatizing, mutilating and inflicting suffering on the members of my entourage," for forcing them to live "in the slavery of that hell," and for "the events that led to the premature death of Solange Boilard." Speaking in his native French, he added that his arrest and incarceration had helped him "to grow as a person" and to realize the error of his ways.

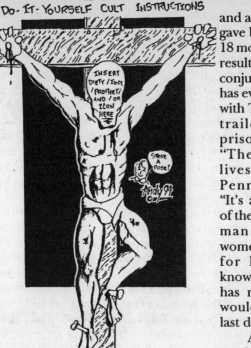

In fact, many of the authorities who have dealt with Theriault's case remain convinced that he still exercises psychological control over some of his followers. One of those investigators is Robert Penny, executive director of the Kawartha-Haliburton Children's Aid Society, which seized 22 of Theriault's children and eventually found adoptive homes for 20 of them. In an interview last week, Penny noted that three of Theriault's former cult disciples — Francine Laflamme, 36, Chantal Labrie, 34, and Nicole Ruel, 35 — now operate a bakery together and live in adjacent rented cabins less than a kilometer from Milhaven's gates. Laflamme, a slim woman with bright brown eyes

and a girlish smile, gave birth to a son 18 months ago, the result of one of the conjugal visits she has every six weeks with Theriault in a trailer on the prison grounds. "The commune lives on," said Penny bluntly. "It's an indication of the power of the man — those women are there for him. Who knows whether he has reformed? I wouldn't bet my last dollar on it."

After meeting a *Maclean's* reporter last week in her three-room cottage, Laflamme spoke to Theriault and gained his consent to be interviewed. But late in the week, the deputy federal Correctional Services commissioner for Ontario, Andrew Graham, banned Theriault from speaking to reporters. A spokesman for the department, Jacques Belanger, described Graham's order as "unusual", but he said that prison officials did not want Theriault to be distracted from the voluntary psychiatric treatment he is receiving. Added Belanger: "There's also a lot of concern about the psychological power he has over some of his people. Former members of his sect could still be influenced by things he says."

Laflamme is clearly among the most devoted of the followers. In addition to the boy born 18 months ago, she and Theriault have had four other children, now aged eight, six, five and three. Authorities seized her first child in 1985 and removed the second from her four days after its birth in 1987. "The Children's Aid gave me two choices: stay with Roch and lose your child, or leave Roch and keep him," Laflamme recalled in an interview. "I decided I wasn't going to leave him, so they took my child. It was a very difficult decision — I wanted to kill those people. But I agreed for personal reasons."

'Monster': Five years after she made that decision, Laflamme remains "madly in love" with Theriault and is anxiously awaiting his release. She says that the cult leader's periods of "craziness" were the products of excessive drinking and an unhappy childhood at the hands of an abusive father. "People try to make Roch sound like a monster, like a butcher," she complained. "But he is not that. Most of the time he was not drinking and performing his operations. He was a marvelous man who was full of passion, intelligence, and originality. He loved to laugh and dance."

In fact, people who grew up with Theriault and knew the family well agree that he had a difficult childhood. Born in a tiny village near Chicoutimi in 1947 to Hyacinthe Theriault, a housepainter, and homemaker Pierette Tremblay, Theriault grew up in Thetford-Mines, an asbestos-mining town 239 km northeast of Montreal. His father, neighbors recall, was a staunch supporter of an ultraright Catholic fringe group known as the "white berets", which opposes liberal trends in the Church. Said Roger Beaulieu, 66, who first met the family in 1962: "Every Sunday, we'd see old man Theriault put on his white beret and troop the family off to their meetings. People around here didn't like that too much."

Castration: Theriault's parents still live in the home where he was raised — a white cement-block bungalow, which now is dilapidated and hidden from the road by overgrown shrubbery. But they have had no contact with their son for years — and display no interest in re-establishing ties. "I don't want to talk about him or hear his name," Hyacinthe Theriault shouted at a **Maclean's** reporter who visited the house last week. "I raised seven children and only one of them turned out like that," he added before slamming shut the porch door, sending two scraggly cats running for cover behind a woodpile.

Leon Vachon, 48, a former next-door neighbor of the Theriaults who remained friends with Roch until the mid-1970s, recalls that the family had little money and that the atmosphere in the household was "abusive." When Roch was a teenager, Vachon said, he and his three brothers would play a game they called "bone" with their father. "They would sit at the kitchen table with their heavy boots on and kick each other's shins until one of them gave in," said Vachon, who recalls witnessing the contest on several occasions. "The mother was no better. You would hear her screaming at the kids from three-quarters of a mile down the road, like no other person could scream."

Perhaps because he wanted to escape the memories of those years, Theriault has since provided several fantastic accounts of his childhood. In a 1983 autobiography published in French, he wrote of growing up in the bush in northern Quebec where he learned to talk to the animals and the trees, and came to regard himself as some sort of medicine man. Interviewed in prison in 1990 by prominent Toronto psychiatrist Andrew Malcolm, Theriault described a childhood encounter that the doctor concluded was "a deliberate attempt at myth-making." Wrote Malcolm in a report to provincial officials: "He said when he was a child he had been gambling in the muskeg in the Far North when he suddenly came face-to-face with a mother bear with two cubs. She rolled him over in the same way that she rolled her cubs and in this idyllic circumstance, he spent the entire afternoon."

Theriault also told Malcolm that when he was eight he discovered that he had the power to heal sick people — beginning with a friend who had broken his teeth. "Following this experience," the psychiatrist recorded Theriault as saying, "he intentionally studied the mosses, the herbs and the plants, and he refined his skills as a healer. He soon was able to castrate cattle and pigs without the loss of any blood."

Satan: In Thetford-Mines, however, Theriault is remembered as a popular teenager who spent many evenings drinking with his large group of friends in local clubs. Several of his former chums use the word "brilliant" to describe him, adding that he had "the gift of the gab." Said Andre Gregoire: "He was a good looking man with piercing blue eyes. He never had any problems getting girls, that's for sure."

In November, 1967, Theriault married one of those girls — Francine Grenier, one of Leon Vachon's cousins by marriage. A talented woodcarver and carpenter, Theriault built a quaint Swiss-style house down the road from his parents, and fathered two boys with his wife. To support his family, he sold a variety of handcarving products: beer mugs carved from tree limbs, ornate wooden clocks and trophies.

But just as his circumstances seemed to be improving, Theriault's behavior became increasingly erratic. Early in his marriage, he had insisted that his wife wear long dresses whenever she appeared in public. But before long, he allowed her to wear miniskirts, and asked his in-laws if he could open a nudist camp on their nearby farmland — a request they flatly refused. An even more puzzling transformation took place in his mid-20s after he underwent surgery in Montreal for an unspecified stomach condition. Gregoire remembers how Theriault began to study medical textbooks "cover to cover", and lectured his friends endlessly about human anatomy. Similarly, when neighbors formed a committee to fight city hall over the issuing of construction permits, Theriault memorized the municipal code "from A to Z," Vachon said. He added: "If there was one weakness in the law, he would find it and exploit it to its fullest. He was good."

Also during his 20s, Theriault joined the local branch of the Aramis Club, a Catholic group that raises money for charity and organizes social events. He soon worked his way up to head of the initiation committee, but gradually his colleagues began to question his suitability for the role. "He wanted to change the rituals," said Gregoire. "He wanted the new members to wear the image of Satan on their backs and all kinds of weird stuff. Roch is a guy who always wanted to become the leader, but just as he would get to the top, people turned on him because he tried to change things and bring in weird ideas."

Stripped of his position in the club, Theriault lost interest in the organization. He announced that he had joined the Seventh-day Adventist Church, and he began to stroll around town in a hooded ankle-length monk's frock. He left the local chapter of the church after a quarrel over the leadership, which he had sought. At that point, Theriault's marriage fell apart. And in 1977, he moved alone to Ste-Marie-de-Beauc, a sleepy town 45 km northeast of Thetford-Mines. He rented space in a two-story clapboard building, opened a homeopathic clinic and began passing out flyers advertising seminars to help people quit smoking.

Almost immediately, Theriault became the focal point of an expanding circle of organic-food enthusiasts and followers of alternative medicine. He married one of them, 26-year-old Gisele Lafrance. Among his other admirers were Maryse and Jacques Giguere, a married couple, both 25, who lived one street away with their newborn daughter. Within a year of meeting Theriault, Jacques Giguere recalled last week, he quit his job as a construction worker and Maryse resigned her secretarial position at the local Vachon cake factory. Drawn by his charisma, they turned over all of their material possessions to Theriault and moved into his house.

Rages: And then one day in 1978, the group disappeared. Theriault had announced to his 17 followers — four men, nine women and four children — that the world was going to end soon "in a shower of boulder-hailstones." The only way to survive Armageddon, he said, was to escape the evils of society and revert back to nature. He led his flock to a remote valley on the Gaspe Peninsula, ordered them to cut all ties with the outside world and assigned biblical names to every group member, taking Moses for himself. Proclaiming himself God's emissary, he told his disciples that the road to heaven would be filled with suffering — but that it was God's will.

The suffering began after the first year of communal life, when Theriault began drinking beer and liquor heavily. While drunk, he flew into violent rages, assaulting adults and children alike. Said Giguere: "He said the children were disobedient and the devil had to be beaten out of them. He justified beating our kids because he said we were too spiritually weak to do it ourselves."

Harem: Indeed, the commune members were worn down both physically and mentally. Working long hours to survive in the wilderness, they suffered from exhaustion and malnutrition and became almost totally dependent on Theriault's erratic leadership. And although Theriault repaid that devotion with savagery, his disciples rarely fought back. Recalls Giguere: "When Theriault sobered up the next day, he'd cry like a baby with his head at his feet, begging God to stop commanding him to commit such brutality." But while he promised that he beatings would stop, they only grew worse. "I think I understand what a battered wife experiences," Giguere said. "She keeps getting beaten, but her husband begs for forgiveness. She wants to believe him and can't bear to leave her family."

The wild recklessness of Theriault's commune came to a head one night in March, 1981. While partying, the members left their children in the care of Guy Veer, a mentally deficient 23-year-old who had disappeared weeks earlier from a Quebec City hospital. They returned to find that Giguere's two-year-old son, Samuel, had been badly beaten. The child was not passing urine, so Theriault "operated" on his genitals. The next day, the toddler died. Theriault blamed Veer for the death and, months later, tried him for murder before a kangaroo court, which found the accused not guilty by reason of insanity. Still, Theriault decided that Veer needed to be taught a lesson — and removed both of his testicles. The commune leader also instructed his followers to tell outsiders that Samuel had been trampled by a horse. But the truth eventually emerged and Quebec police raided the camp. In 1982, seven commune members were convicted of crimes related to the child's death and Veer's castration. Theriault himself served 18 months at Orsainville Prison near Quebec City.

Released in 1984, Theriault collected his followers and moved to Ontario to avoid a Quebec parole order that barred him from associating with fellow cult members. They purchased 200 acres of land in a broad swath of wilderness near Burnt River, Ont., about 100 km northeast of Toronto. Although many of the commune members drew welfare, they also ran a business called the Ant Hill Kids, selling handicrafts and baked goods to locals. According to Laflamme, Theriault chose that name because "we were like busy ants, all working together."

By then, Theriault had established a substantial personal harem. He had gradually made all but one of the nine female members his exclusive "wives", keeping them in an almost constant state of pregnancy. In Quebec, Theriault had presided over the "marriage" of the unfortunate Boilard, who went by the biblical name Rachel, to cult member Claude Ouelette. But she soon became one of Theriault's concubines, and bore three of the leader's children between 1980 and 1986. Ouelette remained in the group as a celibate disciple. "Roch was always telling us that it had to be that way because he was like Abraham in the Bible," recalled a bitter Lavallee, who gave birth to two of Theriault's offspring. "He had to have many wives and children to keep his tribe going."

Apparently, Theriault drew some of his inspiration from Alex Joseph, a polygamist and commune leader in Big Water, Utah, near the Arizona border. Now 55, and a frequent subject of articles in supermarket tabloids, Joseph lives with at least nine wives and their 20 children, and cites the teachings of the Mormon Church and the Old Testament as justification for his unconventional lifestyle. According to police, Theriault made at least three visits to Joseph's colony in the 1980s; during one of them, the American gave the Ant Hill Kids patriarch a gold-colored crown and named him "King of the Israelites" in an elaborate ceremony. Said Ontario Provincial Police Det. Bob Bowen, who investigated Theriault's cult for three years: "It was an extremely important moment for Roch. After that, he began wearing the crown with his robes and acting very imperial."

Meanwhile, commune life in Ontario grew stranger by the week. Lavallee says that Theriault would take two or more of his wives to bed at once and hold contests to see which one would have the most orgasms. In the same competitive spirit, Giguere says that Theriault frequently held outlandish gladiator games for his amusement. He would draw a large square in the dirt and order two naked disciples, men or women, to step inside. At his command, they would fight for three-minute intervals, which he timed with a stopwatch. Said Giguere: "Roch counted the points—one for a punch, minus one for stepping outside of the line. The winners had to fight someone else, and the games could go on for hours."

Perversion: Gradually, however, the isolated commune's activities began to draw attention — and frequent inspections — from staff of the Kawartha-Haliburton Children's Aid Society. Said CAS executive director Penny: "We became increasingly concerned about Roch's mental state. His personality seemed to be disintegrating." On Dec. 6, 1985, CAS workers and police raided the camp and seized all 14 children there. Over the next two years, as Theriault's "wives" gave birth to nine more

off-spring, authorities removed each new infant. According to a 1987 family court ruling that made 21 of the children wards of the Crown, Theriault allegedly forced several of the youngsters to perform sex acts on him. Court records quote a six-year-old girl saying that Theriault "likes me to pull on his penis and make white stuff come out of it. Everybody is doing it, including Mom. Mom and me take turns." The records also indicate that Theriault instructed one boy to masturbate a male adult. And when one of Theriault's sons requested sexual favors from a commune girl, the leader brought the boy to "a prostitute in Toronto to help him."

With the children gone, commune life spiralled downward into a demonic orgy of sexual perversion and violence. According to a statement of facts agreed to by Theriault, and read into court records at the cult leader's Jan. 18 sentencing, the self-styled prophet punished Ouelette for an unspecified minor transgression by placing a rubber band around his testicles. "An hour later," the statement said, "he noticed his scrotum had swelled to the size of an orange and had turned various colors." Then, when Oulette complained that one of his testicles had become infected, a drunken Theriault "made an incision in Ouelette's scrotum, removed a testicle and cauterized the incision with a piece of hot iron."

Murder: Even that gory act pales by comparison with the handling of Boilard's corpse. After her death — caused, doctors say, by digestive acids pouring into her abdominal cavity — Theriault ordered his disciples to bury and dig up her body twice. Court documents say that a rib was removed from the body and that Theriault wore it in a leather case around his neck. And according to police and Lavallee, the cult leader ordered his followers to remove Boilard's uterus and saw off the cap of her skull so that he could ejaculate onto her brain — an act he claimed could restore her life.

A month after commune members cremated Boilard's remains,

Theriault unleashed his destructive energies on Lavallee, ripping out eight of her teeth to treat a toothache. But worse was to come. The following July, in order to "cure" stiffness in one of her fingers, he impaled her right hand to a wooden table with a hunting knife. "I stood there for an hour," Lavallee recalled in an interview last week. "I didn't want to lose consciousness, because if I did I knew he would kill me. He was drunk, of course. My arm turned blue and dark. He decided to amputate it."

In a crude operation with no anesthetic, Theriault hacked off Lavallee's right arm between the shoulder and elbow. "He decided to use a cleaver," said Lavallee, "but on the first try, he didn't do the job because the blade was so dull it didn't chop it. The second time, the job was done." After Lavallee spent the night writhing in pain on the kitchen floor, a fellow disciple stitched up her stump. Days later, Theriault cauterized the wound with a piece of drive shaft from a truck, heated with an acetylene torch.

Terrorized, Lavallee fled the camp and hitchhiked to a hospital north of Toronto, where she told police how she lost her arm. On Oct. 6, 1989, after a six-week search with helicopters and tracking dogs, police arrested Theriault, who had escaped to a makeshift camp where he planned to spend the winter with two followers. Four days later, he pleaded guilty to a series of charges related to his attacks on Lavallee and received a 12-year sentence, later reduced to 10 years on appeal. Only when Theriault was behind bars did a cult defector tell police of Boilard's 1988 murder; he was charged with that offense on Oct. 24, 1989. A publication ban on evidence in that case remained in effect until last month, when Theriault pleaded guilty.

'Psychopath': In a recent prison report, Millhaven authorities described Theriault as "co-operative", adding that he seems "amenable to the rehabilitation process. Indeed, the report even states that Theriault had been offered a transfer to a lower security prison — but that he turned it down because he wanted to remain close to Francine Laflamme.

Meanwhile, most of the cult leader's other victims are trying to piece together their shattered lives. Lavallee, who now has a stainless steel artificial arm, received regular payments from the province's Criminal Injuries Compensation Board — and plans to publish a French-language book on her experiences next fall. Reflecting back on her years with Theriault, she says: "He is a Hitler, a psychopath. He cannot be cured." Another of Theriault's former "wives", who asked not to be named, is seeking legal access to her children, although her lawyer told **Maclean's** that there is little hope of success because of Ontario's strict adoption laws.

Giguere, for his part, has retreated to his roots in Quebec's Beauce region — where he is recuperating with relatives — after serving 18 months in Millhaven for assisting Theriault in Lavallee's amputation. His time in prison helped him to regain his psychological distance from Theriault — and at one point he even considered killing his former master. "I started thinking for myself," Giguere said. "I did not depend on him for food, clothing or sleep anymore." And that is not all that has changed: Giguere, who for more than a decade worshipped Theriault as "Moses", no longer believes in God.

Reprinted with permission from Macleans.

IN THE NAME OF GOD: Part II

Richard Cusick

"The word cult does not further the conversation; it ends it."

— *William Goldstein*
Attorney for
Transcendental Meditation

The story goes that in the 1950's when Scientology founder, L.R. Hubbard, first came out with "Dianetics" the psychiatric profession castigated him. A psychologist would say this was because Hubbard's theories were based on "pseudo science" but a Scientologist would maintain that vested interests feared that Hubbard was going to move in on their highly lucrative turf. Whichever is accurate, the story continues that Hubbard never forgot the pasting he received and set up a major offensive against psychiatry that continues long after his death. Dennis Clark is currently the point-man in that offensive. As chairman of the Scientology-backed Citizens Commission on Human Rights (CCHR), Clark has been a regular on the talk show circuit and other media where he defines the Commission's position on such controversial issues as the dubious benefits of Presoak and the detrimental effects of Ritalin.

The Reverend Heber C. Jentzsch is the President of the Church of Scientology International, a visible and somewhat hyperbolic spokesman. The son of Mormon parents, he has an evangelical bent and demeanor that would have made, had he a more common calling, one hell of a televangelist. But on the evening that he spoke to *Gauntlet* he was calm and composed and convincing.

Herbert R. Rosedale is a crusader of a different sort. As the president of the American Family Foundation (AFF) and an attorney, Rosedale has written letters, represented litigants and has been a consistent source for innumerable articles relating to so-called "cult" activity. Whenever reporters want an expert in "cults" they invariably call Cynthia Kisser of the Cult Awareness Network or Herb Rosedale of the AFF. His name has appeared as a source in *Modern Maturity*, the *Congressional Quarterly* and the *New York Times* to name but a few.

Rosedale wrote a letter to the *American Lawyer* in 1992 following a comprehensive story on Scientology and the law called "The Two Faces of Scientology." The *American Lawyer* is, according to Rosedale, "a muckraker in the best sense of the word" and, his letter stated, in part, "I myself once was asked to appear on a talk show program to discuss the *Time* magazine article but was told by the producer that the format of the program was changed, at the last moment and without notice to other participants, at the insistence of the Church of Scientology and its counsel, to deal solely with the alleged horror stories of people who had taken a Food & Drug Administration-approved drug, whose use the Church of Scientology opposes." Twisted syntax notwithstanding, Rosedale was discrete in the pages of *American Lawyer* and continued to be unwilling to go on the record for *Gauntlet* in this matter. But other persons involved with that talk show were not so reluctant.

On August 19, 1991 the *Geraldo* show taped "The Alleged Cult vs. The Alleged Killer Drug." Apparently on the heels of the *Time* cover story (which came out three months earlier) Geraldo Rivera set out to investigate the Church of Scientology and seemingly bowed to pressure and turned around at the very last minute to make three quarters of the show an investigation of Presoak. Alternately, Geraldo Rivera's staff booked the show in a duplicitous manner and wound up lying to both factions when the heat kicked in. Like Kurosawa's 1950 classic film, Rashomon, truth depends on viewpoint and the nature of reality is liquid.

Down in the front were Dennis Clark of the Citizens Commission and the Rev. Heber C. Jentzsch, president of the Church of Scientology International. The Scientologists brought with them four persons who were allegedly victimized by the Presoak and also dozens of other Scientologists who filled the front rows of the studio audience. "I was told we were going to do a show on Presoak," said Rev. Jentzsch.

"And when we got there I was told that part of this is going to be on the Cult Awareness Network and the American Family Foundation. And that's, you know—It was a surprise that they were going to be there. To me, I mean. I wasn't so stupid as to think there might not be a sandbag."

Associate Producer Cordelia Bowes had lined up a group of professionals to counter the Scientologists claims which included Rosedale, Dr. David Halperin, a noted psychiatrist, and professional exit counsellors Steve Hassan and Monica Pignotti. Geraldo told the television audience, "Stay tuned for what promises to be a heated battle."

Monica Pignotti recalled that she was first approached by the *Geraldo* show about a week before the taping. "Before the show I got a call from Cordelia Bowes . . . I had a very lengthy conversation and we went over exactly the kinds of things she wanted me to talk about." According to Ms. Pignotti, the associate producer told her that there would be a short segment early on regarding Presoak and then the larger discussion on Scientology would begin. That was the show she agreed to do. "And then what happened was we were waiting to go on. And I knew something had happened because the Scientologists had asked to come on. And then all of a sudden . . . Geraldo just sprung this on us."

Steve Hassan tells a very similar story. "The producer came and asked me to do a show on Scientology as a result of the *Time* magazine cover story. And that's what I was told. It was very very bizarre. The whole thing was very strange. About an hour before the show we were there doing make-up and all that, one of the producers came in and said, 'Well, the Scientologists are threatening to walk out. They want us to do something on Presoak', and we said, 'Well, you know let them walk out'? (chuckles) 'They're just threatening to manipulate you.' And they came back in — the producer came back in again and said 'Well, we may need to shift the show a little bit and talk a little bit about Presoak,' and we all objected."

Presoak is a puff piece for the journalist assigned to report on Scientology. Certainly a viable subject for inquiry, it is too often a safe subject to choose to report on because it is a story that Scientology wants to promote. As a result, doing a story of the Presoak controversy is like doing a story on Scientology without doing a story on Scientology.

Rev Jentzsch said smoothly, "I went back to Geraldo and said 'Look, I think that the issue of Presoak is so important that I'm willing to just walk off the set and you can just do a straight show on Presoak. I mean if I'm the lightning rod for this then let's just . . . I think Presoak is far more important than just me talking about Scientology, defending it."

He has a point. The fact that Dennis Clark was there at all suggests that the Scientologists came to talk about Presoak. And Clark brought four alleged Presoak victims with him. (Why were you there then? I asked Jentzsch. "Because I've spoken out on the issue," he replied.) In fact, Jentzsch was the only spokesman from Scientology per se. The chosen opposition, on the other hand, included two exit counsellors, the president of the AFF and a psychiatrist who could and did talk about Presoak in a pinch but who authored a seminal book in "anti-cult" literature. It was never mentioned on the show but Professor Halperin is also on the Board of Directors of the AFF.

"And Geraldo said, 'Nah! Look, why don't we do this? We'll do the first segment with them and then we'll go to the Presoak issue," Jentzsch claims. "And I said, 'Okay, fair enough.'"

Exit counsellor Steve Hassan continues: "Later the producer came in and said 'Well we're all going to go in now.' and kind of walked us into the set and, you know, I've never had — I mean I've done a lot of television shows. I was on *Geraldo* twice before this — It's not like I don't know media — and we walk into the set and Jentzsch is sitting on the stage and they say 'You go up there' meaning me go up on the set, on the stage, and they put Herb and Monica in the front row and then they started filming it . . . and I was floored.

"It turned out to be about fifteen minutes with Jentzsch talking about what Scientology was and me criticizing Scientology, and then the rest of the show was about Presoak. And, in the most unusual weird experience, I & Herb & Monica Pignotti were escorted off the set without any forewarning and we were sequestered in the back."

Pignotti independently told the same story with a few more details. "When they were going to start the second segment," she said, "they asked us to just stay seated in the audience. And . . . Dennis Clark — he's a big tough guy — pointed to me and said 'I don't want these people in the room with me or I'm not going to go on.' And Geraldo just like a little — He just meekly obeyed them. It was unbelievable . . . The reason we were backstage was because Scientology threw us off the set . . . The whole thing was so bizarre."

However, according to the president of the Church of Scientology he saw members of the production team outfitting members of the AFF in the audience with tiny lapel microphones so that their active participation in the following segments on Presoak was assured.

"And," said Jentzsch, "I think Dennis (Clark) made a comment and I affirmed. I said 'Hey, wait a minute, you know, that segment's over. They were miking these people up so it still looked like a sandbag."

Said Rev. Jentzsch, "When the first segment was finished they started to clear the set of the people from the American Family Foundation and the Cult Awareness Network. And they were screaming and yelling and, you know — It was a bit of a zoo."

"I saw as they went off they were screaming as they went down towards the [Green Room]. 'We were promised a full hour!' I have no knowledge of what they were promised. All I know is they were a surprise for me.

"And of course you know the interesting thing is that we still had the psychiatrist, Halperin . . . Halperin was less than forthcoming about his connections to all of this."

Professor Halperin was allowed to stay on the show because of his medical expertise. Halperin, in addition to being a professor of psychiatry at Mt. Sinai School of Medicine is also a board member of the AFF. But Geraldo only wanted to hear from his medical background that day. Dry and reserved, Professor Halperin nonetheless confirmed the essential facts: "Well, as I remember it, other people were supposed to participate more on it. I was on a panel there and I was the only person who really got a chance to talk . . . "

What did you talk about?

"About the positive aspects of Presoak. And the show was not originally supposed to be a pharmacological discussion."

Did you go there to talk about Presoak?

"I didn't think it was going to be exclusively on Presoak. No, I did not . . . I thought it was more supposed to be a broader issue discussion and you know, just simply to discuss Presoak just didn't seem to be what the show should be about."

As Dr. Halperin fenced with Dennis Clark on-camera the associate producer explained to her guests backstage that the decision was made "over her head."

"What was happening," recalled Ms. Pignotti "was Cordelia was talking to us and I think there was another producer talking to Scientology. Geraldo just stepped in and said it himself and Cordelia obviously was in tears."

Steve Hassan confirmed that view.

"The producer that I had dealt with came in — she was in tears — and said 'I'm really embarrassed. I can't believe they're doing this.' She proceeded to tell me that she was leaving the show anyway, and this was one of her last shows."

Monica Pignotti obviously still feels strongly about that day. "I feel if anyone is responsible, it was Geraldo letting himself be intimidated, for allowing the Scientologists to intimidate him. Because there have been other times he didn't allow that to happen. I mean, I don't know if that's what happened, but for whatever reason . . . he went back on the promise that he made with us. That we would have a certain amount of time."

Associate producer Cordelia Bowes did in fact leave the *Geraldo* show not long thereafter and married Geraldo's brother, Craig. She recently had a baby, and she was not available for comment. But the Producer of that afternoon's show was Bill Lancaster, the 'other producer' that handled the Scientologists. Mr. Lancaster remembers essentially the same events with a different spin.

RC: Was the initial direction of that show to be about Scientology and then changed?

BL: Yes, I believe the focus of that show was on Scientology and then when the Scientologists had gotten to the studio they had insisted on talking about Presoak so we basically wove the two. It sort of went back and forth . . . We wanted to hear what they had to say and so we tried to hold the show together as best we could.

RC: Doesn't that sound like Scientology was setting the agenda?

BL: Yeah, that's certainly what they attempted to do but that's nothing new. Virtually every guest who ever comes on any talk show tries to set the agenda . . . So in that sense, yes, I mean they had an ax to grind about Presoak but there was plenty of discussion about Scientology on the show. In fact we had some people who belonged to it and had since quit and had talked about the negative side of [Scientology] as well."

That is not precisely true. The only ex-Scientologist in the house was Monica Pignotti and she told *Gauntlet*, "After everything I had gone over with the producer. . . I got about thirty seconds to talk."

BL: We wanted to talk with them. The discussions of Presoak were all in the context of Scientology. In other words, when they would talk about the drug they would talk about, you know, how their professionals found it or deemed its value. They would talk about the tenets they had about outside drug use because they're anti-drug, anti-psychiatry. So yes there was a discussion of Presoak but it was in the confines of Scientology . . . It wasn't a strict, you know, just talking about the medical end; it was always in the context of Scientology.

In Fact, hardly any of the discussion was in the context of Scientology. Prior the first commercial break Rivera announced that " . . . this is not a show that will dwell any further on Scientology."

And he pretty much held to that promise. A further connection during the next segment was brought out by an audience member ("They miked a few of them anyway," said Jentzsch.) Geraldo was quick to admonish. "No more Scientology," he said. When the next audience member tried to address the former speaker, Mr. Rivera said, "I don't want to talk about Scientology. I don't want to . . . "

Mr. Lancaster continues: "Well, I mean, we do sort of a news show. Our show is a little bit different from most of the talk shows because of Geraldo's background as a newsman. Mine is — myself — I spent seven years in news before I came here. So where we come from — and I can speak for Geraldo and myself, in particular — of the people here at the show . . . The Scientologists — there's been a lot of reports that they cause a lot of harm and have caused a lot of people a lot of problems. And they are a litigious group; that the way they operate is by suing. They refuse interviews and they have a very slick campaign to prevent any sort of interviews or research or reporting on them. So we were anxious to get them and to sit them down and to interview them which is something that few people or few news organizations and people get to do... A lot of media are afraid of them because they are so litigious. So when we were able to get them we were interested in that because it was an opportunity at long last get them to answer some questions. So to include in that the Presoak aspect, you know, we went along with that in order to get them to answer some other questions. If it was a more accessible group we might not have had that interest. It was of greater interest to us and to the public to have these people talk about Scientology, you know, even in the context of Presoak than it would be not to hear from them at all.

You mentioned the litigious nature of Scientology, did that play any . . .

BL: Absolutely not. I mean that's what I'm saying. We were one of the few people who were willing to take that risk with them. A lot of other people, a lot of other groups, news organizations, talk shows, back off from doing that sort of stuff because that's how [Scientology] operate(s).

You don't think that what happened there is backing off?

BL: No. We did what we did to — It was either have these people come on and talk about Presoak and have America take a look at these guys or not have them come on and shed any light on them whatsoever. . . . For example, they would say that Presoak was no good and then Geraldo would say 'Well isn't it true that your group is opposed to psychiatry and that part of the reason being that you would lose millions if people opted for science and psychiatry and chemical treatment?'

That question was not asked. In fact the only question that Rivera asked regarding a context between Scientology and Presoak came after three additional commercial breaks. Rivera allowed himself to question why the Scientologists took on a controlled drug like Presoak rather than illicit drugs and street crime? Far from a tough question, this allowed the spokesmen for Scientology to bring up the Church's highly successful drug education programs. Geraldo asked why the Church has a vendetta with Eli-Lilly and Rev. Jentzsch said, ". . . Because they've declared war on the Church of Scientology." "How did Eli-Lilly declare war on Scientology?" asked Rivera. "Presoak" said Dennis Clark. We ran into Presoak with the Citizens Commission on Human Rights and found out it was killing people." Rev. Jentzsch added, "I started the controversy." Geraldo could not have been more helpful if he were filming an infomercial. After that there was some brief criticism of the Church's viewpoint generated by an audience member but certainly not by Geraldo Rivera.

Bill Lancaster recalled "They came to New York. They got here and they said 'We want to talk about Presoak' and we said, 'We want to talk about Scientology' so our choices were to kill the show and have them walk out of the studio and not tape the show. So given those choices we opted to have them talk about Presoak but that allowed us to interview them and ask questions about their group and what they did. You know, 'Why are you against Presoak?' 'It's a bad drug and we got three people here who said they were harmed from it.' and then Geraldo would ask, 'Well, aren't those people who you paid to come on?' or 'Aren't those three people card-carrying members of Scientology?' And that was the line of questioning. 'Isn't it true that you're opposed to this because you'd lose millions if more people took it?'. . . And that's how it was done."

According to the transcript of the show that line of questioning was *not* pursued. Quite the opposite, Geraldo Rivera went out of his way to make sure that the Church was not discussed in the context of Presoak excepting the examples cited above.

Asked about the concerns of the other invited guests who leveled the charges of intimidation, Lancaster says, "Well, they were given an opportunity to speak. They spoke at the beginning of the show and I believe they spoke at the end of the show."

Monica Pignotti feels that Rivera knew he had done something wrong and that Cordelia Bowes had spoken with him and negotiated a last minute shot to save face. "She was trying to get something done," said Pignotti, "and so [Geraldo] went backstage and gave us this token thing."

Steve Hassan recalls that final "opportunity": "I should also tell you in fairness to Geraldo, the last minute of the show he comes off the set with a portable camera and interviews me in the hallway. This is so bizarre . . . . He says, 'Steve, you have the last word' or something like that . . ."

It was aired at the end?

"Oh, it was aired. and I basically said, 'Well, Geraldo, you promised to do a show about Scientology and I hope that you will do one one day.' Something like that."

With that thought in mind we return to Bill Lancaster.

Mr. Lancaster, have you done any shows on Scientology since?

"Let's see . . . I don't believe so. I don't believe we've done Scientology since."

You wouldn't categorize what happened

that day as intimidation?

"No, I would categorize it as reality."

Rev. Jentzsch recalled pandemonium backstage after the show. "I was walking off the set. I finished and suddenly there's Rosedale and Hassan and Halperin screaming at the top of their lungs. (INTENSELY) 'We want to talk to you!!' I said, 'Look, fellas, I have absolutely nothing to say to you.' And Hassan was yelling and yelling and I said, 'Forget it!' and went down the stairs and Rosedale — Running! Running!! after us, you know.

"I mean the guy was screaming and screaming at me. I mean, what? You know. It was just bizarre!"

That's the word the Reverend used to describe that day: "Bizarre!" That is also the word that Steve Hassan and Monica Pignotti used to describe the experience: "Bizarre." We have a first here. This is the only thing in the world that Heber Jentzsch and Steve Hassan agree on.

No, wait, that's not true. All three agree on one more point: All three agree that they were lied to by the producers of the *Geraldo* show. Either the producers told both factions blatant untruths to begin with or the producers told the Scientologists blatant untruths and then broke their promise of equal time to the other side when the Scientologists threatened to walk. No other explanation fits all the events as indecently described by different parties. It seems evident that Geraldo sandbagged Scientology.

Actually, Dennis Clark has appeared on the *Geraldo* show since the Presoak episode. The chairman of the Citizens Commission on Human Rights was a guest on a show that concerned itself with "Borderline Personalities" that was aired on December 1, 1992. Rivera mentioned in passing that the CCHR was connected to the Church of Scientology and under the circumstances that seems adequate. The announced intention that day was not to investigate the Church of Scientology.

When I asked Rev. Jentzsch if he would consider going on the *Geraldo* show again he said calmly, "No."

When *Gauntlet* first began its investigation of the *Geraldo* show we spoke with Penny Price, a producer on the show but not of "The Alleged Cult vs. The Alleged Killer Drug." We shall return to Ms. Price in a moment but the details of our very first conversation should be reported at this time. I identified myself as a reporter and then said, "A couple of years ago you did a story — a previous story with *Geraldo* and — let me get it right — you had Steve Hassan on."

"Oh, ages ago. Yeah."

"And I'm trying to run down if there was any kind of problems with letters, or litigation . . .

"No."

"Or that kind of thing."

"No, no.

Extremely open and affable, with barely a nod, Ms. Price took the lead. In the opening minute of our first conversation she offered that a deprogrammer had a legal problem with Scientology on another show.

"Huge problem with Scientologists," she said, "On some show he was on."

"Well, that sounds like the purview of what I"m working on."

"Right," said Penny Price. "Because basically, the Scientologists are . . . They — they sue. You mention them — you sneeze — and they sue. And that's why a lot of media doesn't do shows on Scientology because they do that and they have like a zillion lawyers and they — they do that. And they've strong-armed the media for a long time because they do indeed sue whether or not it was bad or not. They just . . . they just . . . they . . . We know that they sue. One time when we did something with Scientologists. we had someone on from [the] Scientologist's administration because we knew that they would sue if we — you know what I mean — If you didn't have somebody saying 'Well, we're not really very bad.' That's the way we have done it when we did it once. That was like ages ago but basically when I've done all the cult shows — and I've done zillions of them — I've just stayed away from Scientologists because there's so many other cults out there." (Laughter).

I spoke with Ms. Price the next day and she expanded on the theme: "Either most shows don't cover Scientology and they do other cults, which is fine, because according to CAN, [Cult Awareness Network] there are like three to five thousand cults, right? Isn't that what they told you?"

"Something like that."

"Yeah, right. So there are many many cults out there. So why focus on — you know what I mean — why focus on something that — there's no reason to . . . "

Do you think that because of the litigious nature of Scientology, as you said yesterday, 'We stay away from them because they sue. If we sneeze, they sue.' Is that intimidation? Is that being intimidated by the litigious nature of the organization?

Her voice falling a measure, Ms. Price said, "I don't — I don't know. I'm not a lawyer. I don't know if— "

I'm talking about intimidation to the media. If you're a producer who makes decisions based upon that, couldn't that be read by a reasonable person as being intimidated by somebody saying, 'I'm going to sue'?

"I don't know how a reasonable person would read it. The word intimidation I would not use until I looked up. I'm telling you it's a fact that people, people don't do stories, I mean because [of] that reason."

Geraldo Rivera was unavailable for comment but Jeff Erdel, a spokesman for the *Geraldo* show, gave *Gauntlet* a statement when the particulars of this article were explained to him:

"It's not unusual for people to threaten us with litigation or worse," said Mr. Erdel, "that comes with the territory. We are not easily intimidated. We have many lawyers at our disposal and Geraldo himself is an attorney. In fact, usually when somebody threatens us we take it as a sign that they don't want a story to be delved into and this makes us all the more interested in the subject matter. Regarding what two of our producers told you, keep in mind that these people do not make the ultimate decision as to what subject areas are examined by the program or how we will approach a subject. Those decisions are made by the senior staff which consists of a senior producer, executive producer and of course, the ultimate authority for us, Geraldo Rivera. These people can not be intimidated. It only makes them more tenacious. And that's my statement."

■   ■

Penny Price seems to be the sort of person that you can like immediately. She is approachable and engaging and intelligent. She has been working in broadcast media since the 1970s and, by her own estimate, she has extraordinary experience in producing shows on "cults". "I mean, there's nobody who's done more shows

exposing cults on national television than I have," she said proudly. "Yeah. I did a show called 'Child Killing Cults: Investigating The Next Waco' around the Waco time. That was terrific. Yeah, I did that one and then I did one called 'Killing In The Name of God' with [deprogrammer] Rick Ross. And I did cults where people had died. Let's see, remember the Longrin case? The cult member? In Ohio . . . And he had a vision from God so he killed like four people? Remember the Ohio case?"

No. I don't actually.

All right. Big big case. And then I had Irene Spencer. She was in a Mormon polygamist group that killed twenty five people and fifty members. She still follows the teachings . . . . And then I had Joan Cogetti, you know, anti-ministry. They're the ones who believe in no medical attention. And her daughter died at four days old because of lack of medical care. And then, let's see what I do — 'Seduced Into Madness — Jonestown To Now'. I did that. I had Pat Ryan on, you know, daughter of Congressman Ryan . . . . And that's one — Oh, that's one that I had Steve Hassan on."

Steve Hassan is an exit counsellor, a deprogrammer, an alleged "kidnapper" or a faith-breaker depending on one's orientation. Those are the highly charged terms used to describe what Steve Hassan does which is contribute to the process by which people leave a system of belief. Penny Price said that Steve gives a "very good definition" of a cult. She further cites the reports from the Cult Awareness Network (CAN) as a reason to promote so many programs on the subject.

"When they report the increase in membership and the increase in the number of cults around the country in the last decade obviously people need to do stories on it."

In an interview with *Gauntlet* Steve Hassan broached a memory of a show he did. "I was on *Geraldo* in 1988 when my book [*Combatting Cult Mind Control*] first came out. This was on the tenth anniversary of the Jonestown tragedy. I had a very odd experience with a producer of the *Geraldo* show, and I want to say Penny . . . Price. That's it. Penny Price.

"I was working with a PR agency at the time and basically they said talk to the producer and, you know, she wants names of ex-cult members. So I talked with her and I said, 'How about an ex-Scientologist?', 'Oh, we don't want to do that. What else do you have?' 'Well how about ex-TM?' 'We don't want to do that.' How about ex-est? 'Well, we don't want to do that.' I said I'll call you back. I got on the phone with my PR person and said, "There's something really weird is going on." Basically they said keep offering until you come up with some people that they want to do. The long and the short of it was, you know, I got former members of different cults together.

"We're doing the show. I'm in the green room ready to go out there and she — Penny — tells me, 'By the way, I wanted you to know that I have received The Knowledge."

"The Knowledge" is a meditation technique that is a practiced by followers of the Divine Light Mission, also called Elan Vital. It is the organization of the charismatic "Perfect Master" Guru Maharaj Ji. The boy Guru was 13 years old when he came to the United States in 1971 to spread his father's teachings. His real name is Prem Pal Singh Rawat and his followers, called Premies, quickly numbered in the thousands. But he fell from Western favor when he married his secretary, bought a Porsch and moved to Malibu. The guru has not been visible in the U.S. since the late 1970s.

Steve Hassan was incredulous. "Here's a producer of a major television show telling me just as I'm about to go on the set that she's a member of a cult which was really bizarre. Anyway we did the show; the show went well.

Why did she do that?

"I honestly don't understand why she did it unless she was just doing it to unnerve me."

What was her manner? Was it friendly? Was it aggressive?

"No, it wasn't aggressive. You know, my take on it at the time was that, like most people involved with cults, they think that other groups are cults but theirs aren't.... Although it certainly unnerved me, it also made perfect sense because of her odd behavior."

Penny Price denies she is a member of a cult and, for that matter, that she is a follower of Guru Maharaj Ji.

"I know a lot of people who have learned how to meditate through his technique. A lot of people love it. Love it."

But asked specifically is she were a follower of the guru, Ms. Price said, "I don't follow anybody.

"We've Western traditions here. In the East they follow gurus; it's very unwestern here.

"I've been meditating for years. It's the one reason most people on daytime television last on a show for a couple of years. And I know that the reason I'm able to be here being as calm and as focused as I am is because of meditation. I do a variety of different techniques."

Pressed to answer if she practiced The Knowledge, Ms. Price concedes, "Yeah, I've learned that technique as well."

Do you think of that meditation has cult-like overtones?

"No, not at all . . . But, do I think that some people can be culty about it? Yeah, I definitely think they can. The definition of a cult which — I think Steve Hassan was really right on when he said: 'For a group to be a cult as opposed to a group it should have three factors,' I believe the three were: One — mind-stopping techniques. And when he said that, I said, 'You're not saying that meditation is bad.' He said, 'No no no, I'm not saying that meditation is bad,' He said, 'It's these three factors only if they're together. Not if one of them exists but if three factors are together.'

"Two is they separate you from family and friends and say 'Don't listen to anybody else. Don't read anything else. Leave your family, leave your friends; we have the one and true and right way. And number three, they preach an Armageddon. They build in fear so that the people become so afraid of the future that then this . . . group says, 'We are the only way'. That's the definition of a cult. If they have all three, then they're a cult. And in all the shows that I've done I really have used Steve's three part identifying factors as things that I have looked at."

Asked if she still practices The Knowledge, Ms. Price was forthright. "I use a variety of techniques currently." she said. "That's one of them."

Do you remember your interest in this system ever coming up in conversation with any of the guests of the Geraldo show?

"I do remember some guest saying something — and maybe it was even Steve, I don't remember. But we were talking on one of the cult shows and one of the groups that he was going to bring up was Guru

Maharaj Ji and really lambasting that [group], and I said 'What's your basis? I know many many people who learned it. It's absolutely false. They learned a meditation technique and that was that. Nobody solicited them. Nobody was on the phone.'" The notion that all practitioners of The Knowledge were members of a cult, says Price, "was garbage."

I tend to agree with Penny Price, but Steve Hassan and the Cult Awareness Network do not. The very experts that Ms. Price depends upon to define the term "cult" would define her as a cult member (Indeed, in Mr. Hassan's case, did categorize her has a cult-member). Ms. Price takes these definitions and then, in her position as a producer of a major television show, make decisions about what group to report on and whom to investigate.

Penny Price is no more a member of a cult than I am, and I do not practice meditation. According to her co-workers, Penny Price is a competent focused professional. The problem is with the definition which is all-encompassing, self-serving and myopic. The "anti-cult professionals" are the masters of this definition, and journalists too readily accept their view without qualification because it simplifies their job and gives them a four letter word that fits neatly into a sound-bite.

Penny Price has never practiced Transcendental Meditation (TM). "I never learned TM," she said. "I mean, why take a few hundred dollars when at that point I had learned a variety of meditation techniques that I had liked." If she had practiced Transcendental Meditation I would have had to add to the list of her critics the prestigious *Journal of The American Medical Association*.

The Cult Awareness Network defines itself primarily as an informational clearinghouse. If you suspect an organization of being a cult you can call CAN and they will tell you what they know about that organization. I asked Cynthia Kisser, the executive director of CAN, if her organization considers Transcendental Meditation as a cult? "The Cult Awareness Network doesn't take that position on any group," she said. "Our purpose is to give information." For twelve dollars, CAN will send you a package of press clippings related to an organization if that organization is on their list.

I put my twelve dollars down and received a hefty blue file of clippings on the TM movement. Whereas the articles were certainly instructive they were also, on the whole, negative and the conclusion was implicit. There were no primary materials, no articles of endorsement (which certainly exist) and no balance. If one were to make up their own mind based on the materials provided by CAN, that viewpoint is a foregone conclusion.

At the very end of the packet was the rather long expose published by *The Journal of The American Medical Association* (JAMA) in its October 2, 1991 edition. The article, written by associate editor Andrew Skolnick, excoriated the TM movement and its related "marketing schemes" and became the focus of a $194 million lawsuit brought by the Lancaster Foundation and the American Association for Ayurvedic Medicine (AAAM). This is a story where vested interests vie for position and where East meets West in a court of civil law.

The story began six months earlier when JAMA, despite its reputation for aversion to holistic medicine, published "A letter From New Delhi — Maharishi Ayur-Veda: Modern Insights Into Ancient Medicine." Seemingly a scholarly report on an updating of Ayur-Vedic medicine "the oldest existing medical system", the Letter From New Delhi" was written by Hari M. Sharma of The Ohio State University College of Medicine, Brihaspati Dev Triguna of the All India Ayur-Veda Congress and Deepak Chopra, MD and darling of the New Age Movement.

Chopra, at one time a prominent Boston Endocrinologist, had become something of a celebrity in recent years by writing best sellers, doing talk shows and, all in all, getting rich in the process. "I've had him on many times," said Penny Price. Dr. Chopra was, until recently, the Maharaji Mahesh Yogi's best western Medicine Man, traveling far and wide to spread the mantra of Transcendental Meditation, and also the most visible proponent of Ayur-Vedic Medicine in the United States.

Auyr-Vedic is a staple of Indian culture with over 300,000 registered Ayur Vedic physicians. It is a system that sounds arcane to western ears, a ancient discipline of herbs and balms and gemstones and cattle dung, of pulse diagnoses, astrology and urine but it is as rife with possibilities as it is with superstition. That's the reason JAMA was interested in an article in the first place. Years of foreign rule over India saw the active suppression of Ayur-Veda and what remains is an eviscerated shell of knowledge.

According to Chopra and his co-authors, Maharishi Ayur-Veda is a revival of complete Ayur Veda in full accordance with the classical texts. This revival is being conducted under the direction of Maharishi Mahesh Yogi and, according to Chopra, the updated system is named after him to honor his efforts. It is this updated system that was the subject of "Letter From New Delhi".

Maharishi Mahesh Yogi is, of course, Sexy Sadie, one time guru to the Beatles before he was cast aside like last nights groupie. But that proscription didn't hurt the swami much. For the last twenty years he has successfully marketed his own personal trademarked form of altered consciousness, Transcendental Meditation (TM) plus a host of related products and services. Current and conservative estimates of his movement's wealth are in excess of $2 billion.

When associate news editor Andrew Skolnick saw an advance copy of the May 22, 1991 edition of *The Journal* it was already too late. Subscription copies had already been mailed and "There was nothing to do to stop it. It was a fait accompli." Skolnick said. "I saw the article and I knew about the TM organization and I was very suspicious"

What made you suspicious?

"Because of the promotion of the flying courses for $3000."

Which you knew from where?

"Readings from various sources. The *Skeptical Inquirer* had articles on the TM movement, and I had seen news release where the TM organization claimed that they had diverted a hurricane away from Texas into Mexico by doing yogic flying. . .

TM-Sidhi, or yogic flying, involves the chanting of Hindu mantras during meditation followed by several minutes of "hopping" in the cross-legged Lotus position. According to Skolnick, adherents claim this to be a form of levitation.

"I knew of their deceptive marketing tactics," said Skolnick, "But I had never heard of Maharishi Ayur-Veda."

Skolnick contacted the National Council Against Health Fraud which sent him a large package of promotional material from Maharishi Ayur-Veda. "And to my astonishment there was Chopra and Sharma and Triguna's name all over this stuff." said Skolnick. "Chopra, of course, was all over. Triguma actually had his picture on the label of one of the products that they were touting in the article!"

"So I presented a memo, clipped it with all the promotional material of Maharishi Ayurveda, of their catalog, and gave it to the editor."

Skolnick took his memo to JAMA editor, Dr. George Lundberg, and suggested that he do an expose and run it in Medical News & Perspectives section of *The Journal*. It took about three months to complete. Skolnick kept digging up more evidence as the offending authors wrestled to spin the Financial Disclosure Correction.

When the final article was submitted all three authors signed a financial disclosure statement which indicated that the authors had no affiliations with the organizations which might profit by the publication of the manuscript. Now it was obvious that that was not true. In fact, the Financial Disclosure Correction which JAMA printed in its August 14, 1991 edition was the longest such correction in the Journal's 111-year history.

The correction for the three authors took up a half page and listed a series of affiliations and relationships, both past and present, which indicate more than a clinical interest in the promotion of Maharishi Ayur Veda. Far from a simple admission, procuring the list from the authors involved lawyers and negotiations far beyond the scope of a mere disclosure. "I have checked with my lawyer," Chopra wrote to the editors, "and would like to inform you that I am not and have not for the past three years been a director or member of Maharishi Ayur Veda Products International Inc. or held any other position in MAPI or any organization related to MAPI." The editors at JAMA had reason to believe that even this record length financial disclosure was incomplete.

"What happened at this point," recalled Skolnick, "I documented as much as I could of their connections and the Journal's decision was to just represent what they will admit to, not what we found."

What Skolnick found was a complex

of schemes and scams, inaccuracies and misrepresentations. In Skolnick's words he found what was a "pattern of deception." Professional alliances were claimed that did not exist. Words were twisted into endorsements. The authors touted Maharishi Ayurveda as a science but the services offered in promotional material pointed to religious ceremonies in India. And the services were not cheap.

The expose enumerated schemes by the dozen to promote a line of trademarked products which include herbs, oils, teas, food supplements, devices, aromas, healing pearls and Jyotish gemstones said to treat or prevent disease; as well as Hindu horoscopes, books, tapes and numerous services under the direction of the Maharishi Mahesh Yogi. The article mapped out a labyrinthine set of incestuous organizations, separate on paper but sharing addresses and phone numbers. Skolnick quoted editor Lundberg, who said, "At the time, we did not know that 'Maharishi Ayurveda' 'Transcendental Meditation' and the 'TM-Sidhi' programs promoted in the article are brands of health care products and services being marketed by the TM movement."

Skolnick quoted from an undated letter from Chopra to 'Friends of Maharishi Ayurveda' calling a blend of more than twenty herbs 'pure knowledge pressed into material form.' At $95.00 for a months supply Chopra urged, that the blend 'should be placed in every home as quickly as possible.' The packaging of these herbs had a likeness of co-author Triguna surrounded by a glowing light.

Chopra and his attorney got wind of the upcoming blast from JAMA and, according to Skolnick, made repeated attempts to be allowed to preview the article before publication and gave repeated warnings that they would sue if they were defamed.

Did you expect a lawsuit?

"I would have guessed a twenty five percent chance . . . Our legal review thought, 'Well, maybe they will, maybe they won't. They can't win. It's libel-proof.'"

Two weeks after the article was printed, Deepak Chopra responded with much outrage and injury. Chopra said in a news release that JAMA "employed the classic tactics of gutter journalism including accusation, intimidation and fear. They wove outright falsehoods and distortions of fact into a fabric of biased and insinuating language . . . "

Chopra published a blistering three page rebuttal: "This attack is an attempt to suppress a viable form of alternative health care on the part of a journal supported by the world's richest and most powerful drug companies . . .

"They accused me and others of infiltrating prestigious journals when all we did was submit articles. Using the buzz word of 'cult' they tried to frighten anyone who had even a remote link with Maharishi Ayur Veda."

As the JAMA expose was mailed out Skolnick published "The Maharishi Caper; Or How To Hoodwink Top Medical Journals" in The Newsletter of The National Association of Sciencewriters. In a very confident muscular prose he recounts the story of the story, repeats most of his charges, and gives some history on fraud in science journals in general. He firmly credited JAMA for backing him up when inevitable criticism hit and the industry snickered.

Dr. Lundberg went on AMA Television in a JAMA Video Editorial which aired on the Discovery Channel in March, 1992. In the video Lundberg warns about the use of non-traditional treatments such as Maharishi Ayru Veda. At the same time, the *Columbia Journalism Review* gave one of its coveted Laurels in its "Darts and Laurels" column. The *Review* called the expose "a fine piece of corrective surgery after a botched operation."

Shortly thereafter Chopra resigned as head of the American Association For Ayurvedic Medicine. Although not known at the time, Chopra had also separated from the Maharishi and set out to work on his New Age bestseller *Ageless Body, Timeless Mind*.

Nine months after the publication of the expose, the hammer came down. "That was sunrising," said Skolnick. "It was nine months later."

In July, 1992 The American Association for Ayur-Vedic Medicine, and the non-profit Lancaster Foundation filed a multi-million dollar defamation suit. The Lancaster Foundation of North Bethesda, Maryland is a family-backed not-for-profit organization which funds and supports TM research. The article addresses the Lancaster Foundation's relationship with Dr. Sharma in one paragraph. The complaint asked for $194.4 million in damages plus expenses. Originally Dr. Steel Belok, a clinical instructor at Harvard Medical School was also listed as a complainant but shortly thereafter when an amended suit was filed Beloc's name was removed.

The complaint was amended again afterward and this time Chopra's name was included as a plaintiff and the American Medical Association was included as a defendant.

The plaintiffs also sought to obtain a injunction against Skolnick and Dr. Lundberg to bar either of them from making public comment. "They tried to gag me from speaking about TM. Or writing or doing any further investigation."

On August 20, 1992 the court declared that the plaintiffs have "little likelihood of success on the merits of the case, that plaintiffs do have an adequate remedy at law and will not suffer irreparable harm, and because we find that the public will be harmed by the chilling of public debate regarding a health care issue in which keen interest has been evidenced, plaintiffs' motion for an injunction is denied."

Unfortunately the "chilling of public debate" was accomplished nonetheless. Skolnick recalled that "At the time of the lawsuit the motion for injunction was denied and so there was no legal injunction on me but what lawyers told me, including my own attorney, is that you don't blow on flames. I was told to stop any further, proactive gathering of information. It was very frustrating," he said with regret. "I had all kinds of things that I was finding out about them."

In October, 1992 Skolnick won the Responsibility in Journalism Award from the Committee for the Scientific Investigation of Claims of the Paranormal (CSICOP). In his acceptance speech the science writer said, "Under the advice of attorneys I am unable to talk about my article or the lengthy investigation behind it." He confined his remarks to the prevalence and questionable quality of SLAPP suits in our society. Like every awards recipient he thanked everyone and his uncle and then, in conclusion, said, "I think it is an outrage that many publications in this land of liberty are not willing to publish articles that are critical of SLAPP-happy individuals and groups. And I think it's outrageous that a journalist in the United States is prevented

from discussing his work at an awards ceremony for that work. I think it is time we started SLAPPing back."

Also in October, 1992 the *Oncology Times*, trade journal for cancer specialist, ran a two paragraph item under the title "Cults Hook AIDS Patient" and reports "Cults, sects and fringe religious groups are finding that there's money to be made and members to be recruited from the large and growing population of AIDS patients. Among the most egregious examples: The Transcendental Meditation (TM) cult of Maharishi Mahesh Yogi is selling a variety of Indian folk medicines as a replacement for the modern medicine it recommends stopping." This was the only reference to TM in the column. It is a particularly insipid string of words leveling serious allegations in the broadest possible language. A little chapter and verse is what's needed here and there is none to be found. The *Oncology Times* did not report, for example, that it had culled this item from Skolnick's expose. The *Journal* article gave a much more informative account of a then on-going investigation into the conduct of two physicians who were prescribing Maharishi Ayur-Vedic treatments.

On December 15, 1992 TM attorney William Goldstein wrote a five page letter to Serena Stockwell, editor of the *Oncology Times*. Goldstein categorized the piece in the newsletter as "malicious statements designed to injure my clients ... It is clear that it is false and defamatory ... " Among the proofs of this alleged defamation, Goldstein wrote "the Maharishi Aryu Veda and Transcendental Meditation organizations in the U.S. do not and never have advocated that patients stop their 'modern medicine'. Absolutely to the contrary, Maharishi Ayur Veda is administered in the U.S. by several hundred medical doctors . . . " (Italics mine). Take note: the *Oncology Times* did not mention the U.S.; Goldstein was careful to mention only the U.S. Finally after five pages of polemic Goldstein gets to the point. "We certainly would prefer not to litigate but rather rationally educate the medical community about Maharishi Ayur-Veda . . . We require a retraction and correction on the noted article. To mitigate the damage caused by your October article, we further require a response piece." Goldstein demands that the article be written by an Ayur-Vedic expert and that it should be a minimum of 3000 words in length. Should the *Oncology Times* not comply with these demands it will result in "continuing damage for my clients, for which we hold the *Oncology Times* responsible."

Gauntlet has obtained documentation that supports the dismal *Oncology Times* piece and now provides details (which is more than the *Oncology Times* did). Surely, Goldstein knew that on October 25, 1991 Dr. Roger Chalmers and Dr. Leslie Davis were censured by the General Medical Council for "Serious Professional Misconduct" for doing exactly what the *Oncology Times reported*: treating AIDS patients with Maharishi Ayru Veda and advising them to "stop using modern medicine." Twenty eight days afterward, Dr. Chalmers's and Dr. Davis's names were removed from Medical Register . . . in London, England.

Both the *Oncology Times* and William Goldstein in his letter to that publication were guilty of sins of omission. But the best defense against libel is to tell the truth — that's Journalism 101 and it's right next to the part about getting the facts straight. The *Oncology Times* item wasn't very admirable but it wasn't very defamatory either.

William Goldstein spoke with *Gauntlet* regarding the threatened *Oncology Times* litigation and said, "The suit has not been filed at this point. There have been some discussions back and forth about a compromise resolution prior to litigation. Quite frankly they wanted to resolve it and I think it's a matter where the parties have discussed trying to resolve it amicably."

But a knowledgeable source at the *Oncology Times* who did not want to be identified said, "It just went away . . . There was some discussion and then it just went away."

Skolnick had no such luck. The JAMA litigation seemed to drag on indefinitely. "It never went anywhere," Skolnick laments. "No deposition. Nothing. Nothing happened. It was very frustrating for me. Nothing happened."

Skolnick thought that some advantage was gained when the gag order was denied and the court declared that the plaintiffs "have little likelihood of success on the merits of their claim."

"I thought the ball was at the two yard line and our attorneys would just pick it up and step over the line and that would be it," he said. "But that's not the way the cookies

crumbled. I don't want to vent my emotions about what happened but I just wanted this thing dismissed. With Prejudice."

RC: How long did it drag on for?

SKOLNICK: From July of 92 till March of 93. The attorneys on both sides kept litigating . . . "

Then in March, 1993 the court broke the stalemate by dismissing the claim "without prejudice." This means that the plaintiff can bring the matter before the court again at any time in the future.

RC: Why was the lawsuit dismissed "without prejudice"?

SKOLNICK: The litigation went on, and the Judge, as all Judges do, wanted it off the docket. So he'd periodically call the parties in and said, 'What's happening?' Finally, the judge said, 'If you all agree I can dismiss this thing without prejudice and you guys can continue talking.' I can't tell you what they were talking about. All I can tell you is, bottom line, there was no settlement.

William Goldstein does not consider the matter settled. Asked to comment on the status of the lawsuit he said, "We put it on hold so we could attempt to resolve it amicably and I don't think it's appropriate to make any further comment."

Several weeks after the dismissal William Goldstein wrote to the editors of the *San Francisco Examiner* about an upcoming column by science writer Keay Davidson. Goldstein was interviewed by Davidson about the item in the *Oncology Times* and Goldstein asked the editors to hold off publication of any opinion because of "delicate" negotiations with the *Oncology Times*. If it were not possible to hold the story Goldstein suggested that Davidson write a masked column where the identities of the parties are not revealed. Mr. Goldstein puzzlingly suggests, "This approach might lend a greater sense of reality to the piece." There was no threat of a lawsuit to the *San Francisco Examiner*.

The next day Keay Davidson's column appeared on schedule. Davidson suggested that Goldstein's five page letter to the *Oncology Times* editor was improper, that to suggest printing a science article to fend off litigation is wrong and intimates intimidation. "In other words," wrote Davidson, "If you don't publish our scientific data then we'll sue you." In the interests of full disclosure Davidson admitted that he was friends with Andrew Skolnick.

Within a week Goldstein fired back a letter to the *Examiner* "A good theme but the wrong facts," he wrote. "Neither I nor my clients asked or now ask that any peer review standards of the publication in question be dropped or lowered . . . This is defamation," declared the attorney. He did not go so far as to accuse Skolnick and Davidson of collusion.

William Goldstein recently told *Gauntlet* that he is exasperated by what he feels is a double standard from the press. "[The media] always gets on lawyers for being litigious. The alternative (to a response piece), which is litigation, is not satisfactory to any party. Here lawyers who are making attempts to eliminate or avoid litigation are being attacked. . . I think it is ultimately to everyone's advantage [not to litigate]. It is to the public's advantage and the parties advantage. It creates a remedy which is more appropriate and satisfactory.

"You know what?" he concludes, "Money doesn't do much towards untarnishing a reputation that's been damaged. The truth is what you want . . . In our legal system they award money; they don't award the truth. In other words they don't require somebody to print a correct."

But columnist Keay Davidson maintains a different view. "I'm a science journalist who has to rely a lot on what I see in scientific journals," he told *Gauntlet*. "They do have a certain standard that I think is higher than any other kind of published [material]. . . It doesn't mean that it has to follow anyone's particular scientific ideology, just that it should be that something gets into print for the right reason and not because it was litigated into print. If it's litigated into print then all of the sudden the standards of scientific truth cease to be scientific and then become legal, and I think it's a very dangerous precedent particularly when one's dealing with issues of medicine and health and psychology."

Goldstein counters, "All we're asking is to be judged scientifically. The reality that we encounter is a bias, a non-scientific bias, by scientists who look at something called Transcendental Meditation and think it is mystical. And we just want to be judged on the merits scientifically. And when we are, when journalists take the trouble to look at the scientific research that's available, they'll realize that this is a valuable program and that it's not anything mystical and it's not anything religious."

Your detractors say that there is a hidden agenda for Hinduism?

"It is not Hinduism nor is there a hidden agenda," Mr. Goldstein says emphatically. "There's nothing hidden about this program. It's highly publicized and published. There's no merit [to say] there's a hidden agenda; that it's Hinduism is even more ludicrous because you have clergy and people from all religions practicing these techniques. Not [just] Hindus. I'm Jewish. You have Hindus practicing it, you have Jews practicing it. If its a religion it's the only religion in the world I know that you can practice along with another one."

But Davidson is unconvinced. "There's something about this [scientific] enterprise where there's a certain belief. It isn't written down anywhere — there's no Constitution of science — but there's a basic belief that you have to have a very very high standard for facts because those facts are the basis for the operation. It doesn't always uphold that standard but it's got to be the ideal . . . I think it's very dangerous. Particularly when the litigators are from an organization dedicated to medical world views that are, to put it mildly, far from the mainstream.

Goldstein is weary of that attitude. "We find we often encounter among certain individuals, certain people who think in a certain way, this kind of reactive anti-intellectual and anti-scientific attitude. That is I think at root the problem, with regard to the *Oncology Times* and the JAMA piece."

I asked Keay Davidson about a perceived collusion between Skolnick and himself. "All I can tell you is I think very very highly of Andrew Skolnick," he said, "and a lot of medical writers and science writers in this country do. He's a really courageous, very capable guy and you know I may not have necessarily written that column if it had involved the work of someone else. I mean, even if I had not known him personally I think I would have been compelled to write it because of the quality of what he does."

In July, 1993 a spokesperson for the TM movement announced in Washington DC that the movement was no longer endorsing the work of Dr. Chopra. This announcement came a full year after the actual split with the Maharishi. Nonetheless Chopra was referred to as "our dear friend."

It is said that Deepak Chopra still practices and recommends Transcendental Meditation but sources have also said that the split with Maharishi was less than amicable and this is the real reason why the lawsuit is stalled. In order to press the suit successfully Chopra's visible cooperation would be necessary and, according to knowledgeable sources, Chopra is unwilling to expose himself in that arena any more. He is now the author of seven books with a combined sales figure of over two million copies. His latest book, *Ageless Body, Timeless Mind* has sold over 800,000 copies.

In his book *Return of The Rishi* Chopra wrote, "In my own mind, I had joined the mainstream of medical science. My ambition was to equal or surpass my American colleagues." No matter what Keay Davidson, Andrew Skolnick or *The Journal of The American Medical Association* have to say, it is undeniable that Deepak Chopra has realized that ambition.

In late 1993, Dr. Chopra joined the staff of Sharp Memorial Hospital, one of six hospitals operated by Sharp HealthCare, a not-for-profit community health care provider in the San Diego area. Sharp announced two new programs focusing on mind-body medicine, the Institute for Human Potential and Mind Body Medicine and the Center for Mind Body Medicine, founded to sponsor research and base patient treatments on controversial alternative medicine theories. Chopra was named the executive director of the new institute. Although the Mind Body Center will utilize other alternative techniques such as bio feedback, Ayur-veda will be the prime basis of treatment. It is interesting to note that the salutation "Maharishi" has been dropped. It is a bold move by a mainstream health care facility and most certainly driven by hard economics as much as by conviction.

A Harvard Medical School research team estimated that in 1990 Americans spent $10.3 billion out of pocket on alternative medical treatments compared to $12.8 billion out of pocket for conventional treatment. And in the current political climate where the health care initiative is encouraging an emphasis on preventative rather than intraventative treatment, a forward-looking institution like Sharp may well find an alliance with Chopra to be both politic and profitable. Critics of Aryu-veda say the folk medicine has not yet been subjected to rigorous scientific study to determine its potential and Sharp says that this will be the stated goal of the new Mind Body center.

On November 19, 1993 Chopra appeared on the *Phil Donahue Show*. But, if you didn't catch that episode when it originally aired, you're out of luck because *Gauntlet* has learned that that edition of the *Donahue Show* was recently placed on legal hold and is no longer available to the general public. At press time there is no explanation for this action.

And Penny Price — remember her? The television producer with the highly selective definition of the word "cult"—In this debate, Penny Price, without much provocation, falls squarely on the side of Deepak Chopra. "What he wants to do at where he is now at Sharp is that when patients come in, he wants to do controlled studies. 'Let's do a study using western medicine or holistic medicine or Ayur-vedic medicine or whatever and let's find out what works on different patients."

Ms. Price believes that Chopra was limited by his association with the Maharishi. "And it benefits him to [be independent]. I mean, he's an extraordinary doctor and for him to be limited because of only being able to practice Ayurvedic medicine . . .

"There was an award winning, I think, Pulitzer Prize winning journalist and he wrote a book that I read last year and he was talking about visiting various people in the New Age. It was very interesting. The chapter on the Maharishi International University Iowa was dreadful, Absolutely dreadful.

"Oh, I mean, very controlled," amended Penny Price, "and afraid and hierarchical. I mean, one would not want to go there. So perhaps it was cult-like. And this was a really good journalist.

"So when that kind of stuff comes up, Deepak doesn't mean that. I mean, he's in a whole other field. He separated himself from that."

Yes, he has separate himself from that. With a little push from Andrew Skolnick and *The Journal of the American Medical*

Association.

"Ayur-veda was pre-scientific; Maharishi Ayur-veda is pseudo-scientific," says Andrew Skolnick. "It came about in a culture that was Pre-western science. There may be a lot of useful things in there which by trial and error they picked up and continued. But there's also a lot of superstition and ineffectual treatment, of course. And also a lot of potential harmful things. To be fair it may have some very interesting and very useful stuff and that's why JAMA — in the interests of looking at traditional medicine and looking at the stuff of worth — that's why the [original] article was published. That's what I think about Ayur-veda. There may be some potentially dangerous stuff. They are pre-scientific. They did not evaluate their claims in a rigorous enough way. Their experiments have not been replicated by others."

How do you feel about holistic medicine?

"Holistic medicine is like New Age, It's a nonsense term," he says. "All good medicine is holistic. You know what it's like, it's like saying 'Oh, I'm not a reporter. I'm an investigative reporter. All good journalists are investigative reporters — should be. All good doctors are holistic doctors. You treat the patient; you don't treat the disease. It's an artificial dichotomy: the New Agers claim there is holistic medicine and there's conventional medicine. Nonsense."

In June, 1994 Andrew Skolnick won the Morris Fishbine Award for Excellence in Medical Communications for Health Professionals; from the American Medical Writers Association.

INTO THE MAINSTREAM: THE NEW WORLD OF CULTS

Marcia R. Rudin

Jews and Jewish organizations are tired of hearing about cults. They want to put their attention and money into new problems. After nearly twenty years of working to combat cults, I'm tired of them too, and I'd like to move on to something else and get on with my life. But unfortunately the families, "significant others" and friends of cult members aren't tired of this problem; their rage and pain is fresh.

Cults have not gone away. On the contrary, the numbers of cults and those affected by them are mushrooming. I know this from the volume of cries for help I receive regularly on two telephone hotlines, and from the huge increase in calls after major media stories about cults, such as the Branch Davidian crisis last spring.

My colleagues and I in the counter-cult field don't have exact statistics, but we estimate there are three thousand to five thousand groups and two million to three million people who have been or are members. Cults are everywhere throughout the United States and the world, including Israel. Recruiters are rushing into the former Soviet Union and other Eastern European countries to snap up converts in a new, ripe marketplace. Cult-education organizations now exist in countries throughout Western Europe and in Japan, Canada, South Amer-

ica, Australia, Israel and the Caribbean. We receive anguished calls for help from all over the world. Sometimes people asking assistance bypass the phone and mail and just appear, desperate and in tears, in our offices.

People joke that Branch Davidian leader David Koresh was the "wacko from Waco." But Koresh wasn't crazy. He was just acting like a typical cult leader, pushing his power to the limits with followers conditioned to hand over complete control of their lives to him. Dying for — or at the hand of — David Koresh was a logical conclusion to a situation that contained the typical ingredients in a recipe for cult disaster: an authoritarian leader, an ends-justifies-the-means philosophy, and followers who submit themselves totally.

But Koresh and his group did NOT typify the kind of cults most common today. Many are not religious groups and most cult members don't live communally. To the degree that we continue to think of cults along such lines, we miss the dangers they present. Today there are a wide variety of cults that attract followers by offering mass mind-empowerment, psychotherapy, business opportunities, and political activism. Rather than promising spiritual salvation or ultimate meaning, they skillfully market themselves to a new clientele by offering financial success,

I DON'T MIND GIVING UP ALL MY WORLDLY POSESSIONS, BUT CAN'T I AT LEAST GET A TAX WRITE-OFF?

WARDLE '94

happiness, social success, and self-ful-fillment. And more often than we are aware, they appeal not to the young "counterculture" seekers of the 1960s and 1970s but to older, affluent, established, "normal" people.

In short, cults have main-streamed themselves. Today's cult members come from every ethnic and religious background and include young adults, the middle-aged and elderly, and children. Entire families join or develop within a group. Thousands of small children are raised within cults, and often ex-perience nothing of the outside world. The number of small children in Koresh's Branch Davidians and the abuse and neglect they suffered se-cretly is replicated in hundreds of other groups.

What makes these diverse groups cults or cultic is their leaders' use of deception and sophisticated mind-control techniques to recruit and keep adherents, and their ma-nipulation and abuse of members. Beliefs are not the issue. Cults spring from all ideologies.

The Branch Davidians' fiery con-flagration was a spectacular horror, but smaller, quieter, unnoticed hor-rors take place in cults every day. In

their closed, unmonitored societies, cult leaders violate the human rights of their members, especially those of women and children. Members are forced to cut off contact with outside friends and families; even when fami-lies are members of the cult, relation-ships are often disrupted or severed. Living under totalistic conditions, cult members lose their decision-making abilities, and it is not uncom-mon that they give up school and careers to devote all of their time and energy to the group. And they fre-quently suffer medial neglect and physical, psychological and sexual abuse.

Ex-cultists spend years recover-ing from the intellectual and psycho-logical effects even if they were in a group for a short time. Experts be-lieve these scars may never fade. Some are lucky enough to find help within counter-cult networks such as the ones I work with. Others who leave cults on their own — we call them "walkaways," and they are now the majority of former cult members, experts believe — receive no help at all. Because ex-members tell us they must constantly have their recovery process reinforced, we provide recov-ery workshops attended by old and young alike. But there's such de-mand for this help that we have to turn people away. I'll never forget hearing one young man weep on the telephone when I told him that the registration for one of our workshops has just closed and that he would have to wait until the next one began.

Cults say counter-cults such as myself infringe on freedom of belief and religion, that we are bigots or parents who are unhappy that our children have made choices we don't like. They are skillful at getting this message out to the general public in order to discredit us and to avoid responding to the charges against them. They harass us personally with surreptitious surveillance, which invades our constitutional right to privacy, and with specious lawsuits against one cult-education organization; so far they have launched about fifty. Even though the cult has never won in court, it costs hundreds of hours and time and thousands of dollars to fight these suits.

Cult propaganda claims we are the threat to cultural and ideological pluralism and to democracy because we want to quash unpopular "new religious movements" and "alternative lifestyles". but it is the authoritarian, totalistic cults that threaten freedom of choice by pressuring recruits into committing to their group without full knowledge of it and by harassing critics, including journalists who write about them, in order to silence the truth. One journalist told us he would never do another cult story because of the harassment from a group he wrote about.

Some cults threaten our democracy also because of their political agendas, which span the spectrum from right to left. A few groups are so wealthy that they've been able to buy expensive attorneys and influence our government and large media outlets.

How does this affect us as Jews?

On a broad scale, we know that extremist political agendas, whether on the right or the left, never bode well for Jews. Many of the new political cults are anti-Semitic in their ideas and teachings, as are some of the older, more traditional-style religious cults.

On a personal scale, Jewish families are impacted by cults in proportions far larger than our two percent of the population. Because many of the new religious cults are Christian in theology, Jews don't join these in large numbers. Instead adult, middle-aged, elderly and affluent mainstream Jews are consumers of business, mass-mind empowerment, therapy, political, and new-age cults which pitch happiness, success and self-fulfillment.

And the mass mind-empowerment cults present a challenge to our traditions as Jews. These are based on a monistic philosophy that teaches that you are divine. The only thing keeping you from enlightenment or from realizing your power or divinity is rational thought. There is no right or wrong; you should do only what feels good to you. And with the correct mental outlook, you can do — or be — anything. Such thinking, based on Eastern religious thought, is contrary to the Jewish concept of morality and the essential separateness of humans and God. Hence, while these newer kinds of cults are not anti-Semitic, they are a challenge to Jewish identity. In addition, the selfishness that results from this philosophy runs counter to Jewish concepts of community, concern about others, and working toward a better world for all.

The Jewish community has drastically cut its financial and personnel commitment to fighting cults. We must pour more, not fewer, resources into fighting this serious problem. We need to educate our rabbis, mental health professionals, social service workers, physicians, attorneys, youth, and their parents and grandparents who are also cult-recruitment targets. And we must offer Jews a sense of community and a personal and vibrant belief system that will speak to the loneliness, despair, and isolation that may make them vulnerable to cults.

Reprinted with permission from PS: The Intelligent Guide to Jewish Affairs. Marcia Rudin is director of the International Cult Education Program.

The Brother Julius Cult

Judith A. Gaines

The Messiah has returned to earth and is preaching in New England, according to about 100 people who call themselves the followers of Brother Julius.

They live in central Connecticut and their savior is "Brother Julius" Schacknow, 69, a doomsday prophet also known as a "sinful Messiah." He says he intentionally demonstrates the evils of the world so they can be overcome. As he put it in a rare interview, God told him "He wanted me to know what it feels like to be a Commandment-breaker, so I would be a just judge when the time came for me to judge."

Former-cult members say the sins Brother Julius demonstrates include polygamy, sexual abuse of women, labor fraud and more. They claim his son sexually abuses children. They call Schacknow a blasphemer, a charlatan, an exploiter, and worse. Many feel deeply betrayed. Said one ex-follower who was devastated by his cult experience, "I haven't been able to go to church since then. I've put religion on a shelf. It's something I try to forget."

Devoted disciples just as fervently deny the allegations, stressing that Jesus was wrongly scorned and vilified during his first earthly appearance, too. They claim Brother Julius has healed addictions and illnesses and brought meaning to their lives. In the words of one disciple, "He's a great teacher of Truth." They call him, simply, "The Lord."

The fiery end of the Branch Dividian sect in Waco, Texas, last year heightened interest in the estimated 2,500 cults operating in the US today — groups that differ from other organizations mainly in the degree of control exerted over the membership by a leader who claims a special mantle of authority. This control often includes efforts to isolate followers from family and friends outside the cult, and other practices normally considered to be private, such as dictating sexual arrangements.

Most of these groups go their quiet and secretive ways, calmly countenanced by civic authorities, observing their rights to privacy and freedom of religion. But their existence raises the question that was so unsatisfactorily resolved in Waco: At what point does society have the right to intervene?

The U.S. Constitution guarantees that all Americans can practice whatever religion they prefer. "It's when cult practices break the law and infringe on people's basic human rights that society has an obligation to investigate," observes Steven Hassan, a Somerville, Massachusetts resident and author of *Combatting Cult Mind Control*, who has counseled about 15 former members of Brother Julius's group.

Has Brother Julius stepped over

this line?

Society has stepped into the world of his cult, also known as "The Work," on many occasions. In civil lawsuits, two women accused Schacknow of having sexually molested them. The suits were settled out of court for undisclosed sums. At least one labor fraud suit has also been settled out of court. And Schacknow's son, Daniel Sweetman, was convicted of sexually abusing children.

After the U.S. Labor Department accused two of Schacknow's "apostles" of having looted the pension plans of 130 employees in one

cult-run business, the two agreed to reimburse $1.8 million and to waive their rights to an additional $300,000. The state of Connecticut also currently is suing another cult-run business for a range of environmental violations, including illegally altering and polluting a stream and destroying wetlands.

In the face of such charges, Brother Julius is implacable. About 5'7" tall, overweight and balding, he has a long grey beard, piercing blue eyes and a deep, resonant voice. In a four-hour interview at the offices of the *Boston Globe* — the only interview he had granted in six years — he declined to discuss the allegations against him, calling them "smears" and "smut" and saying he had been repeatedly misunderstood. He mainly read at length from the Bible and explained this by saying, "I can't improve on my own word, I just quote scripture."

But current followers said the allegations are unfounded. "He's brought nothing but good into my life," said one employee at the cult-owned Northwood Real Estate Office, in Bristol, Ct. The charges against Schacknow "are distorted out of proportion," she said.

Taking a positive tack in the interview, Brother Julius tried to explain why he believes he is the Messiah, why he has come to New England, and some of his prophesies for the future.

Schacknow was born August 21, 1924 in Brooklyn, New York, into a poor Jewish family. He had no religious training, never went to college, and said he "knew nothing of God" until 1946, when he was a sailor in the US Navy.

In a "living vision," he said, he "was taken up into heaven, and I stood before God, who looked at me with eyes of love and called me by my name, Julius. I thought, holy smoke, God knows my name!"

Then he said God told him: "You are a very special predestined chosen vessel to help me close the world and your generation of evil, and I will make you a light for the gentiles and hope for my people of Israel . . . When you return to earth, read nothing but the Holy Bible for five full years. You are my son. All things will be made known to you in the future."

There were several subsequent visions marked by divine appearances and reaffirmations of Schacknow's surprising status. He began earnestly studying the scriptures, where he found his true identity, he said. He was Jesus, the one and only. He cited chapter and verse showing that God would be made flesh, that Jesus only fulfilled part of the Messiah's mission, and that he would come again at the end of the world.

"Think of how it feels to be me," he said. He had come to earth as Jesus and now he's back again, but despite all his teachings humankind was still doing the same old things — "cheating, stealing, lying and sodomizing."

"I'm disgusted," he said. "And I'm warning all the inhabitants of earth: change your ways, turn back to God, or divine destruction is coming."

After two unsuccessful marriages, Schacknow wed Joanne in the early 1960s and the couple moved to Dover, N.J., where he worked as an employee of the Federal Electric Corporation and began preaching to his fellow workers at lunchtime. In 1968, he resigned the job, saying he had a religious calling.

He led a small Bible study group and began preaching to whoever would listen. Early in 1970, he declared his identity to his followers. Ron Loncar, of Windsor Locks, Ct., one of Schacknow's followers at that time, said he was at a meeting in Trumbull, Ct., when Brother Julius "announced to everybody's shock and amazement that he was Jesus Christ."

Some members of the group were flabbergasted and left his circle. But others believed his claims and gradually his following grew. Schacknow expanded his territory, moving particularly into central Connecticut and seaside towns in southern Massachusetts — Marshfield, Scituate, Weymouth, Cohasset, Norwell, Hanover, and Duxbury. His doctrines of divine

justice and love and the healing power of faith seemed like heaven-sent balm to many who were feeling lost and unloved, and who were looking for uncomplicated answers. The idea that he might be The Lord was awe-inspiring.

"The possibility that the actual Messiah was in my midst completely overwhelmed me," recalled Rick Keegan, a recruit from Weymouth, who dropped out of college to join Julius' select band. "The authority with which Julius spoke combined with the vivid detail of his heavenly visions was so engrossing that you felt as if you were there with him. Julius would quote scripture after scripture confirming the claim of his Messiahship, mixing in some near Eastern philosophies, healings, and fatherly attention which I drank in like a thirsty child."

Stephen Mehl, a former follower now living in Nantucket, remembered the first time he saw Schacknow. "He was wearing a long blue robe and preaching on a hillside overlooking a lake," Mehl said. Brother Julius was a charismatic speaker with an inspiring command of the scriptures, "and when he prayed over people, they'd fall on the ground and shake or go into convulsions."

"A lot of young people were impressed," Mehl continued, "and I couldn't stop thinking about him . . . In college, many things had made me despondent about the material world and I was ripe for spiritual messages." Soon Mehl was Schacknow's "South Shore Apostle," recruiting Massachusetts members living south of Boston.

For a few years, all went well, Mehl, Keegan and others said. Schacknow arranged marriages — most members were aged 16 to 22 — provided jobs, and gave their lives "vast meaning and purpose," Keegan said. "After all, we were hand-picked by the Messiah himself to help him close the age! The uncertainty and melancholy of my life had given way to a euphoric sense of belonging."

Members did not live communally but occupied separate apartments or houses in the Connecticut towns of Southington, Plainville, Meriden and vicinity. They worked at the cult's expanding, multi-million dollar real estate and construction businesses and donated a hefty portion of their weekly paychecks to The Work.

They also allowed Schacknow unusual power to enter into many aspects of their lives. For instance, he and Joanne approved all marriages. Cult members also were actively discouraged from maintaining contact with former friends or family. Said Keegan, "We were taught that a man's enemies would be of his own household."

Members also were taught that they were "living words of God." They were given new names by Brother Julius to define who they would be for eternity. The word was said to represent the member's most angelic quality, such as "joy," "peace,"

"tenderness," and so on. The words also were the basis for the seating order at meetings, with the "most pure" members placed closest to Julius and those out of favor put in sections said to correspond to limbo, purgatory or hell. Disciples who displeased Schacknow risked having their word changed for the worse or eliminated altogether, effectively excommunicating them.

Pat Goski, a former member now living in New Jersey, explained that having their word downgraded or removed was "a very severe punishment in the eyes of members: it's tantamount to having your angelic life and identity taken away. The member must then endure the disgrace of being looked upon, and addressed, as a mere human, and as someone who is failing God!"

But God, it seemed, soon began failing his followers.

Although some continued to revere Julius as an "exhilarating teacher of truth," in the words of one believer, others saw the situation slowly deteriorating.

Goski remembered one Sunday when Julius wanted to illustrate the importance of parents using adequate discipline with their children. When a child, about 4 years old, began whining at the meeting, "each member of the family, including parents, was then required to take down their pants, including underpants, and bend over Julius' knee to be spanked."

When members tried to question these or other humiliating tactics, she said, "they were told that the word 'why' was considered a devil. You were never supposed to question Julius or his commands, because that was rejecting God. They had a formula for casting out evil spirits. You repeat these words, 'In the name of Julius and JoAnne, you devil, you spirit of doubt, I cast you out and bind you until the Day of Judgment."

In several interviews, former members said Julius and Joanne, who was also known as "The Holy Spirit," believed they had the right to ask certain followers for sexual favors. One former follower, who asked not to be identified, said that when she was 19 and new to the cult, "Julius came to me privately and said I was ready to receive the divine seed. It would help me be more Godlike."

Another said Joanne made sexual advances at him, saying he had been "called to be one of her men." One youngster, who was born in the cult and left with his father at age 17, said some of his close friends were abused by Daniel Sweetman. "He tried to do it with me, but I ran out of the room," he said.

In civil suits filed in 1986 and 1988 and settled out of court, two women, including one of his stepdaughters, accused Schacknow of sexually molesting them when they were children. Daniel Sweetman was sent to prison for a year for sexually molesting two boys, then ages 9 and 10, from different families.

And many members were stunned when Julius announced not only that he intended to take seven or eight wives and several concubines, but that other men in the group might be required to have sex with women other than their wives, or to swap wives.

Some members charged that they were being exploited financially, paid subminimum wages and forced to engage in fraudulent labor practices. Pat Goski said she worked six days a week, 12 hours a day, and never received more than $60 a week. She also said many laborers were officially "laid off" but were still expected to work full-time at cult businesses. They were paid the difference between the unemployment benefits and their normal wage.

A former member whose word was "Clearness" was one of several who sued Brother Julius' enterprises for back wages and damages. He settled out of court for $25,000.

Despite threats that they would become depressed, diseased or damned if they left, disillusioned members began departing in droves. Membership plummeted from at least 600 at its peak to the approximately 100 stalwarts who remain today. Some say the total is even lower — with as few as 50 true believers left.

Today, the remaining followers keep to themselves in a disciplined life that centers around Bible study at group meetings and work at one of the cult's businesses. These include a realty, an insurance firm, a construction company, a quarry operation, and a "truth center" which publishes writings by cult members.

Schacknow's main residence is located in the town of Berlin — a small, white wooden house with yellow shutters and a flower-filled heart cut into the front lawn. "He thinks he's Jesus," said one young neighbor, with a sneer. "What that means is, he wants you to mow his lawn and not take a penny for it."

Schacknow and Joanne have divorced, and she has remarried Paul Sweetman, the cult's chief apostle, who oversees business affairs. The eleven other apostles each represent a sign of the zodiac and look after members born under their sign.

For a time, many parents removed their children from public schools in favor of a large cult homeschool, known as Eastgate. But that was discontinued because of financial difficulties and after school officials pressed parents to seek psychiatric help for some of the children, according to former members.

Several cult businesses have been closed or gone bankrupt. The U.S. Labor Department charged Paul

Sweetman and Alfred Dube Jr., another apostle, with bilking $2 million from the pension plans of workers at the cult's County Wide Construction Company, and the two have agreed to reimburse the bulk of the money. The Connecticut Department of Transportation has sued another cult business, variously known as Quarry Associates or Fairfield Resources, charging that it has filled in wetlands, diverted a stream, built an illegal dam, and pumped so much water from the pit that nearby residential wells have gone dry.

And Brother Julius reportedly has been ailing.

Police in several communities where the cult operates said they had investigated allegations of inappropriate activity over the years, but had not found any criminal violations recently. Neighbors described the cultists as "unfriendly" and "tight-lipped," and Brother Julius as a "charlatan," but had no serious complaints.

"Only the Lord would know what he knows," countered one current member, who claimed Julius' healing power was so strong she has "hardly had an aspirin in the 17 years I've been with him." She dismissed the defectors as "people with a gripe, something to complain about."

But Hassan said he is "extremely concerned" about the remaining members.

"It's got to be devastating to watch long-term followers fall away and leave the fold," he said. "And to see Julius ill is very disconfirming to all their years of indoctrination."

Hassan says he worries that the members "are at high risk for suicide or nervous breakdown, because their whole belief system is crumbling," and many cultists long ago severed their ties with family and friends outside the group who could provide support. If they don't have mental breakdowns, the probability is high that "they will find some other totalistic group to switch allegiances to, so they can continue their black-and-white thinking patterns."

An amazingly large number of such cults are popping up now, he added. And their numbers will only continue to grow as the end of the millennium approaches.

*This is an greatly expanded and updated version of an article that first appeared in the **Boston Globe**. Judith A. Gaines is a journalist at the **Boston Globe**. As **Gauntlet** does not have space constraints of many dailies for a comprehensive article, we have afforded the writer a venue to fashion her piece as she would have wished. We invite other journalists who would like to expand upon stories they have covered for dailies or other periodicals to contact us.*

THE NEED FOR DEPROGRAMMING

Rick Ross

Destructive cults and their related tragedies seems to be a recurring episodic nightmare marring our American dreamscape. Some on the growing list are the Manson Family in the 60s, the SDA political cult that abducted Patty Hearst in the 70s, Jonestown in 1978, MOVE of Philadelphia in the 80s and now the Waco Davidians. First, we are shocked and then fascinated by each event, but later they just become another sound bite in our collective consciousness.

The Waco story seems to be nearing its conclusion. The jury acquitted all eleven Davidian defendants of murder, but found five guilty of voluntary manslaughter regarding the four slain ATF agents. Perhaps the five convicted were really guilty of involuntary manslaughter. David Koresh totally controlled his followers. They were completely dependent upon him for almost every decision. When the shooting started in the compound everyone must have obeyed his commands. Within that milieu Koresh was king and disobedience meant betrayal, not only of him, but God.

Why were the Branch-Davidians willing to sacrifice their lives and children for the "lamb of God" (Koresh)? Most of us would prefer to believe that they were insane, disturbed or simply stupid, refusing to accept the reality that the mind can be controlled. Denial makes us feel safe.

However, both the American Psychological and Sociological Associations have passed resolutions acknowledging thought reform. *The Encyclopedia of Sociology, Merck Manual of Diagnosis* and *Therapy and the Diagnostic Statistical Manual* of the American Psychiatric Association have included discussion of this subject. Dr. Robert Jay Lifton published definitive research in his book, *Thought Reform and the Psychology of Totalism* and further proof was offered by Dr. Flavil Yeakley Jr. in his book, *The Discipling Dilemma*.

I learned the details about David Koresh's methods of mind-control through successfully deprogramming two of his victims. Deprogramming is a process of unraveling the group's program through dialogue and education about the cult in question, cults in general and the techniques of thought reform. This is done by sharing information through discussion, films and written material. Hopefully, this results in reactivated critical thinking, accomplished largely by providing an alternative frame of reference.

Cults oppose deprogramming because it works. 80% of my cases result in members leaving the group. This often causes other members to doubt and reconsider their commitment and may allow important information to leak out about abuse, finances or criminal conduct within the cult. In an effort to keep members and information under their control cult leaders will say and/or do almost anything.

Destructive religious groups often claim their "religious freedom" is under attack whenever anyone attempts to criticize their motives or behavior. However, the First Amendment does not protect ANYTHING done in "the name of God." Their propaganda also frequently includes attacks against deprogrammers and deprogramming. This is done partly to induce unreasonable fear in their followers by describing the process as torture, abuse and "faith-breaking". Members may run as a direct result of this conditioning if their families attempt an intervention.

About 10% of my cases have been done on an involuntary basis. That means physical restraint was exercised by families to keep their child from leaving during the deprogramming. Many of these cases included minors, but others were adult children. Some reasons families chose an involuntary intervention were possible death, sterilization, essential medical treatment, and sexual and/or physical abuse.

Recently, I was charged with "unlawful imprisonment" re-

garding a failed involuntary deprogramming. Numerous cult groups urged a prosecutor to refile a case that had been dismissed in 1991. The jury returned a verdict of "not guilty" after only two hours of deliberation. It seems they realized that when families make the choice of involuntary deprogramming, they are often running out of time and hope.

After more than a decade deprogramming cult victims I know that those who fight cults will be targeted. My life and family have been threatened, I have been stalked, physically attacked, slandered, sued, libeled and maliciously prosecuted. However, each year I receive many calls, cards, and letters from former cult members I have helped. They express joy, relief, happiness, hope and most of all freedom. This more than balances the scale.

IN GOD WE TRUST

UNLIMITED COMMOTION AT UNLIMITED DEVOTION

Joseph A. Gervasi

[Editor's Note: The following two articles provide differing perspectives of a small cult in Northern California. They were submitted by Gauntlet subscribers after reading cults were to be our focus topic of this issue. These writers do not know one another and their viewpoints make for an interesting juxtaposition.]

I first became aware of the Church of Unlimited Devotion when two friends of mine, Sanders and his wife Sandy — who I knew from when they lived in New Jersey — extended an offer to me to come stay with them at the Church's Community in Philo, part of Mendicino County in Northern California, when I passed through the San Francisco Bay Area on part of a trip I was taking in the spring of 1992. All that I knew of the Community was told to me by a mutual friend who had spent some time with them on a trip he had taken just a few months before I was to leave. He had a great time there, and while my idea of fun wasn't necessarily spending a few days with some "very religious, gentle hippies", I felt that this would be a rare opportunity to observe these individuals as more of a sympathetic friend of one of their own than an outsider who might not be trusted.

It wasn't until I was picked up by Sanders and Sandy on Haight-Ashbury and on the way up through the sleepy Northern California towns that I really got the low-down on the Church of Unlimited Devotion. The Church had been founded by a man named Joseph just a year before. Previously, some members of the core group of fifteen members had been together for seven years. Their religion was a fusion of Catholicism and Krishnaism (called *veda-ism* by them). The women (called *mas*) of the Community dressed almost like nuns, complete with habits and heavy, formless dresses. Most of the men wore monk-style shirts with tiny crosses embroidered on the chest. They didn't eat meat or "spicy" vegetables such as mushrooms, onions or garlic (because Prabhupada, a deceased Krishna spiritual leader, said they "ignite the passions" or something to that effect), and did not consume alcohol, yet many of them smoked marijuana up to three times a day in "puff circles" (a "religious ritual") off in the woods. The puff circles once took place in the center of the Community — which is located atop a very mountainous area near another well-known "alternative community" (at least in that area), the Haywards — until the media began to sniff around, so they moved them into the surrounding woods.

In the morning the Community chanted "Hare Krishna" and danced around in what's called *Kirtan*; at night, before eating, they recited the Rosary in their temple. The men and women lived in separate buildings called *oshrams*, unless they were married, in which case they were permitted to live together.

At the time I was there, the church owned a cow and a calf, a horse and chicken I never saw. They

Sandy & Sanders in the
Prayer Room - Spring 1992

sibly most importantly — peddle the garments they made back at the Community in Philo.

The Church of Unlimited Devotion's primary source of income, it seemed, was from the sales of the huge volume of clothing they made in the "spinning room". They wove and dyed pants and shirts and long hippie- dresses, all in the Guatemalan style so popular among Grateful Dead fans. Each day after *Kirtan*, while some members of the Community would sit about and read or get in little groups to "philosophize", the women would gather in this spinning room, which also served as the dining hall at night, to sew and listen to the hundreds of Grateful Dead bootleg tapes they amassed.

At the time that I arrived at the Community, there was a quiet revolution going on. Their "spiritual leader", the aforementioned Joseph, was being ousted and turmoil was feared by Community members in his wake. There was a whole laundry list of torrid allegations against him (none of which I can confirm): While he was married to a much-loved member of the Community, Annie, he was having intercourse with another member of the Community, Konjari, in his office while the other devotees prayed the Rosary. To top it off, he forced his wife to watch on many occasions. One time he supposedly had Konjari give him oral sex while his wife drove the two of them somewhere. But this was only the tip of the depravity iceberg. Allegations abounded that he beat Annie (in the shower, so the blood would run down the drain) before the church was formed, and that he had forced her to get an abortion and paid for it with Church funds. Even the very nature

had another cow not long before I arrived, but it overate sixty pounds of food. They refused to have a vet look it over, as they shun modern medicine, and it died. They prayed the Rosary over it's carcass, then buried it by the cabin Sanders and Sandy were living in. I was told they also had a couple peacocks at one time, but they escaped when they were put in a cage with a massive hole in it. The food they consumed either came from their own gardens or were donated or acquired from dumpsters. To my knowledge, they purchased nothing.

Where the Church was most famous was in the close-knit inner-core following that the Grateful Dead had trailing them about the country. In this circle, the members of the Church were known as "the spinners" because of the whirling dervish style dance they performed at Dead shows. These shows served several purposes for the Unlimited Devotees: 1) To recruit new members among the legions of fans who would attend the shows, many of whom worshipped The Dead as sort of demigods and could, perhaps, be convinced to join the ranks of fellow deadheads who served another set of gods. 2) To enjoy the music of a band they felt had a spiritual link to. 3) To — posof their marriage was in question — I was led to believe that they got married to get a lighter sentence on a drug bust.

The night I arrived, his "trial" was taking place in the spinning room/eating hall. The group was reading Joseph's sins and a confession written *for* him by his wife, Annie, who temporarily left the community so as not to have to face him and, in turn, be manipulated by him. I found out his trial had been going on since early morning. They accused him while he knelt before a crucifix begging forgiveness. Upon my entrance (shoe-less, as their rules demanded), thirty or forty pairs of eyes fell upon me. They didn't like having an outsider present, apparently. Several raised their voices in protest, so I left with Sandy while Sanders stuck around.

The next morning I got clued in on many more of the allegations levied against Joseph. I was told about books on mind control and handcuffs he kept hidden. A story was related to me about how a man — whose hand I shook the night before — was punished for supposedly having an affair and was beaten by Joseph until he fell down. Then Joseph ordered a group of females that he brought with him to kick him.

What was most ironic about this was that Joseph, who apparently had a strong hold over everyone in the Community, enforced very strict laws to keep the unmarried men and women apart. Free love was not permitted (unless of course you were, like him, beyond reproach). After the trial ended, I witnessed the Community members tentatively begin to loosen up. Some men and women would lie together in the sun, not worried about being chastised for their feelings.

The end result of Joseph's "trial" was never made clear to me. From what I was told, he was taken into town and put on a bus back to his parents (though he was at least in his late twenties), head cast down in shame. I did get to see Konjari taken away, but at the time I didn't know it was her. All I saw was a veiled woman, also with her head down, being led to a vehicle to, presumably, be taken to town.

It seemed to me that the devotees of the Church of Unlimited Devotion were there of their own free will. While a few were saucer-eyed and zombie-like (especially the drug casualty that shared the cabin with Sanders and Sandy), most were seemingly happy and very friendly to me despite my appearance (I'm obviously not a hippie). There was no forced labor, just a division of tasks based on skills. Each member of the Community performed a service that would benefit the entire Community. Sanders' job, for example, was to tend to the compost heap, which he felt was a fair trade for his being able to live there.

The main problem I perceived was the presence of two children. The first was a boy of eight or so. He belonged to the zombie-like woman who shared the cabin with Sanders and Sandy. He didn't seem to be an unhappy child, but he rarely wore shoes (even through the mud) and from what I heard definitely didn't go to an outside school or get any home instruction. The other child was a girl, age (approximately) three, who belonged to a devotee couple. She toddled around barefoot most of the time and, from what I was told, didn't have regular doctor's exams (Joseph allegedly said he'd rather she die than see a doctor).

After my stay of a few days, Sanders and Sandy drove me back to San Francisco and we parted on very friendly terms. I left a Community about to make a lot of changes — for the better, they hoped. And while several members of the Church felt that one man, much older than the rest, was making overtures to lead them (despite their resolution not to have a set leader), they were hopeful and ready to move on. I returned to New Jersey and wound up getting an article entitled, "The Church of Unlimited Devotion: An Outsider's Inside Look", published in the *Anderson Valley Advertiser* (A.V.A.), Medicino County's renowned local newspaper.

Sanders felt that I had betrayed him by writing the piece "behind his back", though I had told him all along that I intended to have my experiences in the Community published. What occurred as a result of the publication came to me in only scattered bits through a mutual friend. I was told that Sanders came into the center of the Community, one morning, to find several devotees gathered in a circle crying. He went to see what the problem was and discovered they were reading something in the newspaper. As it turned out, it was the article that I had written. He was not only hurt, but was put in a position whereupon he had to explain that he had no idea what I was "really" up to — the destruction of their Community. Not long after, he moved away with his wife so that she could have their baby at the home of his parents.

Until recently, I had only heard

about the article's aftershocks from others. Then I spoke to Bruce Anderson, the editor of the A.V.A., to find out what really happened. According to him, the article helped to kill the Church of Unlimited Devotion. While some members are still up there (eight or so, I was told by a neighbor I spoke to), they disbanded after the local Department of Social Services and Health and Building Inspectors began to investigate them. He said it took them that long to intervene (though they were more or less aware what went on up there) because in such a small county they prefer not to spend money on things unless they absolutely have to. Another problem arose from the hostile takeover by an enemy of Joseph's who bought out the remaining shares in the land. According to a neighbor of the Community, he allowed the members to stay, but their resentment of him drove many away. As for Joseph, I was told he encountered some problems on the East Coast, but Mr. Anderson was unsure exactly what they were.

There was no doubt that the Church of Unlimited Devotion was (is?) a cult, but while abuse took place, the members seemed to be free to come and go as they pleased. Mind control may have occurred, but as adults the members were exercising their Constitutional right to choose their own religion. As for the children, however, a great injustice was being perpetrated upon them, and for that reason alone I'm glad the Church has, for the most part, disbanded. I only hope that the situation they are growing up in now is safer for them than the Church of Unlimited Devotion was.

Joseph Gervasi is editor of NO LONGER A FANzine. A sample copy is available for $2 (cash only) at 142 Frankford Ave., Blackwood, N.J. 08012.

Unlimited Devotion

AM I HOLY YET?

Stacy Cancelarich

moment. My head feels like a pinball machine; each thought rushes to the top, then ricochets around, before crashing through a hole to my stomach. The truth will go away or change, or as it is supposed to — belong to someone else, I do not wish to own this truth, I do not want it to be mine. The truth — my sister is in a religious cult. I say this aloud, more frequently now, hoping if I say it often enough, it will penetrate my mind a little deeper.

This is not a new revelation; my sister has been a member of The Church of Unlimited Devotion for several years. Her involvement and resulting metamorphosis have deepened over time, and the group has grown in size. My parents and I have known for years that she is involved with a peculiar group of people. At first, our knowledge was limited. It is easy to condemn those with an alternative lifestyle, and we did not want to be judgmental.

"Maybe we should give her credit for escaping the rat race," I would say.

"I don't care that she's a vegetar-

"Just take a look and let me know if you want to go. Dad and I are going, so just read it over, you don't have to go if you don't want to," my mother says, after placing a pamphlet on my glass coffee table. "Do you think you're interested?"

"I don't know, Mom, I just don't know," I say.

My parents have left, and there it is — the pamphlet, describing the Cult Awareness Seminar, to be held April 5th, at the Holiday Inn.

I can only stare at it. I do not want to touch it. My brain is frozen, the impenetrable steel wall rising once again, to protect me from the excruciating, yet inevitable decision I must make. I am unable to face reality at its worst, and most pressing

ian, or follows the Grateful Dead. I just wish she would take better care of herself," my mother would say.

But with each passing phone call or visit from California, it became clear that her mind was no longer her own. For Lori, "me," "myself," and "I" has become "us" and "we." She is unable or unwilling to make her own decisions. My little sister, the person I grew up with is gone. Someone or something has taken her place.

Through her admissions, my eavesdropping, and a network of other group family members, I have learned much more than I want to know. The group has a doctrine, and a hierarchy of members, who make rules and pass judgment when needed. High-ranking members hold counsel with those who have doubts, or need help following the way of the Lord. They pray throughout the day, perform various rituals, sleep on the floor, do not believe in doctors, and eat only what they need to survive. This group of twenty has a mind of one. Everything is done for the greater good; there is no self, no individuality. Members are made to feel weak and are filled with self-doubt. All of their answers, their "guidance," comes from Joseph — he is their self-proclaimed leader. You must aspire to his wishes; he knows the way. His approval is the ultimate praise, although I know he can never give it. Like other powerful leaders, he must keep his members, his rank and file, filled with the idea that they are no good.

My sister was visiting me when I heard her sobbing these words on the telephone, "I know that I'm weak. Yes I want to perform the highest order of service." I have since heard these and many other frightening conversations take place between my sister and her "brothers and sisters."

The members make progress on their path to being holy, but they will never get there. Deprivation, and the lack of all creature comforts, make them weak. Any desire for this comfort confirms their weakness, and their need to work harder. This is how the cycle of mind control takes hold, until there is seemingly no way out.

> This group of twenty has a mind of one . . . there is no self, no individuality.

My sister always spoke of their celibacy, their desire to be free of this worldly and common human act. You can imagine our surprise when she arrived home six months pregnant, on the eve of Yom Kippur in 1990.

My mother entered her home, and found my sister standing in the living room.

"I didn't want to tell you on the phone," she said.

My mother begged and pleaded with my sister to see a doctor. Finally, my sister conceded, after Mom promised that the doctor would only look at her. When my sister told the group what she had done, and why (to save my mother's sanity), her loyalty, decision, and the strength of her devotion were called into question. Her weakness was revealed and her mind further shattered.

I suppose the arrival of an innocent baby propelled my parents to the path they are now traveling. They attend a support group for the families of cult members. These meetings with other parents, and a counselor, have helped them to cope with the situation. It has provided them with possible actions they can take to change the situation.

They brought home some literature on the behavior of cult members, and how to recognize them. Denial had carried me this far, but after reading the books I realized it wouldn't carry me much further. The descriptions, while not about my sister's group, *were* about my sister.

"I would like you to come with us to a meeting, Stacy," my mother said.

I wanted to run far away from these words. But how could I say no? This was my family, and my parents had done so much for me and asked so little in return.

I sat there hoping no one would ask me to speak. I listened to the parents, to their pain and their shock, their guilt all laced together throughout their words. I heard the stories of their normal children, drifting off to oblivion. Some were no longer in contact with their children, others hung precariously on a high wire — afraid if they made one wrong move, they could lose contact forever. My insides shaking, I wondered how I ended up here, and wished I was someplace else. These parents were in agony. Powerless, their search for answers, was with them twenty-four hours a day.

"Stacy, we're thinking of starting a sibling group, the counselor says. How do you feel about that? Would you be interested in attending?"

"Well, um, I'm really not sure." I could barely choke out these six pitiful words.

Don't tell Mom and Dad what only I know. Is this not the solemn pledge that siblings carry throughout their life? For me, it is not so easily discarded. I don't want to be a rat, a snitch. I want to help my sister. I think she needs my help, but the truth is buried in a thick, heavy fog, lifting at times, and then quickly blinding me again.

"We're meeting with an exit counselor, to find out more about the exit interview. I really want you to come," Mom said.

The *exit interview* — a new and kinder phrase for kidnapping and deprogramming.

"We no longer take people by force," the counselor said. "It is a voluntary intervention."

I listened to him talk about this process for two hours. An ex-cult member, he discussed the preparations, the actual intervention, and post-intervention therapy.

"I will mail you a 10-page questionnaire about your family, and the group member. Don't omit anything, because it always comes out during the intervention," he said. "You have to decide where it will take place, and how you will get the group member there. It can take up to a week, and you have to be prepared for all the consequences."

Question number seven: Which family members are willing to take part in the intervention? Which are unwilling?

"Stacy, do you want to be there or not?"

My parents now await my answer to this question.

It is a question that requires a yes or no answer. It is the end of the road, and there are no more doors through which I can escape. No more avoidance, no more denial; no matter how loud I scream, no matter how hard I fight.

This unraveling of my family's past, this psychological meltdown, is going to occur. I've seen it documented on television programs, and have watched the pain of strangers. They lay the pieces of their mind on the table, and unravel their history like a skein of yarn, until they reach a core of memories, which dissolve into tears.

It is decision time. There is a canyon to be crossed, and I know that my family cannot reach the other side without me. It will be a journey of four, and I hope we all make the trip safely.

[Editor's Note: Subsequent to the writing of this article we were provided with additional information about the Church of Unlimited Devotion. The group disbanded March 30, 1992, of its own volition. After Joseph was expelled the group discovered "coercive mind-control" material as part of his possessions. The remaining members felt they had been duped into following a "false idol" precipitating the decision to disband.

Lori married in the summer of 1993, is making a fine recovery and is in regular contact with her family. She and her husband have started what looks to be a successful business. Other former members have also begun rebuilding their lives. As for Joseph, after his expulsion he came to Massachusetts, then returned to California to recruit new followers. Failing this, he has himself sought counselling, although it cannot be confirmed whether he received any. No criminal charges were ever filed; members of the cult and their families deciding against pursuing revenge. We will have a further update as more information becomes available.]

SEASON OF THE WITCH

Michael Newton

She was known to members of the ghoulish cult she served as *La Madrina*—"The Godmother"—or simply as *La Bruja*: "The Witch." She occupies a prison cell today, because of her participation in a string of grisly human sacrifices, executed in pursuit of cash and magic powers that would help her followers elude police. The cash was there, and plenty of it, but the magic failed when it came down to making members of the cult invisible and bullet-proof. That failure, in the end, would bring the gruesome sideshow to a close.

Sarah Maria Aldrete Villareal was born on September 6, 1964, the daughter of an electrician in the Tex-Mex border town of Matamoros, Mexico. She crossed the border to attend Porter High School in Brownsville, Texas, where her teachers remember Sarah as "a real good kid". She maintained her star-pupil status in secretarial school, instructors urging her to attend a real college, but hormones intervened. On October 21, 1983, Sarah married Brownsville resident Miguel Zacharias, eleven years her senior. Two years later they were separated, moving inexorably toward divorce.

Late in 1985, Sarah applied for and received resident alien status in the United States. Her next step was enrollment at Texas Southwest College, a two-year school in Brownsville. Admitted on a work-study program that deferred part of her tuition, Sarah began classes in January 1986 as a physical education major, holding down two part-time jobs as an aerobics teacher and assistant secretary in the school's P.E. department.

By the end of her first semester at TSC, Sarah stood out physically and academically. She was tall for a Mexican woman, at six foot one, and her grades were excellent. She was one of thirty-three students chosen from TSC's 6,500-member student body for listings in the school's Who's Who directory for 1987-88. Aside from grades that placed her on the honor roll, Sarah also organized and led a booster club for TSC's soccer team, earning the Outstanding Physical Education Award in her spare time.

With the breakup of her marriage, Sarah moved back to her parents' home in Matamoros, constructing a special outside stairway to her second-floor room in the interest of privacy. She was home most weekends and during school vacations, looking forward to completion of her studies and the transfer to a four-year school that would bring her a P.E. teaching certificate. Attractive and popular with men, she was currently involved with 20-year-old Serafin Hernandez, Jr., a criminology student at TSC.

One scorching Sunday in July of 1987, Sarah was driving through downtown Matamoros when a shiny new Mercedes cut her off in traffic, narrowly avoiding a collision. The driver was apologetic, suave and handsome. He introduced himself as Adolfo de Jesus Constanzo, a Cuban-American living in Mexico City. There was instant chemistry between them, but Constanzo did not "make a move" at first. It was enough for them to meet and talk, becoming friends.

Constanzo was a native of Miami, born to Cuban immigrant parents on November 1, 1962. His father left the family within a year of Adolfo's birth, and his mother moved to Puerto Rico for a time, there acquiring the second of her three husbands. In Puerto Rico, Adolfo embraced the Catholic faith, becoming an altar boy, but it was only a phase. Back in Miami as an adolescent, he began to display "psychic powers" — at least to his mother's satisfaction — around age fourteen. She put him through rigorous training with several witch doctors in South Florida and the Caribbean, Adolfo picking up the fine points of voodoo, santeria, and the more sinister palo mayombe (which makes use of human remains to invoke demonic entities). A confirmed bisexual at age twenty-two, he moved to Mexico City, supporting himself as a fortune-teller who also performed *limpias* —"cleansing" rituals— for clients plagued by "curses" or bad luck. A price tag of $4,500 for one of Constanzo's ritual cleansings was not unusual.

Perhaps the most peculiar aspect of Constanzo's new career was the appeal he seemed to have for ranking law-enforcement officers. At least four members of the Federal Judicial Police — the same force later implicated in the murder of a Mexican presidential candidate — joined Constanzo's cult in Mexico City. One of them, Salvador Garcia, was a commander in charge of narcotics investigations; another, Florentino Ventura, retired from the *federales* to lead the Mexican branch of Interpol. In a country where bribery — *mordida* — permeates all levels of law enforcement and federal officers sometimes serve as triggermen for drug smugglers, corruption is not unusual, but the devotion of Constanzo's followers ran deeper than cash on the line. In or out of uniform, they worshipped Adolfo as a minor god in his own right, their living conduit to the spirit world.

Constanzo's rituals involved animal sacrifice, and he prepared a full menu, ranging from roosters and

"IN A CORNER OF THE SHED, ASWARM WITH FLIES, A METAL POT — THE DREADED NGANGA OF PALO MAYOMBE — CONTAINED A STEW OF HUMAN BRAINS AND ANIMAL INGREDIENTS..."

WITCH'S BREW

goats to zebras and African lions, depending on a client's ability to pay. Soon, his followers included Mexican celebrities and superstitious drug dealers, all seeking spiritual guidance. Extreme cases called for human sacrifice, the souls of murdered victims viewed as captive messengers to the "other side", and Mexican police suspect Constanzo of at least six ritual murders in the year before he met Sarah Aldrete.

Even that meeting was not the simple accident it seemed to be. In fact, Constanzo had been watching Sarah's lover, well aware that Serafin Hernandez, Jr., was part of a major drug-dealing family. His meeting with Sarah was carefully stage-managed, as was their burgeoning friendship and Sarah's introduction into the occult. By summer's end, her TSC classmates found Sarah dramatically changed, an overnight expert in witchcraft and magic, eager to debate the relative powers of darkness and light.

Constanzo finally took Sarah to bed, but the sexual side of their relationship was short-lived. Adolfo preferred men, and Sarah did not seem to mind. She offered no objection when he ordered her to dump Serafin Junior and concentrate on older brother Emilio, a troubleshooter for the family's narco trade. It was Sarah who arranged the introductions, putting Constanzo one step closer to his goal of controlling a personal smuggling network.

As it happened, the Hernandez family was ripe for a takeover, torn by internal dissension and threatened by outside competitors. Using every trick at his disposal, Constanzo persuaded Emilio, his brothers, and even patriarch Serafin Senior that palo mayombe could solve all their problems. Enemies could be eliminated in the course of magic rituals; those rituals, in turn, would keep the family safe from harm. If they were faithful to Constanzo, his disciples would become invisible to the authorities. In return, all he asked was 50% of the profits . . . and de facto control of the family.

Incredibly, the street-wise dealers bought it, falling back on peasant superstition in their hour of need. Even Serafin Junior went along for the ride, abandoning his college studies and returning to the fold as a disciple of Constanzo, willing to accept the wizard's rule and murder on command.

Sarah Aldrete's role in transforming the Hernandez family from a gang of border smugglers to a homicidal cult remains a matter of debate. From prison, with a vested interest in proclaiming innocence, Aldrete claims she never witnessed or participated in a human sacrifice. Surviving members of the cult say otherwise, insisting that *La Bruja* joined Constanzo in the torture-slayings of numerous victims, inventing new refinements to prolong each victim's agony. She also picked a lurid horror movie, based on santeria, *The Believers*, and required each member of the cult to watch it several times, as an example of the powers they would gain by following Constanzo's strategy.

Striking first at the competition, Constanzo and company orchestrated the massacre of the Calzada family in Mexico City. In early 1988, nine members of the drug-dealing clan were tortured, mutilated, and dumped in the Tula River, parts of their bodies retained as "sacred" relics for future rituals. (In June 1989, a member of Constanzo's cult who doubled as a Mexican policeman — one Vidal Garcia — was charged with participation in the Calzada murders).

Other deaths followed, beginning in Mexico City's homosexual quarter, the "Zona Rosa", where Constanzo recruited his male lovers. One such victim, transvestite Ramon Paz-Esquivel, was found on July 2, 1988, his body cut into twenty-one pieces, consigned to four separate trash bags. Cult members blame Constanzo for the murder; in 1989, Sarah Aldrete was charged with criminal association and obstruction of justice, for trying to conceal the crime.

When Mexico City began to heat up, Constanzo and Sarah shifted their base of operations to Rancho Santa Elena, twenty miles from Matamoros. In the twelve months between May 1988 and April 1989, at least fifteen human victims were sacrificed at the ranch, their cruel deaths mixing business, religion, and sadistic pleasure.

The first to die at Rancho Santa Elena were middle-aged locals Moise Castillo Vasquez and Hector de la Fuente Lozoya, reputedly killed for their marijuana stash. Another victim of greed was 30-year-old Ruben Vela-Garza, reported missing on February 14, 1989. Eleven days later, the cult kidnapped 14-year-old Jose Luis Garcia de Luna; the youth had been slaughtered before Elio Hernandez recognized his own teenage cousin. Cult member Jorge Valente del Fierro, yet another ex-cop, was sacrificed for using cocaine in defiance of Constanzo's standing order to abstain. Other past or present lawmen murdered at the ranch, some of them known to moonlight as pushers, included Saul Salceda Galvan, Gilberto Garza Susa, Joaquin Manzo-Rodriguez, and Robert Rodriguez (no relation). Matamoros farmer Esquivel Rodriguez Luna was abducted as a matter of convenience, while Ernesto Rivas-Diaz was killed for his stockpile of drugs. Three other male victims, unearthed by police in April 1989, remain unidentified today.

It was Constanzo's urge to sacrifice a *gringo* that finally led to cult's undoing. Texas pre-med student Mark Kilroy was kidnapped in Matamoros on March 14, 1989, driven to the ranch and sacrificed. His disappearance in the middle of Spring Break prompted a search on both sides of the border, and the manhunt was still underway four weeks later, when the roof fell in on Constanzo's coven.

Serafin Hernandez Jr., was driving out to Rancho Santa Elena on

Sunday, April 9, when he passed a police roadblock without stopping. Hernandez thought himself to be invisible, a quirk that led him to ignore the squad cars following him in hot pursuit. Arriving at the ranch, police arrested Sarafin, his brother Elio, and three more members of the gang. The raiders confiscated several guns and found the shed where drugs were stashed beside a bloodstained alter. In a corner of the shed, aswarm with flies, a metal pot — the dreaded *nganga* of palo mayombe — contained a stew of human brains and animal ingredients required for personal communion with the spirit world.

In custody, the suspects named Constanzo and Aldrete as the leaders of their cult. By April 17, fifteen mutilated bodies had been unearthed at the ranch, including one identified as Mark Kilroy. Adolfo and his witch, meanwhile, had been spotted in Brownsville on April 11, cruising the streets in an $80,000 luxury sedan, but from there they disappeared without a trace.

The dominoes began falling in earnest on April 17, with Serafin Senior's arrest in Houston on outstanding drug warrants. The same day, police raided Constanzo's palacial home in a suburb of Mexico City, finding an altar, occult paraphernalia, and stacks of homosexual pornography. They also found Sarah Aldrete's purse, passport, and airline tickets, prompting brief speculation that Constanzo may have killed her to eliminate a potential witness. On April 18, a federal grand jury in McAllen, Texas, indicted Constanzo on conspiracy charges; a week later, Adolfo, Sarah, and nine of their disciples were hit with new counts involving narcotics violations and the kidnapping of Gilberto Garza Sosa.

By early May, manhunters were seeking Constanzo and Sarah as far north as Chicago, where their reputed customers included members of the Windy City Mafia. In fact, the fugitives were still in Mexico City, as revealed on May 6, when a women matching Sarah's description tried to pay her grocery tab with an American $100 bill. Police were summoned, and they found Adolfo's Chrysler parked outside a nearby apartment house. A stealthy approach was out of the question, as someone saw them coming, smashing out an upstairs window and hosing the street with submachine-gun fire.

The battle lasted forty minutes, Constanzo doing most of the shooting for his side, wounding one patrolman on the street below. At last, surrounded, *El Padrino* stepped into a closet with his male lover, Martin Quintana, and ordered cultist Alvaro de Leon to kill them both. When de Leon hesitated, Sarah reportedly urged him on from the sidelines, shouting, "Do it! Get it over with!"

In custody, Sarah insisted that she had been Constanzo's hostage in the shootout. She even claimed credit for bringing police to the scene, referring to an SOS note she allegedly dropped in the street, but police saw a different side of *La Madrina* when the television cameras took their leave. "She would talk like a witch," one officer said. "She never cried. She was cold. Cold." For her part, Sarah described an all-night session of police torture, during which she was "almost raped." A self-described practitioner of "Christian santeria," she denied any participation in human sacrifice or other black magic rituals, blaming the various murders on Constanzo. Charged in a total of seventeen slayings, plus various narcotics violations, Sarah was initially tried on two counts. She was acquitted of Constanzo's murder, but convicted on a charge of criminal association, for which she received the maximum six-year prison term.

Four years later, in May 1994, Sarah and four male disciples were finally convicted for the murders at Rancho Santa Elena. Aldrete was sentenced to sixty-two years, while her cohorts — including Elio Hernandez and Serafin Junior — drew prison terms of sixty-seven years.

The cult of blood and pain, meanwhile, endures. Police in Mexico City investigated the ritual slayings of sixty adults and fourteen infants between 1987 and 1989, with a similar outbreak reported from Veracruz. It was tempting to clear the books by blaming Constanzo and company, but in fact, the murders have continued since his death and the incarceration of his followers. A relative of Martin Quintana told police, in June 1989, that Adolfo's first *madrina* was still at large, practicing her blood magic around Guadalajara.

And from jail, before he died of AIDS, cultist Omar Orea said, "I don't think that the religion will end with us, because it has a lot of people in it. They have found a temple in Monterrey that isn't even related to us. It will continue."

Prosecutor Guillermo Ibarra agrees. "We would like to say, yes, Constanzo did them all," Ibarra says, "and poof, all those cases are solved. And the fact is, we believe he was responsible for some of them, though we'll never prove it now. But he didn't commit all those murders, which means someone else did. Someone who is still out there."

Michael Newton is the author of **Raising Hell: An Encyclopedia of Devil Worship and Satanic Crime** *(Avon books)* *and* **Hunting Humans** *(Loompanics).*

ROTTEN TO THE C.O.R.: CULT ACTIVITIES WITHIN THE CATHOLIC CHURCH

Paul Wardle

Cults come in many different forms. Though the Catholic Church can be accused of many things — being old-fashioned, repressive, male-dominated, out of touch with the modern world, the list goes on — still I doubt even its most staunch critics would level the word "cult" at this age-old religion.

In early 1985, a close friend of mine named Diane, then in her late teens, was going through some personal traumas. Similar problems were also troubling her best female friend, whose mother suggested she and Diane attend a weekend retreat she had heard about that operated through schools and churches. These retreats were said to help troubled teens deal with emotional problems through group discussions, fun activities, meditation and prayer. Though not terribly religious herself, Diane's parents were ardent Catholics and were in favor of the idea. The next Friday evening, Diane and her friend attended what was known as a C.O.R. weekend.

C.O.R. stands for Christians On Retreat, suggesting that other sects besides Catholics may be involved. Yet I am sure the events I am about to describe do not coincide with most people's idea of Christianity. What follows is Diane's account of what transpired on her first (and last) C.O.R. weekend. For those who may be skeptical, let me just add that Diane is one of the most honest and straightforward people I know and would have no reason to invent or exaggerate any of the following details. She originally told me the story the day after it occurred and its effect on her was so damaging that she remembers every detail of it to this day.

Diane and her friend arrived at C.O.R. headquarters on a blistery Friday night in the middle of winter. It was a large multi-roomed structure located in Markham, Ontario (a small Canadian town just north-east of Toronto). Upon entering, the organizers of this "retreat" (who introduced themselves as COCO-MOMs and COCO-DADs, protecting their own anonymity) immediately sought to separate the two friends, taking them to opposite sides of the main hall to interview them in private. All these COCO-people had the same glazed look in their eyes, the kind you see in cult members who just seem too happy for their own good.

After rounding up the 30-40 high-school kids in a "corral-like" enclosure, the organizers said that the weekend would be a lot of fun but that certain rules had to be observed. Everyone was asked to surrender their books, magazines, radios, walkmans, wristwatches and rock music as well as any food or snacks they had brought with them. This as a way to keep them from getting sidetracked from the planned activities. However, Diane soon noticed that there wasn't a clock, a phone, a calendar or any other reminder of the outside world in the building. Was this a retreat or a prison sentence?

Unbeknownst to the youths participating, the organizers had asked the parents and other family members of the participants to write them very personal letters expressing feelings they had never expressed before, full of love and sentiment. Their first activity was to go to their dorm rooms, unpack their gear and read these letters. This was an emotional experience for the students, causing tears in some cases. One of Diane's letters concerned a brother of hers who had recently been killed by a speeding train.

The youths barely had time to finish reading these letters, let alone the time to deal with their emotional impact, when they were shunted out of their rooms into the main hall. Once there, all lights were turned out and boxes of tissues were strategically placed around the room in anticipation of cathartic crying jags to come.

It was then that the "COCO-nuts" put the first phase of their draconian plan into action. With everyone in an unstable emotional state due to the aforementioned letters, few were willing to discuss their feelings. Yet slowly, one by one, the kids began to open up and tears began to flow freely. At first, the kids who confided were those that had been indoctrinated at previous C.O.R. weekends. In a style similar to an Alcoholics Anonymous meeting, these inspiring self-admissions were designed to make new recruits more talkative. Since none of the new kids knew anyone, and were prevented from talking amongst themselves, they assumed it was the atmosphere alone that had created this willingness to open up to total strangers. Soon, the neophytes were discussing their innermost thoughts with COCO-MOM and COCO-DAD.

After what seemed like hours, (though having no timepieces it was impossible to tell) it was announced that dinner was served. However, the students were not simply allowed to eat in peace. Every time someone put their elbows on the table, one of the regulars would jump up and shout, "I saw so-and-so with his/her elbows on the table!" This signalled the start of a "game" in which the offending youth would have to get up and recite a poem or sing a

C O R

CULT

CANCEL
OUR
RESISTENCE

WARDLE '94

song or some such nonsense, after which everyone would run around the table. This occurred relentlessly amid much laughter and playful embarrassment, but it achieved the goal for which C.O.R. had included it. No one got to eat much. Physical sustenance is the one thing that might have guarded these unfortunate dupes against the brainwashing that was in store for them. This combination of psychological manipulation, hunger and strenuous physical activity left the students physically and emotionally exhausted until finally they were allowed to sleep.

The C.O.R. people kept them up Friday night and woke them very early the next morning. How early, Diane had no way of knowing, since there were no clocks. She felt as if she had very little sleep. The next day progressed in a like manner. A strict regimen of physically taxing games, emotionally draining discussions, church masses and very little to eat.

Later that day, Diane discovered that one of the other new girls shared a mutual friend with Diane, a friend who had tragically died of leukemia. This girl was unaware of her teen-age friend's death, having lost touch with her years before. Diane felt obligated to be the one to break the sad news to her, and, not wanting to do it in front of everyone, took her into the girls' bathroom where they could talk in private.

The news was a shock and the girl began to cry for her dead friend when suddenly, COCO-MOM burst in, loudly berating them for breaking away from the group and demanding to know what they were up to, what they had talked about, etc. Privacy, it seemed, was a valuable commodity on these C.O.R. weekends. Crying was apparently not allowed unless sanctioned by a C.O.R. group discussion. The incident in the bathroom upset Diane very much and she was

continually being chastised for not participating and not being fully part of the group. Mainly, she was not buying into their bullshit and they knew it.

That night, the inmates of this asylum were promised a relaxing evening to themselves. But this chance to unwind never came because shortly thereafter, the plans were changed. Everyone was piled into a bus and taken on a road trip out to a barn in the middle of nowhere. Far from relaxing, they were instead treated to about three hours of non-stop squaredancing. On the way back, completely exhausted, the students were anxious to get back and catch up on much needed sleep. Suddenly, on a dark country road, the bus broke down. This unexpected anxiety startled awake the fatigued children and when it was announced that the bus was fixed, the anxiety turned into relief. Now wide awake, they chattered away happily, unaware that this whole mechanical mishap was a ploy to keep the group on a high energy level and an emotional roller-coaster at the same time. In fact, there was no breakdown at all.

The organizers further capitalized on this adrenaline rush by making the exhausted teens write letters to themselves before the mood faded. The letters would be full of mindless ramblings about all the new friends they had made, all the fun they were having, etc., and would be mailed to each boy or girl's home address. Designed as a clever trick to keep the same kids coming back every week, the self-addressed letters were an important part of the hold that C.O.R. had on these kids. Since they were not allowed to exchange addresses or phone numbers with any of their "new friends", regular attendance was the only way they could keep in touch. In Diane's case, reading this letter she had written to

THE OUTSIDE WORLD IS A HORRIBLE PLACE, BUT AT LEAST WE'RE HAPPY AND DON'T HAVE TO ACKNOWLEDGE ITS EXISTENCE

WARDLE '94

herself had a different effect. It read like the rantings of an insane person and even her own handwriting was drastically altered.

On Saturday, they were up at the crack of dawn for more emotionally draining mental exercises, physically taxing activities and meals they never got to eat. Again they were promised a relaxing evening to do what they wished and were encouraged to stay up as late as they wanted with the promise that they would be allowed to sleep late on Sunday morning.

Having secretly violated the anti-rock rule, Diane had held on to one of the cassettes she had brought with her, and not realizing how seriously C.O.R. takes its rules, popped her Pink Floyd tape into a portable tape-deck. The effect of the music on these kids was staggering. It was the first reminder of the outside world they had been exposed to all weekend. Grooving to the music, they started to feel like maybe they hadn't been having much fun after all and what the hell were they doing there

anyway? This revelation was shortlived however, since COCO-DAD, upon hearing the heathen rock and roll, stormed into the room, ripped the tape out of the player, and launched into a furious oration against breaking the rules. Seeing the reaction of the teens to his outburst, he immediately calmed down and, reverting to his nice-guy image, explained away the incident with the usual double-speak. It just doesn't fit in with our plans . . . it distracts from what we're trying to do here . . . and on and on. Still, they saw a chink in his armor of contentment and realized, as is usually the case with these kinds of things, that he wasn't quite as happy as he pretended to be.

Even worse, after all the promises made, the kids still didn't get a chance to sleep in on Sunday. After a few hours, the organizers came into their rooms, burning candles and singing hymns. Once again it was the breaking of one of C.O.R.'s sacred rules that revealed the truth. One girl had kept her watch and checked it to see how late they had slept in. It was 4:00 A.M.

From then on, it was back to the big, dark room and plenty of Kleenex while each of the kids, in turn, spoke about how wonderful this weekend had been, how much they had learned about themselves, and other positive, but misguided words. There was much crying and soul-searching and revealing of inner secrets. Diane and her friend had been saved for last because it was known that they would be the toughest nuts to crack. After listening to hour after hour of kids breaking down and saying how wonderful the experience had been, Diane succumbed to the weekend of brainwashing and told them what they wanted to hear. This submissive gesture created a watershed of new tears from the entire group and Diane immediately regretted her words, having realized that they had been used to cement the programming of these unfortunate kids who were tired, hungry and in an extremely vulnerable emotional state.

Diane, her friend and a boy who had been stoned throughout the whole weekend, viewing the proceedings as one big joke, resolved to escape the closing ceremonies. They were glad they had met this boy because his rebellious attitude had helped them keep the bizarre behavior in perspective. For the first time they had a means to get away as the doors were opened to admit the parents who were to be reunited with their children in a tearful, emotional ritual. As the three dissenters listened to the proceedings from behind a closed door, what they heard was terrifying. The programming was complete. The C.O.R. people and Diane's parents were upset by her absence at these closing ceremonies but even Diane's mother (a deeply religious woman) was ap-

palled at the effects of this so-called retreat. For four days afterwards, Diane slept most of the time and was an emotional wreck when awake. She fought off repeated calls by C.O.R. to return, and her mother finally told her to remove the crucifix C.O.R. had given to her to wear around her neck. It had seemed to be symbol of the hold they still had on her. Even after all that had happened, Diane had been feeling guilty that she had not been able to achieve the contentment that the others had, as if there was something wrong with HER!

To be fair, people I spoke to within the Catholic Church don't seem to be aware of what really went on at these weekends, assuming them to be regular retreats. Several of those to whom I spoke had never heard of C.O.R. and some that had couldn't even tell me what the initials meant. The general consensus seems to be that the retreats are no longer being held, but this may be a cover-up. The same thing could easily be going on under another name. I have recently learned that similar activities took place in the province of Nova Scotia under the name CHALLENGE weekends. I plan to delve further into this matter, hopefully find out who was behind it and how it was funded. Anyone reading this who has been to a weekend of this kind and would like to tell the story can write to *Gauntlet* to be forwarded to me.

It is not clear what sinister purpose this group had for brainwashing teenagers. Whether the motivation was political, religious or criminal, the restriction of free thought should be considered a crime in and of itself.

Paul Wardle's wit can be seen in the many editorial cartoons he has penned for **Gauntlet**, *in this and previous issues.*

THE HITLER CULT IN AMERICA

MOSHE PHILLIPS

Introduction

There is a movement in the United States that is anti-American and anti-Christian, yet it claims to be more Christian and more patriotic than anyone else in the nation. Neo-Nazi organizations, that have had a very long history of violence in America, are now more widespread and radical than ever before. They claim they are going to save America from the Blacks, Jews, Communists, immigrants, homosexuals, Catholics, Free Masons, and others that threaten the existence of America as a national home for White Christians. The Neo-Nazis worship Adolph Hitler as the greatest hero the White Race has ever produced. The leaders of the Neo-Nazi groups have attracted a large following of young, violent Skinhead gangs. White supremacist groups have set up armed compounds throughout the nation where para-military training is conducted and armed fanatics wait for the start of a future "Race War".

Today's Neo-Nazis are far from being the insignificant and basically harmless bunch of lunatics that they are sometimes characterized to be. Neo-Nazis are much more dangerous than David Koresh and his Branch Davidian cult in Waco, Texas was. The Neo-Nazis want nothing less than the violent overthrow of the United States government and the creation of the Fourth Reich in America. The members of these various groups have proven that they are prepared to wage a war of terrorism. Their armed camps have the potential to be the sites of tragedies far worse than the Branch Davidian disaster in the Spring of 1993. Neo-Nazis have shown that they are more than willing to die as martyrs for their cause.

The Origin of the Neo-Nazi Movement in the United States

The American Nazi Party (A.N.P.) was founded in 1958 by George Lincoln Rockwell. Rockwell openly called for the murder of Jews and for Black Americans to be "sent back to Africa." Rockwell's headquarters were in Arlington, Virginia. His frequent public demonstrations and marches in nearby Washington D.C. featured Nazi banners and protesters in Nazi stormtrooper uniforms. The marches gained Rockwell a certain following and notoriety. Rockwell openly proclaimed Adolph Hitler as the hero of the "white race".

Rockwell was assassinated by a fellow Nazi in 1967. His official successor was "Commander" Matt Koehl. Koehl introduced many changes into the A.N.P. including the decision to downplay publicity stunts and concentrating on organizing and leadership training. Koehl was one of the first Neo-Nazi leaders to stress the need to recruit young men. Koehl eventually changed the name of the A.N.P. to the National Socialist White People's Party (N.S.W.P.P.) and later to the New Order.

During the early period of Koehl's leadership many Neo-Nazi splinter groups formed throughout

WARDLE '94

the U.S.

Skinheads: Neo-Nazi Street Warriors

Neo-Nazi Skinheads first began to surface in the United Sates over ten years ago. Their appearance is now familiar: shaven heads, Neo-Nazi tattoos, Doc Martin steel tipped work boots, and flight jackets. Many Neo-Nazi leaders were quick to realize the value of recruiting angry young White people into their movement. Tom and John Metzger of WAR and the leaders of the Aryan Nations and the Church of the Creator are all active in recruiting Skinheads. The Skinheads have earned a reputation for violence and are responsible for the murder of many innocent victims throughout the country.

The main supplier of Neo-Nazi literature, promotional items and paraphernalia for Skinheads in both the United States and Europe is the Lincoln, Nebraska office of the NSDAP/AO (the National Socialist German Workers Party/ Overseas Organization). The NSDAP is run by Gerhard (Gary) Luack. His newspaper, *The New Order* features advertisements for stickers that show a swastika and read "Fight crime . . . Deport Niggers".

Other Neo-Nazis are attempting to reach young new recruits through the use of new methods such as Skinhead rock music, Nazi video games and computer networks. The Neo-Nazis are using Computer Bulletin Board Systems (BBSs) to attract a more intelligent element to their ranks.

The Los Angeles area based White Aryan Resistance (WAR) organization is led by former Ku Klux Klan leader Tom Metzger and his son John. John Metzger first gained national attention when he and other Skinhead leaders appeared on the Geraldo Rivera's syndicated television talk show *Geraldo*. The show turned violent as a melee broke out on stage and Rivera ended up with a broken nose. The White Aryan Resistance's newspaper, also known as *WAR* featured an article that stated the principles of WAR's ideology, which says that the White Race cannot depend on Christianity, which it calls a "Jewish religion" or on any other organized religion but can only depend on White Power for the survival of the White Race.

The Neo-Nazis have also targeted for recruitment white convicts. Several members of the Neo-Nazi terrorist group the Order were ex-convicts. The Neo-Nazi Aryan Brotherhood (A.B.), the Whites only prison gang, has been active in the California prison system since the late 1960's. In the early 1970's Robert Beausoliel, a convicted murderer and an accomplice of Charles Manson, was the leader of the Aryan Brotherhood at San Quentin Prison.

An Important Lesson to Learn from Waco

There are at least three other heavily armed compounds in the United States that are very similar to the Branch Davidian compound that was outside of Waco, Texas. The difference between the Branch Davidians and the other three is that the other three are teaching their members that the coming "Apocalypse" is going to be caused by Jews, and therefore Jews are to be hated and killed.

Immediately after the Branch Davidian cult's compound near Waco, Texas burned down, United States Attorney general Janet Reno was asked by reporters if she had any information about other similar cults. Reno failed to respond positively. This is very understandable, as her main concern at the time was to defend the FBI's actions that day.

However, in fact, there are at least three other armed camps, that have many characteristics in common with the Branch Davidians sect's compound. The three camps are all heavily fortified and their members are believed to be heavily armed with automatic weapons. The compounds' members have come from throughout the nation and belong to non-mainstream Protestant Christian sects. The Bureau of Alcohol, Tobacco and Firearms and the Federal Bureau of Investigations have already investigated the groups that own the complexes as well. The other fortified complexes like the one in Waco, are also led by charismatic individuals who call themselves Christian ministers and believe that "the end is near" and that the "Day of Judgement" is coming soon. These groups, like the Branch Davidians, house children within their compounds.

These similarities alone should be very frightening, but what is different about the other three armed compounds is that they are owned and operated by Neo-Nazi groups with a long history of terrorism, violence, and murder.

The oldest of the three compounds is at Hayden Lake, Idaho, near Coeur d'Alene. The compound is operated by the Aryan Nations and was first organized in 1974. The head of the compound is the Reverend Richard Butler, who founded the Church of Jesus Christ Christian, the largest group in the white supremacist "Christian Identity" movement. Butler teaches that white Christians are the true "Chosen People" and that the Jews, who control the government and the media, are the children of the devil.

The Aryan Nations compound resembles an Army base, with a guard tower, barracks, armory, security fence and a main gate.

The Aryan Nations compound has been the scene of the Aryan World Congress, the annual national convention of Neo-Nazis, Skinheads, Klan members, and other extremists. The purpose of the Aryan World Congress was to forge a united Neo-Nazi movement.

Members of the Neo-Nazi terrorist group known as the Order were often guests at the Aryan Nation's compound. Members of the Order were prosecuted for the murder of Jewish Denver talk radio show host Alan Berg on June 18, 1984. Members of the Order are believed to have received paramilitary training at the compound. Besides Berg's murder members of the Order were convicted of robbing Brink's armored trucks throughout the Northwest. The heists netted the Neo-Nazis millions of dollars.

Another armed compound is in

Otto, North Carolina, and is operated by a group known as the Church of the Creator. The leader, Ben Klassen, also calls himself a Christian minister and his Neo-Nazi doctrine is similar to the Aryan Nations' ideology of hate, violence and preparation for a future "Race War".

The third compound is in Mill Point, West Virginia, and is operated by the white supremacist group the National Alliance. Dr. William Pierce, a longtime Neo-Nazi activist is the leader. Dr. Pierce had been George Lincoln Rockwell's chief aid in the 1960s. Dr. Pierce is the author of the 1978 novel *The Turner Diaries*, a novel which he published under the pseudonym Andrew MacDonald. The novel is about a white racist revolutionary leader who leads a terrorist campaign against the Jews and the United States government. The Order allegedly used *The Turner Diaries* as the blueprint for its attacks.

These three are the largest compounds, but other, smaller Neo-Nazi organizations have their own similarly armed and fortified sites in other parts of the country. The most notable of which is in New Berlin, Wisconsin, and is owned by former American Nazi Party leader Matt Koehl. Koehl is currently the head of the Neo-Nazi group the New Order.

Another disaster like the one in Waco can be prevented. The FBI and the ATF must intensify their investigations of these Neo-Nazi compounds and the individuals and organizations that are associated with them. Ms. Reno's important task is to insure that the leaders of the Neo-Nazi compounds do not follow in the footsteps of David Koresh and cause the death of innocent children.

There is an important lesson to learn from the standoff in Waco. Armed extremists must not be allowed to build fortress like complexes and cause violent confrontations to develop where innocent children will be killed by a fanatical, hate-filled leader.

Case Study: The Weaver Family Standoff

In August and September of 1992 ATF and FBI agents surrounded the home of Randy Weaver and his family in Idaho. Randy Weaver was a fugitive who was wanted on charges of illegally selling firearms. In the ensuing battle a Federal officer and Weaver's son and wife were killed. A family friend of the Weaver's Kevin Harris was seriously wounded. Weaver, a special forces veteran, was involved with the Aryan Nations he and his family were well armed with semiautomatic assault rifles and pistols. Weaver and his family had moved to the mountains of Idaho in order to live alone in the woods and escape what they

saw as the self-destruction of society. The standoff finally ended after eleven days. Populist Party candidate Bo Gritz talked Weaver into surrendering to the authorities. A crowd of over one hundred friends and supporters of the Weavers, including Skinheads, were there when Weaver gave up. Five heavily armed Skinheads had been arrested during the standoff, when they tried to join the Weavers.

Conclusion

What are the limits that the United States can put on Neo-Nazi propaganda and Neo-Nazi activity without violating the laws of the United States Bill of Rights and the Constitution?

The Neo-Nazi organizations that advocate violence and the mass murder of fellow Americans must be made illegal. It is not a Constitutional right to plot genocide. Genocide is murder and conspiracy to commit murder is illegal. All the talk about the Constitutional right to free speech must be kept in the context of remembering that it is illegal to yell "fire" in a crowded theater because it is dangerous to innocent individuals. It is much more dangerous for individuals to speak about putting people in gas chambers and ovens. The question that Americans must ask is "Are Neo-Nazis entitled to free expression?"

Moshe Phillips is the Education Director of the Jewish Defense League of Philadelphia. The JDL can be contacted at P.O. Box 6664 Philadelphia, PA 19149. The Jewish Defense League Computer Bulletin Board System (BBS) can be reached at (215) 464-5174.

INSIDE "THE FELLOWSHIP:" THE TRUTH ABOUT ALCOHOLICS ANONYMOUS AND OTHER 12 STEP PROGRAMS

PART I OF II

John Henry Biedermann

The media is full of stories about addicts beginning new lives through 12 step programs like Alcoholics Anonymous. Celebrities open up regularly about breaking "denial" and finding happiness through "The Fellowship". It would seem natural that if you, or someone you care about, develops a problem, A.A. is the answer.

Or is it?

Today A.A. has over 1 million members in the U.S., spawning over 200 varieties of 12 step programs, from Narcotics Anonymous to Prostitutes Anonymous, including family members ("co-dependents") with groups like Adult Children of Alcoholics. Some of the strangest incarnations are Clutterers Anonymous and Alatot (for infants of alcoholics).

A.A. keeps no records, but its surveys recently state " . . . that about 1/2 of those coming to A.A. for the first time remain less than 2 months," and outside efforts indicate that 1 to 10% of those who try A.A. achieve durable sobriety through it.

Yet proponents resist change. Addiction care facilities utilize the steps, and courts mandate A.A. meeting attendance or 12 step-based counseling for offenses like DUIs. Alternative programs allege the program ineffective and often harmful, but critics' voices are curiously muted alongside advocate's praise.

"I tell my friends about the problem," says member Mary, "and some say, 'Gee, it's a shame I never had an alcohol problem. The 12 steps sound great for everybody.'" With such fervency and such a poor success rate, the public should know more about Alcoholics Anonymous. How do you work the program?

"There was nothing to work," says Chuck Gottmann, a former attendee, "It's like going to a holiness revival."

The most common complaint is religiosity, with some alleging A.A. a cult. In the hundreds of mediums dealing with 12 step recovery, its methods remain secret. This article unveils the true nature of "The Fellowship."

Most of this information pertains to Alcoholics Anonymous, but the "alcohol" can be interchanged with whatever problem a group addresses.

THE INITIATION PROCESS

Before meetings, members congregate for coffee and chatter, going out of their way to comfort newcomers. There are dozens of catch phrases, such as "All that's required is a desire to stop drinking," but individuals may say anything.

"The first time I went, I was edging over by the coffee, and a guy comes up and says, 'Cup of coffee?' I said, 'Sure.' He says 'Meeting's gonna start in 10 minutes, wanna sit down?' Sat down at the table and he looks at me and goes, 'I turned my life over to God,' at which point I got up and moved two tables away."

Chuck's experience is not standard, but religious undertone reigns. A "speaker," (member with year or more A.A. sobriety) addresses the gathering, half his spiel detailing the hell of drinking, the rest raving about A.A. After a break, the soapbox proceeds around the room. Members relate current problems and compliment the program.

Step One: *We admitted we were powerless over alcohol — that our lives had become unmanageable.*

This is all that's expected of newcomers, to break "denial", and admit having incurable alcoholism. This "disease" must be fought "One day at a time." A sponsor (long time member) will guide them further.

Alcohol is described "Cunning, baffling, and powerful." Members are warned that without the program, they can expect "Jails, institutions, or death." Little is said about HOW to give up drinking, but there are many references to God. Meetings end with group recital of the "Lord's Prayer," but you'll be told A.A.'s "spiritual, not religious" and "For all faiths."

The Program itself will show you otherwise.

THE PROGRAM

Step Two: *Came to believe that a Power greater than ourselves could restore us to sanity.*

Step Three: *Made a decision to turn our will and our lives over to the care of God AS WE UNDERSTOOD HIM.*

Objectors are told to substitute anything outside themselves for "God". Quad A (A.A. for Atheists and Agnostics) substitutes "Wisdom", and A.A. itself is suggested for newcomers. Folklore describes a member using his bedpan. Turning your life over to any of these seems ludicrous, but they're considered *temporary.*

Dr. Albert Ellis, inventor of Rational Emotive Behavior Therapy (REBT), president of the Institute for REBT in New York, an addiction therapist for over 50 years, considers this harmful. "The *worst* illness is thinking 'I *can't* empower myself to beat this.' It becomes very often a self-fulfilling function. Dependence is a serious emotional problem."

Suppression is furthered by a blatantly anti-intellectual nature. Quips like "Your best thinking got you here," and "You can be too smart for the program but never too stupid," discourage questioning, disturbingly similar to the Moonies' "you think too much."

Step Four: *Made a searching and fearless moral inventory of ourselves.*

Step Five: *Admitted to God, ourselves, and to another human being the exact nature of our wrongs.*

Step Six: *Were entirely ready to have God remove all these defects of character.*

Step Seven: *Humbly asked Him to remove our shortcomings.*

Step Eight: *Made a list of all persons we had harmed, and became willing to make amends to them all.*

Step Nine: *Made direct amends to such people wherever possible, except when to do so would injure them or others.*

While the first three steps garner a hopeless nature, four through nine spotlight "sin". Morality and amends are "cures" for a hopeless nature, leading a 1984 Wisconsin court ruling of A.A. that "beyond a doubt. . . religious activities, as defined in constitutional law. . . (are) a part of the treatment program. The distinction between religion and spirituality is meaningless . . ."

Step Ten: *Continued to take personal inventory and when we were wrong promptly admitted it.*

Step Eleven: *Sought through prayer and meditation to improve our conscious contact with God AS WE UNDERSTOOD HIM, praying only for knowledge of His will for us and the power to carry that out.*

This lifelong battle completes a philosophy identical to "original sin." Cult's commonly lure members with "God as you understand him" while delineating a very specific one. This bait and switch is explained in A.A.'s Serenity Bible "We may start as agnostics. We may then come to view

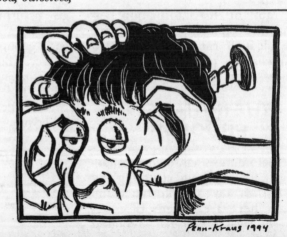

the group or recovery process as our Higher Power, looking to other people for strength. Gradually, we accept a vague notion of God, which grows to a more specific monotheistic God. Eventually we come to know the one true God."

Alcoholics Anonymous, the book, serves as scripture, referred to as "The Big Book." It contains the steps, elaborations on their meaning, and dozens of member's stories. "I don't care how much time has passed," member Rick asserts, "I hope they never alter the Big Book." Its chief authors, founders Bill Wilson and Bob Smith, are regarded as saviors. Nothing else is needed to qualify A.A. a religion.

The differences between spiritual and religious remain to be explained. John Houlihan, director of the 12 step chemical dependence unit at Chicago's Grant Hospital, provided a reply of nearly 10 minutes without a concrete answer. "It's like the difference between sex and love. You can have both together and you can have them separately . . . Good question . . . But I don't think that religion and spirituality are the same thing. Matter of fact, in some cases I think they're mutually exclusive . . . I think it's spiritual and people want to um, whatever it may be . . . something that's good for your spirit, those things that we can't see . . . The spiritual is of responsibility and values . . . but I don't see the argument . . . Some people get their hair up every time you mention God . . ."

The "Big Book" calls the steps *suggestions*, and members are advised "Take what you want, leave the rest." Houlihan explains, "The steps are paradoxical," and "I know lots of people who've gone there, used A.A. for 2, 3, 4 years, are very well — and don't go to meetings anymore." These assertions put the program in better light, but paradox and ambiguity are questionable assets for mental health programs.

The steps are supplemented with 12 traditions providing recruitment by "attraction rather than promotion." Members preach "Live and let live," but the final step renders them dogma.

Step Twelve: *Having had a spiritual awakening as a result of these steps, we tried to carry this message to alcoholics, and to practice these principles in all our affairs.*

This explains 12 step growth. Since 1935 members, having cleaned up lives, embark on new careers "helping" addicts. The National Council on Alcoholism (NCA) was founded by member Marty Mann in 1944, and from there addiction care has become ruled by A.A.

Designed for evangelism, phrases like "half coming to A.A. get sober right away" need no proof. Dedicated to the program, members need to believe, assuming anybody else can do as they have. "I agree that A.A. doesn't work for everybody," Houlihan states. "Not everybody will go and expose themselves to it."

"The facts show (that) most people give up alcohol without any support group, psychotherapy, or other help," maintains Dr. Ellis, but this doesn't fit A.A. philosophy and begs explanation. People attaining sobriety without A.A. are called "dry drunks", fighting addiction tooth and nail, fundamentally unhappy inside. If that doesn't fit, they aren't "alcoholics" — they abused alcohol, but lack the "disease".

Behind a non-religious facade, A.A. converts more unbelievers than any other movement today. Through court acceptance, it's responsible for possibly the greatest rape of church/state separation in U.S. history, but the question remains: Does it cross that fine line into culthood?

ALCOHOLICS ANONYMOUS: A CULT?

A.A. utilizes deceptive recruitment, pernicious dogma, and anti-intellectual, evangelically religious methods, but its lack of authoritarian hierarchy or leader set it apart from cults. Other cultish attributes exist, largely through the tentacles of the 12th step work. This amorphous nature proves beneficial quashing critiques — the "official" organization *is* humble and definitely not a cult. But despite formalities, outside incorporation occurs through members, making the distinction between organization and outside followers meaningless.

A.A. has no enclosed structure, but when court ordered, the effect is similar. And treatment centers are arguably compounds — where else in the 20th century can you enter a hospital and be given a cure via "spiritual awakening?"

From 12 step dances to businesses hiring only members, A.A.'s separatist society needs no compound. Members are encouraged to avoid "people, places, and things" of their former lives. Assumed to be drinking, ex-members are described as "Out There" — in regular society. A phrase even exists to identify the status of strangers: "Are they friends of Bill Wilson?"

The resultant 12 step community, "Exercises unreasonable control over people's lives," says Dr. Ellis. "A.A. members aren't supposed to start an intense love affair, start a business, or any other serious undertaking for the first year sober."

While A.A. does not employ

"IT'S REALLY BEAUTIFUL BUT I'LL JUST HAVE THE ELVIS STAMP."

brainwashing techniques like starvation or beatings, effects are similar. Members hear A.A. philosophy repeatedly in rooms where nobody openly questions. "I consider myself a fairly intelligent person, but after a while, this stuff starts to work on you," says Chuck Gottmann.

Keep in mind the typical alcoholic's mental state: Lives in ruin, fuzzy minded and willing to do anything for sobriety, members enter meetings or hospitals "ready hazed." Would anyone mentally healthy perform the "therapy" prescribed Sandy? "I expressed reservations about the program, so they drove me out to a nearby farm and had me shovel sheep manure to learn humiliation."

Similar experiences are common — R.R.'s (Rational Recovery — an alternative treatment group) journal publishes a regular section, "Tales of the Untold," chronicling hospital injustices. Hospital methods are kept secretive — John Wootton, addictions director of Northwestern Memorial Hospital, missed the interview appointment for this article and refused to return calls afterward.

Although the support group is free, again its incorporation has led to cultish economic exploitation. The state rakes in millions on DUIs, and with hospital rehabilitation typically lasting two weeks, addiction is big business. And where there's money alongside evangelism, violence can appear.

For a period, Chuck Gottmann ran R.R. meetings in Chicago and served as regional coordinator. "When I started coordinating, I got death threats full of 'step-talk'. I mentioned them to the group then threw 'em out. I'm not gonna buy into that hate shit. You get as nuts as they are after a while." Gottmann also reports calls from people seeking refuge from recruiters through stalking laws, and one ex-member claims to have witnessed Nazi slanted groups.

Evidence concerning such events is lacking, but groups have mutated before. Synanon began as an A.A. group, declaring itself a church in the 1970s. Soon it engaged in practices like mass vasectomies and attempted murder of critics.

But 12 step addiction groups are probably more dangerous *because* they don't condone violence. Their means are indirect, making it difficult to prove harmful. Members are kept from alternatives and instilled with self-fulfilling predictions of disaster. Unable to work a religious program, ex-members launch into the debauchery they've been prophesied, leading often to vehicular deaths and suicide.

Although within addiction's nature, benders are by no means necessary. "When I read some R.R. materials and got away from A.A.," former member Carlos asserts, "I screwed up but realized I didn't *have* to 'hit bottom', like A.A. says. A couple times I limited my relapse to a night—one night I even stopped after three beers."

But A.A. continues promoting monstrous relapses. As the ruling addiction theory for over 50 years, the concepts promulgate society. "The American public wants people to believe in the 12 steps, even though they don't want to follow them themselves," explains Jack Trimpey, president of California based Rational Recovery. "People love to hear about the A.A. style of recovery. Hopeless people, surviving only by the help of other people, calling each other for support in the middle of the night. It's all so touching. The media likes to hear about people having 'spiritual awakenings' and such, it makes a better story than just quitting."

Although apparently not exactly a cult, A.A. is a dangerous religion that's managed to creep into widespread acceptance. It's as if this socially palatable, evangelical religion was designed for deceptive success.

Which, in all reality, it was.

Part two, concerning the true history of A.A. and efforts to quash other treatment methods, will appear in the next issue of **Gauntlet**.

[Editor's Note: While we have attempted to commission a rebuttal of this article, A.A. did not cooperate. Anyone wishing to rebut this piece should query **Gauntlet** *with a SASE.]*

John Henry Biedermann is a freelance writer, volunteer editor of Rational Recovery's **Midwestern Update***, and is a* **recovered** *alcoholic. He is currently seeking an agent and/or publisher for his novel,* **'Hab***, which takes place inside a 12 step drug and alcohol rehab. He can be reached at P.O. Box 14127, Chicago, IL 60614-0127.*

DON'T CALL US MOONIES

Peter D. Ross

I can remember occasional nocturnal adventures going home from the club-house after an afternoon's rugby and an extended evening of camaraderie. As freshmen in college, it was not unusual for my friends and I to pass a *rozzer* (Dublin slang for a policeman) at his post and "moon" him from a speeding car! Emboldened by the ingestion of copious pints of Guinness, we were anesthetized to any possible offensiveness with which such conduct might be received by the innocent and hard-working officer, never mind anyone else who happened to witness the crude exposure of an Irish tush!!

Later as a full-time missionary for the Unification Church when I began to be accosted with verbal barrages of "fuck you *Moonie*" from speeding cars, I realized that some youthful indiscretions had caught up with me. Purgatory had for some unknown reason begun prematurely on earth! Upon hearing that other church members had been subjected to the same abuse, I questioned them as to what sports they had played in their youth and what the accompanying social life was like. It was only then that I realized that this name calling had nothing to do with any occasional youthful disregard for authority but that it had all to do with my religious affiliation.

The term "Moonie", as a reference to a member of the Unification Church, was not coined by Unificationists. Rather, it is a drive-by shot from the coward in the speeding vehicle intended to harm and to injure. Like the paintball fired from an air-powered gun in mock battle, it impacts and splats, leaving the modern-day version of the yellow cross impressed upon the *conversos* (a term referring to those Jews in the Middle Ages who were forced to "convert" to Christianity and who were then required to wear identifying yellow stars). The coiners of the term "Moonie" knew full well the impact of the suffix "ie," and its informal, disrespectful, and derogatory "register" (a term of art for any linguist). Add to that the prurient undertone, and the coiners of the term, the editors at the *Washington Post*, had landed a keeper in February of 1974. Not known for any overt displays of affection towards Unificationists, the *Post* has perpetuated the use of this term until today. When challenged recently to finally let it go, Leonard Downie, executive editor at the *Post*, wrote to me and stated that "we do not agree that the term is pejorative and offensive and therefore allowed its use . . . "

In the intervening years since the *Post* first introduced the "Moonie" term, their editors have ceded any exclusive rights and this offensive epithet came to be generously shared with anyone seeking to exhibit their own naked prejudice. And so "Moonie" came to be added to an undistinguished list of similar terms, such as, "nigger", "kike", "fag", "chink", "jap", "mick", "guinea", "spick", etc..

After its inception and adoption by the movers and shakers of our social mores, the editors and the TV anchors, the term was picked up by those detractors of the Unification community. In particular it was seized upon by those who elected to turn their animus of the Unification Church into a profitable career. The use of "Moonie" came to be persistently used in order to blind-side any project, activity, or initiative, undertaken by the Reverend Moon himself, by any single Unificationist, or by the Unification community as a whole. Call it a "Moonie such-as-such" and any consideration or regard for the matter at hand is justifiably and expediently excused. Call the individual a "Moonie" and the listener or reader is immediately endowed with all there is to know of the individual being discussed.

The *New York Times*, in an editorial "Winking at Baseball's Racism", criticized the suspension of Marge Schott from baseball for one year as being too lenient. The *Times* questioned why Ms. Schott did not receive the same punishment as Al Campanis who was forced to leave the game forever for stating that blacks "lacked the necessities" to manage baseball teams. A more recent example is the public outcry over the comments of the New York Yankees' community affairs liaison officer comparing his Bronx neighbors to "monkeys" whom he contended did nothing more than hang on basketball rings. Such insensitive and offensive rhetoric incited universal indignation in the press and along the hallowed hallways of the major networks.

One can only wonder how long

Unificationists must bide their time before their sincere petitions regarding the offensive use of the term "Moonie" will finally be acknowledged. I consider twenty years to be enough. Any short-term anesthesia has long since worn off and it really hurts to be so persistently abused. Unification Church members have been derided as "Moonies", then mobbed and beaten. In New York city, a seven-months pregnant woman was beaten and sent to the hospital as a result of irrational hatred of "Moonies". Members have been abducted, imprisoned, assaulted and abused. In many instances the perpetrators were not charged by the authorities or even admonished by society because their victims were only "Moonies". Hatemongers are depicted as "expects" on this subspecies called "Moonies" and all too often they are provided free air-time to express their moonophobia with impunity.

While I am familiar with the saying that there is always someone out there who doesn't get it, I do hope that at least one ol' die-hard finally gets it! And so I invite Leonard Downie to step forward to do the decent thing and hit a vestige of the *Washington Post*'s own religious bigotry out of the ballpark! And then I promise not to show my Irish tush around the offices of the *Washington Post* ever again!!!

---

*Peter Ross is a lawyer for the Unification Church. [Editor's note: Mrs. Ross provided us with a number of letters from news publications which indicated they would refrain from use of the term "Moonies." **The New York Times**, for example in 1991 indicated it would not use the term as it is "pejorative." Reuters also "banned" use of the phrase in 1991. Recently the **New York Post** ran a story using the phrase. Mr. Ross has fired off a letter, but as went to press the paper had yet to respond.]*

"NEK-KID" PHOTOGRAPHS CAUSE BROUHAHA IN COBBS COUNTY, GEORGIA

Martin M. Stone

Tuning forks. They have always amazed me. Take one and tap it. You will hear a tone — the vibration actually. Waves. Up and down. Another tuning fork nearby — if matched to the first — will begin to vibrate. Sympathy. This wave physics thing is a recurring theme in nature. Waves and the sympathetic transmission of information. That's a very fancy way of describing a particular process of communication.

Not surprisingly language, music and all kinds of artistic media enable us to communicate through sympathetic transmission. Some people are so deeply affected in this way that a spiritual experience results. Others, because they are not 'tuned' to the information, simply don't understand what all the fuss is about. The message just does not move them. Some are confused and confounded. Still others are so profoundly upset that the mere existence of the information threatens their well being.

There is a little bit of each of these types in all of us. How we interact, act and react to our environment and the information around us determines where our sympathies lie—and if they are rigid or flexible.

As an artist, I am moved and challenged by many divergent 'voices.' I am particularly affected by metaphor, symbolism and the unconscious mind. From the very start, my photography has been subject to attack for not being 'politically correct'; for being 'sexist'; for my various depictions of the nude . . . *ad nauseam*. In fact, I have managed to stir things up on both sides of the ideological fence simply through the exploration of themes, cultures and images that interest and inspire my muse.

I have also been the victim of attempts at censorship. The story that follows was my first experience with censorship.

It was 1987 and I had not been photographing long. A figure model I had been working with told me of an exhibition opportunity at a local county sponsored arts center. I called and scheduled a meeting with the assistant director. She viewed a sample of my portfolio and agreed to give me a exhibition. I had about five months to get over twenty-five photographs printed, mounted, matted and framed for exhibition. There was a lot of work to do.

After printing the exhibition, I went back to review the prints with the arts center guild and the assistant director. When I arrived at the Steeple House Arts Center I was met by both the director and assistant director. There would be no review by the guild. Instead, I was to receive special treatment. You see, the director of Cobb County Arts and Cultural Affairs had heard that my work included studies of the nude.

Everything was going just fine until we got to the nudes. A pile of rejected photographs began to form. Not all the figure studies were dis-

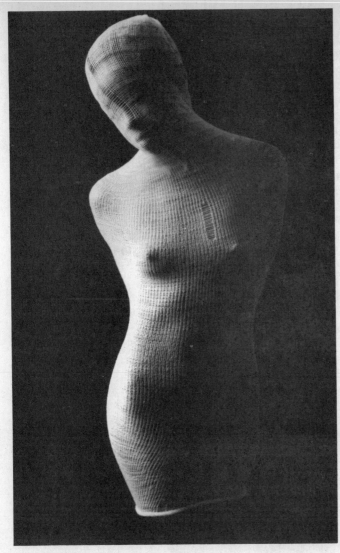

Enraged both conservatives & liberals. Caused accusations of being "sexist" & being into "bondage."

weeks until the opening, I could not come up with nine new images to fill in the exhibition. She mentioned that I could go before the Cobb Arts Commission, but that she hoped I would be able to work around the censorship and print some other images. She confessed that she was in trouble for approving my exhibition in the first place. She was afraid of losing her job.

As I drove home, I tried to sort it all out. I was ready to quit — screw the exhibition and screw the arts center. It's not worth it, I thought. I decided to call the model who had first told me about the exhibition opportunity. He was surprised by the censorship. After all, the arts center offered figure drawing, painting and sculpting classes — complete with undraped (nude) models — of which he is one.

I decided to go and speak to the Cobb Arts Commission.

Composed of judges, lawyers, doctors and others with an interest in the arts (music, theater, visual arts, etc.), the Cobb Arts Commission is an all volunteer advisory board. They provide advice and direction to the Cobb County Commission and the Department of Arts and Cultural Affairs on arts policy. Their next sched-

carded — just the "naked" ones (pronounced: nek-kid, for those unfamiliar with southern speech). The unacceptable photographs were "naked"? I was in shock.

With a Cheshire cat grin the director left. I found out later that this was not the first time she had censored an art exhibition.

The assistant director began to apologize. She didn't see why some of my photographs had offended the director. I complained that with two uled meeting was in a few days.

At the meeting, I was asked to speak of what happened to me. I also had some questions for the commission. I wanted to know why an art center that teaches figure drawing, painting and sculpting would have a problem with figure (nude) photography? Why was the director of Arts and Cultural Affairs so personally interested in my work as to review and censor my exhibition? Why didn't the guild get to see my work? Where did the director get the power to act as the county art censor? And just what is the difference between "naked" and "nude"?

My questions went unanswered. The Arts Commission decided to study this matter further before making a recommendation. They also decided to personally review my exhibition — to judge for themselves if the censorship was uncalled for. Another meeting was scheduled for the following week.

Little did I know that my complaint was about to be used against the arts center and the arts community.

The next day, I got a call from my model friend. All the figure classes are being cancelled! "What?", I said. "Why?"

"Because of my complaint," he said, "all the models will have to wear bathing suits in the figure classes. Some teachers are cancelling their classes altogether."

I felt sickened — and then mad! He suggested that I call the local newspaper — and I did.

Over lunch, I told the newspaper reporter what was going on. I had not brought my art work to show her, so I couldn't tell what she was really thinking. I hoped for the best. I couldn't believe that my little exhibition was about to become a media event. I wasn't ready for this.

Front page in the local morning paper (*The Marietta Daily Journal*) was the first story on the figure classes and the covered-up models. In two days, the *Atlanta Journal/Constitution* picked up the story and expanded the coverage. In fact, the story was picked up by the wire services and by newspapers all over North America. A reporter from the *Miami Herald* came to sit in on the next Arts Commission meeting.

At the meeting, it was decided that nude figure models would be acceptable in county supported arts centers and that my exhibition of photography would be held without any censorship! But the battle was not over. The county bureaucrats now wanted specific guidelines on what was acceptable art and what was not.

I decided to avoid any Cobb County funded art centers or art exhibitions.

It's been six years and things have recently gotten much worse. After a few complaints about a local award winning theater company's production of "Lips Together, Teeth Apart", in which a reference to a homosexual couple is made, the Cobb county Commission (under the ceaseless prodding of commissioner Gordon Wysong) drafted and passed a resolution condemning "the homosexual lifestyle" (among other things) and then totally eliminated all county arts funding for the upcoming year (about $110,000 worth). It was another media circus with demonstrations and counter demonstrations.

What really happened was another victory for the ultra-conservative Christian right and another loss for the community and its artists.

A portfolio of Martin M. Stone's work follows.

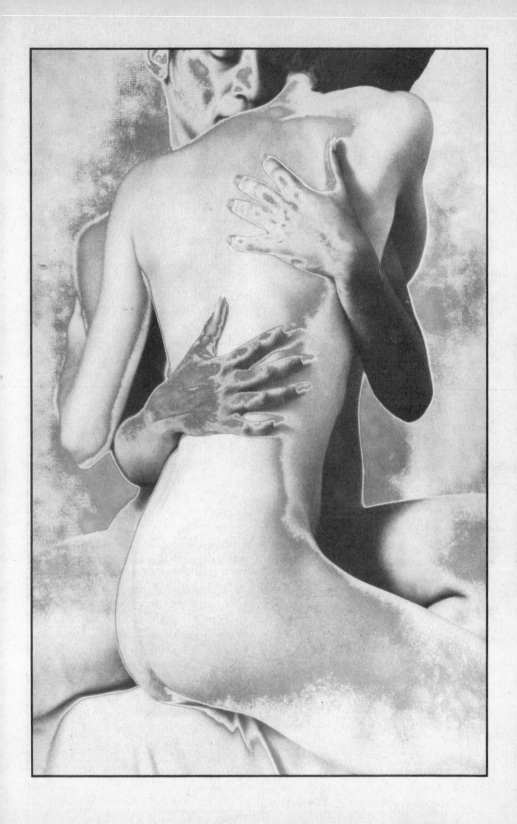

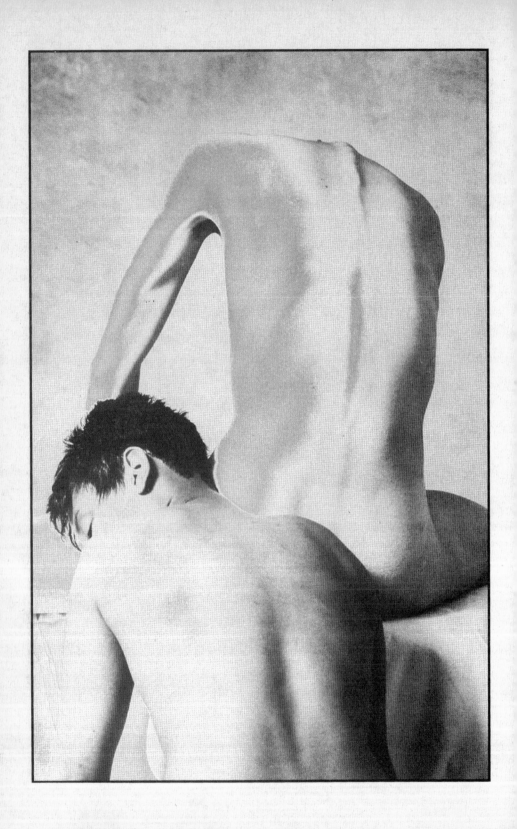

"Curva Couture"

"The Crux of Fiction" In response to uproar over
the movie ***The Last Temptation of Christ***

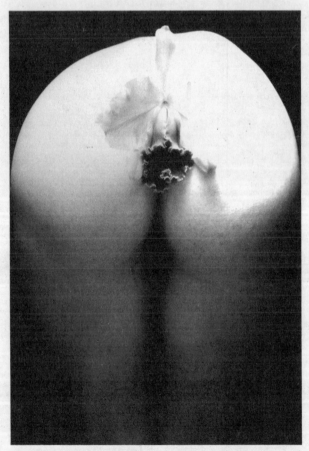

"Nude with orchid." My apologies to O'Keefe

BODYPAINTING: AN ARTFORM NOT FOR EVERYBODY

Mitchell J. Poulouin

My artistic form of shamanism is an assimilation of many cultures honoring the magicks of their ancestors. The tribal influence in my designs seem to tap into the subconscious of the painted model, and evoke a personal sense of transformation for them. I paint masks and body-covered amulets on my subjects . . . I don't do face painting. My artwork is an active energy exchange between artist and subject and the transformationally experience is mutually felt by both.

As an erotic artist, I recognize the tightrope between "pornography" and "fine art" and I tend to walk a conservative rope between these judgements. As a shaman, I am humbled to be permitted to paint my transformations on such loving and trusting souls. Just as an artist's studio is considered "sacred space", my work environment establishes a "safe space" for my subjects no matter if it happens to be a gala, special event, private party, or portfolio-oriented photography session. Most artists working with a nude subject have a distant and impersonal rapport with the model. Rarely does the opportunity arise that allows a more intimate relationship to develop. I recognize the unique situation created with bodypainting. My subjects come to me willing to offer their vulnerabilities in exchange for my magick. They are rarely disappointed. Even the most ardent feminist has drifted off into dreamland under the application of my paintbrush, due to the safe and sensual (yet not sexual) scenario.

What constantly appalls me as an artist is the possessive reaction exhibited by many of the paramours of my models. The intimacy that is shared between artist and model is experienced as a creative trance-like convergence between one another, yet as permanent as a sand castle. This artistic collaboration apparently can unintentionally threaten a loosely-woven relationship by the mere consideration of participating in a body painting session. This is a more common threat to men of heterosexual relationships and typically evokes rather strong feelings toward the need to assert control over the actions of their partners. I have encountered similar insecurity-oriented conflicts within alternative relationships as well. This is not a conflict limited to race, financial status, employment position, or age. Often the model explains the disappointment

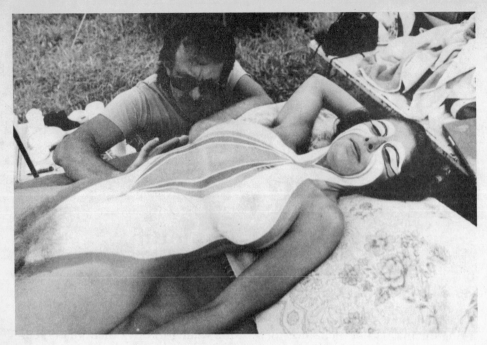

Artist Mitchell Poulouin at work

of cancelling the bodypainting project with sincere embarrassment.

When I approach female exotic entertainers to collaborate on experimental art projects, I encounter interest yet reservations, shyness, mistrust and a lack of sincerity. When I contract professional models for collaborative portfolio projects, I am surrounded by enthusiastic subjects that are limited by "recognition" conflicts associated with nudity. When I set up my portable studio at clothing-optional events, I am besieged with beautiful people with open hearts of all shapes, sizes, ages, and cultures. These prospective models are attracted by the creative possibilities, intrigued by the sensual experience, and captivated by their own innocence.

Even though I work in an erotic art forum, I consciously establish a non-sexual environment, striving to create a safe space for my subjects. When I am working with my company's staff of special effects makeup artists, I inspire a sacred atmosphere for my subjects to feel honored and empowered. We pressure no one and celebrate everyone . . . and everybody has a real good time.

Why deny anyone (especially your paramour) from having a good time in a sacred space, with artsy people, without a stitch on, covered with bodypaint, while listening to New Age music, and surrounded in a cloud of incense and love? Well?

Mitchell Poulouin holds a Bachelors of Architecture with minors in Filmaking and Set Design. He is currently working as a Technical Theatre Director and Glamour Photographer, when he isn't soliciting body painting projects for his makeup troupe, S/FX network. For further information, contact him at his studio: P.O. Box 612 Claymont, DE 19703.

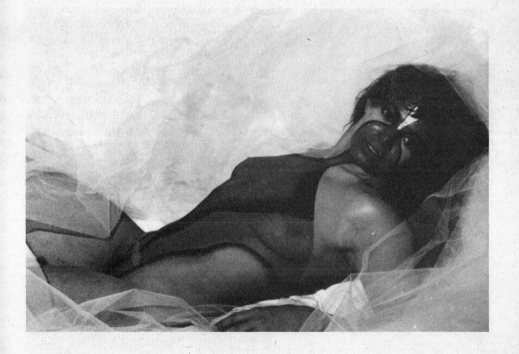

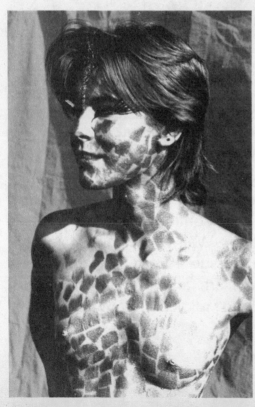

IN OUR NEXT ISSUE . . .

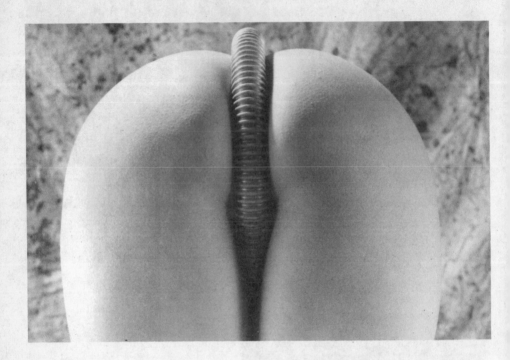

Former-*High Society* and *Penthouse* model Justice Howard now operates on the other side of the lens, as the most controversially erotic photographer to shock the art world since Robert Mapplethorpe. Her signature untitled high contrast black and white visions of lust often juxtapose soft, female sensuality with the harsh confines of urban reality — and latex. Watch for porn critic Wally Wharton's explosive interview with Ms. Howard in issue #9 of *Gauntlet*, as they discuss feminism, censorship, art, and the darker side of sexuality. An extensive portfolio will accompany the text.

Sugar And Spice; Pin-up Art By Women

Lisa Petrucci

Beauty is in the eye of the beholder. We've all heard that before. And yet, this is a right that is constantly being challenged by both extremes, feminists and right-wing conservatives, when it comes to representations of the female form whether it be in pornography, advertising, print media or fine art. The visual continues to be a point of controversy when it comes to women's bodies, and no one can agree upon correct and proper ways of portraying them.

Recently, there has been a resurgence in nostalgic images of women, particularly the pin-up genre that donned many magazines, calendars, postcards and a wide array of printed material from the thirties to the sixties. Copies of the magazine covers and assorted ephemera are now available in trading card sets, books and magazines surveying the various artists and publications who popularized the pin-up as well as numerous collectibles being produced to reintroduce these sugar-coated images to new eyes.

As you may imagine, pin-up art has been criticized as being sexist and exploitive, given that the pictures exaggerate idealized aspects of femininity—focus is on a fresh, beautiful face (preferably smiling or pouting) and a curvaceous and buxom figure (big breasts, tiny waist, full hips and long legs in most cases). I'm not here to either criticize or defend the art—but to look at a new generation of artists, and in this case, *women*, who are cur-

rently making art inspired by or examining pin-ups.

To begin with, I am guilty of liking this type of art — probably for the same reasons I'm drawn to horror movies and comic books. They're all about fantasy, tapping into the imagination and childhood part of the brain. I can remember when I was a little girl being fascinated with pictures of beautiful women from fairy tales and other sources. Many young girls spent hours during their childhood drawing horses, rainbows and princesses. We weren't told that it was wrong, so when confronted with these images again in adulthood, why should our reaction be any different than it was then? The attraction is still there, lying dormant until faced with some sentimentally-charged eye candy.

Let's try to see this appropriation of pin-ups by women as a reclamation of the genre, some whose view is celebratory and others taking a critical approach.

The historical background of the pin-up begins during the early part of the century with the rise of Hollywood — glamorous pastel portraits of movie stars were mass-produced for fans in magazines and postcards. World War II took hold of the country, and American GIs were sent overseas to fight for democracy, taking with them pictures of their sweethearts and wives, along with reproductions of their favorite actresses or idealized illustrations of wholesome-type American girls for

"Stiletto" by Olivia, 1993

moral support. For better or worse, pin-ups became an integral part of our culture, and began appearing on printed materials of all sorts. Many artists were well-known for their particular vision of the "perfect" woman — Gil Elvgren George Petty, Alberto Vargas, Earl Moran, Enoch Bolles among the top illustrators who created notions of "the girl next door", having just the right amount of niceness and sexuality. Basically this was a woman who exuded a cheerful personality, and was unaware of her own sensuality.

Interestingly enough, two renowned artists during the golden age of pin-ups were women, Zoe Mozert and Joyce Ballantyne. Both did work for magazines, advertising and calendar publishing companies; and were praised for their technical abilities and sensitivity to their subject. It makes sense that a woman artist would have an instinct and familiarity with female bodies. Mozert even

posed in the mirror for many of her paintings!

As times changed, pin-ups became dated and obsolete; being replaced by more revealing photographs of actual "real" women (of the Snap-On Tool calendar variety). Values and media changed, and so did perceptions of what ideal women look like.

Perhaps the most visible artist working in the commercial erotic art scene these days in Olivia DeBerardinis. Her dazzling, airbrushed paintings have appeared in numerous men's magazines including *Playboy*, and are also reproduced on everything from posters, prints, calendars, trading cards, CD ROM programs, t-shirts, magnets, you name it. Olivia's original art has been exhibited at the Tamara Bane Gallery and Robert Bane Editions in Los Angeles, as well as locations internationally. She's known by a wide cross-section of art lovers, porn readers, comic book fans and others; and recently an artbook of her pin-ups was published called *Let Them Eat Cheesecake – The Art of Olivia*.

Like many of the women artists we'll look at, Olivia drew a lot when she was young (and guess what she would draw — sexy women in tight clothing!). She went on to The School of Visual Arts in New York, and then began working as an illustrator for some men's magazines. Early on she was interested in erotica, and even went to visit Alberto Vargas on her honeymoon with husband Joel Beren. Over the years, Olivia gained a reputation for her style which at times seems reminiscent of Vargas, but more often having a bolder, contemporary edge. Although the execution is delicate and flawless, these women she portrays have a strength and power that seems missing from many male artist's depictions. The models are very much in charge of their own sexuality and not an object to be possessed. In an interview Olivia did with pin-up dealer/historian Marianne Ohl Phillips, the artist said, "I do like modern aggressive women. The bolder the better; but people find them very intimidating. I enjoy painting all different types of women. They are all fascinating and beautiful in totally different ways."

Olivia also reports that at least a third of the collectors who buy her paintings and prints are women. When questioned by a writer from the *New York Daily News* about her work, she said "Sure pinups exaggerate the female form, but I think all artists exaggerate. I mean, look at [Michelangelo's] David. That's pretty great beefcake."

Throughout history, the human body has been molded into various shapes and sizes depending on the ideals of the culture. It is unlikely that many people looked like the classical Greek sculptures of antiquity (or that they were expected to aspire to do so). Something to think about. . .

Another West coast artist who began drawing pictures of women as a youngster is Christine Karas. Growing up in a household of women, she says that she was accustomed to dealing with female issues as these were familiar to her. Christine went on to art school and pursued fashion illustration as a means of validating her desire to make art about sexy women. During the last semester at school she tried painting on canvas and realized that this was the direction that she wanted to continue in, though previously she felt guilt towards this subject matter, as it was somehow trivial and not a legitimate means of expression.

Since then Christine has had numerous exhibitions (including Tamara Bane Gallery and La Lux de Jesus) as well as illustrating men's magazines and other projects. Response to her work is mixed. In a recent exhibition at an L.A. coffeehouse, she told me that some feminists complained about paintings, claiming that they were degrading to women, because of the blatantly sexual context. One woman invited Christine to a radio show she hosted to discuss and explain the work on air. Perhaps misconceptions were cleared up at that time, but when it comes down to it everyone is entitled to their opinion.

Though the paintings may appear to some as objectifying women — many other viewers find them empowering, seeing them as icons of voracious female sexuality. The

Diana Bolton "More, More, More," 1992. Enamel on metal.

model is surrounded by things that have personal or metaphorical meaning to Christine — color has significance as do the objects that clutter the canvases. A tattoo on the woman's body may mean something. Another interesting aspect of her work is the method of its execution, the seemingly amateurish quality of painting is quite intentional — they really do go after a cheesy, thrift store look or perhaps closer to the illustrations on a cheap, vintage pulp cover.

On the other hand, conceptual artist Lutz Bacher uses the traditional pin-up imagery to comment on cultural and sexual politics. She recently had an exhibition at the Pat Hearn Gallery in New York which was met with confusion by most who saw the work. To many, the paintings appeared to be copies of Vargas Girls from *Playboy* (which they were but with a subtle and ironic twist). On the surface, they were familiar, but upon closer inspection revealed a deconstruction of the nostalgic image, having taken it out of it's original context to expose other issues at work.

The "Playboys" series was conceived when Lutz discovered a three ring binder in a thrift store which was filled with torn out sheets of Vargas

"Betty's Favorite Hobby"
Christine Karas 1992

Girls, placed in plastic sleeves. She saw these images as being representative of Vargas' oevre during the time he worked at *Playboy* (1957-78) — they depicted a variety of cliched poses. At this point, Lutz had a commercial artist recreate and tamper with the original illustrations in a series of large-scale paintings and drawings. She chose materials that were unlike Vargas' watercolors, using acrylic and gesso (both materials from plastic) which also lend an artificiality to the women. Because of the enlargement of the figure, these models tend to be more confrontational than they were ever intended to be. There isn't any room for intimacy. Given the plasticity of the women, they appear to be made of generic head, breast and leg combinations; much like rubber sex dolls with interchangeable parts.

Added to the static relationship of the women to the cold white background they exist within, are textual one liners referring to historical events during the time the pictures were originally published ("Peace Sign" is based on an illustration published during heated protests over the U.S. invasion of Cambodia). Her examination of cast-off American popular culture would make Vargas roll over in his grave.

The first time I saw Diana Balton's paintings was at the Tony Shafrazi Gallery in New York, I was at once thrilled and delighted to see an artist's work with hearts and flowers motifs, and ambiguous, though optimistic texts. I thought to myself that she must have really enjoyed making these. They were large, human-sized commercially produced metal signs of cut out shapes, stuck on the wall like a happy face decal. One of them had a reclining woman (which I was later told was from a Victoria's Secret catalog) surrounded by lush flowers and simultaneously exclaimed

"Kisses & Wishes" and "I Like My-self!" I felt she communicated a vul-nerability that many women experience — that of the responsibil-ity of nurturing others while trying as hard as possible to convince oneself of her own worth.

The logo-type design Diana cre-ates around the models is con-structed from "sugar and spice and everything nice" imagery. On this giant scale however, the paintings are anything but dainty, becoming pow-erful symbols of female culture.

When I asked Siiri Howard why she liked pin-up art, she giggled and said "They're pretty!", but continued to explain that when she was little she had seen Vargas Girls in her uncle's *Playboys* and thought that she wanted to be like them. She went on to col-lect George Petty prints and decals with pin-ups on them when she was a teenager. Siiri grew up and contin-ued to be attracted to these images, but incorporated them with her love of other things like car culture and tattooing. Her paintings are a pas-tiche of her loves and obsessions, never at all apologetic or embar-rassed. She uses the materials and language of traditionally women's crafts (needlepoint, crochet, cake decorating tools, etc.) and combines them with subversive imagery and content. Teddy bears and naked girls frolic under rainbows, another work is a loving tribute to Betty Page done in needlepoint and laced-up leather. These paintings are celebrations of pop culture, and really don't care what anyone thinks about them. And I like that!

I curated an exhibition of pin-up art a few months back at the Bess Cutler Gallery in New York, and re-ally didn't know what to expect as far as people's (especially women's) reac-tion to the art that defiantly hung on the walls. Surprisingly, nearly every-one who came to the show enjoyed

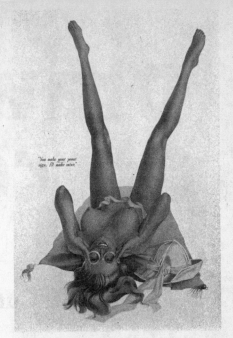

"Playboys" Peace; Lutz Bacher, 1991

what they saw, saying that it was re-freshing to look at something beauti-ful for a change. A writer from *The New York Daily News* told me that she came to the show expecting to feel hostile towards the pictures, but went away actually liking a lot of the art. Even NYU art historian Linda Nochlin was quoted by the writer as saying "You hardly want them as your role models, but I hope no one could take them very seriously. They're cute."

During the next year there are a number of opportunities to become more familiar with the whole pin-up phenomena. Pure Imagination (the publisher of *The Betty Pages*) will be introducing a new magazine called *Tease!* which will be devoted to pin-up art and other cultural nostalgia of a sexual nature.

Lisa Petrucci is a curator, artist and writer living in Los Angeles (as of this printing!). Her articles on popular cul-ture, art and film have appeared in Ax-cess, Sin International, Tease!, Baby Boomer Collectibles.

Drawn to Obscenity

Scott Cunningham

From 1987 until 1990, Mike Diana published an obscure little 'zine called *Boiled Angel*. At the height of its popularity, his comic anthology boasted a whopping 300 subscribers. Before the cops called on Mike Diana, he was just another desperate 'zinster: quiet and shy, spending all his spare time at all-night copy shops, xeroxing his punky doodles about rape, murder and incest. Let's just say he was compelled to do it. Artistically raised on reprints of *Zap Comics* while listening to the Butthole Surfers, he drew ugly things to gross his way out of a bland existence in poor white trash suburbia. Who could blame him?

But when Florida state troopers stumbled across a copy of *Boiled Angel* in the apartment of a "Gainesville Murderer" suspect (a high profile local case starring a serial murderer with a taste for college girls) Diana became caught up in the region's broad and sweeping manhunt. Intelligence officers in Pinellas County, where Diana lives, even tested the cartoonist's blood to see if it matched the blood found at the crime scenes.

While the investigation of the suspect who originally owned *Boiled Angel* was eventually dropped for lack of evidence, Diana was sternly warned by officers to stop publishing his evil 'zine.

One of the local "intelligence" officers became obsessed with Diana'a publication, posing as a fellow 'zine fan and corresponding with Diana through the mail — eventually ordering the next two issues of *Boiled Angel*. Ironically, these were the only copies of Diana's 'zine ever sold in Pinellas County. Flash forward two years later to Stuart Baggish, Florida's assistant state attorney, who suddenly decides to prosecute Diana on three counts of publishing obscene material. On March 26, 1994, Florida state decides to reward Mike for all those years of standing in front of a photocopier: he was found guilty of all three charges.

Diana'a lawyers went into court feeling that their client might be found guilty on obscenity charges and fined, but confident that the three years of jail time Baggish was asking for would be seen by Judge

Walter Fullerton as clearly overkill. But Diana and his lawyers woke up to the harsh reality of the Florida criminal justice system when the cartoonist was forced to spend four days in jail awaiting sentencing, since bail wasn't allowed to be set. When sentencing finally came on Monday, everyone on Diana'a side let out a collective sigh of relief when the judge released him on probation. Then the man in black started reading the conditions attached to his freedom, and the collective mood in the court house went from elation to depression: the probation was for *three years* (for each of the three counts against him); he was fined $3,000, which must be paid in payments of at least $100 per month; he was forced to work 1,248 hours of community service at the local Salvation Army (which translates into 8 hours per week for the entire three years — he also has to pay $6.00 for worker's insurance per 8-hour session); he must work full-time (meaning that he is *mandated by law* to log a 48-hour week, once you've factored in the community service); he had to seek out psychological evaluation within 30 days of sentencing; he was supposed to take a course in journalistic ethics (at his own expense).

Okay, now catch your breath because there's more amendment-bashing coming, including a "stay away" order from minors which means Mike must not come into close contact or intimate conversation with anyone under 18. Pretty tricky, since he works at his dad's convenience store and has to wait on people of *all* ages (after all, this is a democracy). At the sentencing, the judge explained to Mike that he had to stay behind the counter and speak only when spoken to, if he suspects one of his customers is an innocent underager. One assumes he's not supposed to flash any of his drawings at them either.

And now the real clincher – he is not to draw or write anything that may be deemed obscene, *even for his own personal use*, and he's subject to unannounced searches of his apartment by his probation officer to make sure he's not doing any dirty drawings. The state of Florida has made it illegal for Mike Diana to make his

Getting "Ahead" in FLA.

art. They have rendered an official order that is the equivalent of thought-crime; George Orwell was only off by a decade, folks.

Is Mike's work obscene? Is it art, or sick and prurient material meant to excite child molesters? For the record, when I first saw Mike's work in 1989, I thought it had a primitive power and energy that made it stand out from the crowd of gore-loving 'zines swelling in the serial-killer subculture (the equally obsessed *Answer Me* currently holds this title-and not surprisingly, Mike has done illustrations for it). Keep in mind, in '89, Mike was only 19, and I was impressed by someone his age putting out a 'zine regularly in some god-forsaken place where I'm sure there was zero encouragement. That was one of the wonderful things about the 'zine movement of the eighties: it was an outlet for artists, writers and musicians in all those little "normal" towns across the country to connect with other weirdos and odd-balls. Over the years *Boiled Angel* continued to grow in size and complexity and I came to respect it, in some crazy way, because it was so over the top. Eventually, I started to contribute to Mike's 'zine, and in fact my drawings and comics are included in the two

anthologies of *Boiled Angel* that have been deemed to be utterly without any artistic merit (one of the conditions necessary to have any material declared obscene). At the same time Mike was producing *Boiled Angel*, he was also making homemade "live-action" gore videos and contributing to a number of other underground publications. He was a busy and ambitious guy — someone who took his art-making very seriously. And over the years his work has shown real growth both in technical and conceptual ways. In the last year he's appeared in a number of top-flight comics and 'zines like *Snake Eyes, World War 3 Illustrated, The Brutarian* and the aforementioned *Answer Me*.

If you're still trying to figure out how all this happened, don't try. It wasn't logic or perspective that ultimately influenced the jury's decision — it was the highly inflammatory rhetoric employed by prosecutor Baggish that moved them. In his summation to the jury he exclaimed: "Pinellas County has its own identity. It doesn't have to accept what is acceptable in the bathhouses of San Francisco, and it doesn't have to accept what is acceptable in the crack alleys of New York." Baggish reminded the jury that Mike's tiny list

Meanwhile across town Mike's girlfriend Suzy was devising a plan to fix Baggish for good!

Don't worry honey, I got a plan! I'm going to make a brainwashing machine!

Suzy worked for hours all to save Mike! Being no angel with the State of Florida she understood his prediciment!

of 300 subscribers included people in France, Australia and Africa. Then he said, "It goes all over the world and it says, Largo, Fla. Nice reputation for Pinellas County, don't you thing?"

I think the reputation of being a *fascist state* is worst, but then what do I know — my mind's been addled from all that crack I've been smoking in alleys.

Diana went before a judge over a month ago and his lawyers were able to have his probation overturned once a $3000 bail bond is paid. It is July 12, 1994 as I write this, and due to bureaucratic bullshit with the courts, Diana'a probation conditions remain in effect.

IN HIS OWN WORDS . . . MIKE DIANA SPEAKS

There must be some reason why certain kids draw certain ways. It was interesting, when I started having to explain this stuff to the lawyer. I had to ask myself "Well, why did I draw this," because I had never really given it any thought before. And I tried to remember where I was when I drew this. At the time, I was just trying to make it [my art] as sickening as possible, and trying to make it offensive.

And I wanted people to look at it and think it was ugly, but also funny at the same time. I was trying to gross people out, basically. So it was hard to talk about in court.

I'd watched a lot of films that had gore. I always liked John Waters movies — his early 70s ones. That was a big influence, because it sort of gave my work a kind of place that I could start from. My drawings were always pretty weird and gross, but after seeing his movies, it made me want to add bad taste to it too. He would make things funny, but unspeakable at the same time. I think all the other old underground cartoonists were real influences. People like Rory Hayes and S. Clay Wilson. Especially Wilson, he had a lot of violence and drugs — guys getting their dicks ripped off and stuff like that. A lot of people seem to think it's a fantasy that I draw and jerk-off to. But, I wanted to do something really disgusting and that's what I thought up. For myself, it's enough to know that I enjoyed drawing something I knew was nasty. I don't know why I'm drawn to it, I haven't really figured that out.

During the summation was when I got the most nervous. I was the last one to take the stand. For

about six hours I was talking. I got to feeling I was giving a lecture at a university, because I had to explain almost every line I drew while doing the picture.

My lawyer got out there and talked about what a good guy I was, and talked about how the state's witness art "expert" was really from Eckerd College—a local Catholic College—and he admitted himself that I was an artist but my work was not art. And then the prosecution got out there and started talking about serial killers. Danny Rollins had just confessed to the Gainesville murders and this was all over the television and news the whole week. So Stuart Baggish starts talking about serial killers. He tried to scare the jury into prosecuting me, telling them I'm a monster. At that point, he was cheating, really, because he wasn't saying that my work wasn't art, he was saying I was trying to get people to kill. I can't imagine anybody seeing my art and going nuts and killing somebody, or seeing it to provoke them to kill. If anything, I think it would even help to . . . what's the word . . . deter.

After the closing arguments, the jury went and deliberated for about ninety minutes. They came back and said: "Guilty on all three counts."

And, you know, it felt just like on T.V., when they read the guilty verdict and people start crying. It didn't seem real at that point. I couldn't believe it, to hear the lady read off "You, Michael Christopher Diana, are hereby found guilty of the first count of publishing obscene material," . . . and then count two, and count three. I just looked at the jury as they walked out, really neatly, and thought to myself, "You fucking bastards."

They brought me into the back room and frisked me and handcuffed me. Walking out the back door of the courthouse into a paddy wagon, there was this news camera waiting out there for me. And as I'm walking past in handcuffs, he asking me, "Well, did you ever think it would come down to this?" and "What do you think now?". The whole strain of the trial, and now to know that I was going to jail. They're taking pictures of me in handcuffs, getting into the paddy wagon. I didn't even want to look at the camera.

I was put in maximum security. The place has a long hallway, with cells on both sides. Little cells. And everybody would roam around the hallway in and out of the cells in this big room all day. And, of course,

there's nothing to do in jail. They just throw everybody into this one room and you're just sitting around and that's it. There's no T.V. or books. You're just sitting there doing nothing. It just happened that the cell I got in was the solidarity confinement cell. The other cells had doors with bars, so you see through them, but mine was a solid metal door, with just a little Plexiglass window way at top, that I couldn't even reach to see out of. All night being stuck in this room — just four walls all around me. I tried to tell myself it would be okay and that I'd get out. But my lawyer was worried too; he was saying that the judge didn't have to put me in jail over the weekend. I was thinking I'd go back to court on Monday and he'd say, "Well, six months in jail."

On Monday when I got out of jail and went into sentencing, next to the judge's table there was this big stack of letters. He put his hand on it and said, "These letters are from concerned citizens of Pinellas County. They all want you to go to jail." He must have had 200 letters up there. I don't know if that was true or not — it might have been junk mail — but that's what he said. He told me he wasn't going to give me any jail time, but he was going to give me as much as the law would allow him to put on me, which was a year probation and a $1000 fine for each count. So it was 3 years probation and a $3000 fine, instead of going to jail. I had to get a psychiatric review. They ordered me to take a journalism ethics class so I could learn about "serious journalism" instead of writing about the type of trash that I was. I have to do eight hours a week community service and have to keep my 40 hour a week job. So I'm working 48 hours a week.

Another condition was no contact with minors, which just purely came out of their fears and imaginations. I never had anything in my record, or never been charged with any crime with children. Of course, the worst thing was they ordered me not to draw anything that could be considered obscene — even for my *own* use. And that a probation officer could come to my house, *anytime*, and check and make sure I'm not drawing anything obscene. That's the one that really bugged me, because I was already pretty much working a 40 hour a week job and drawing in my spare time, and here they were telling me I had to work 48 hours a week and also not allowed to draw. So, I was getting the whole punishment. They really were stopping me from doing

my art, by giving me so much work to do. I couldn't draw at home because I was afraid of the probation officer showing up at any moment.

After the sentencing at the trial, after I came home, we had to get all the "obscene" material out of the house and hide it. I had to get rid of all my drawings. The ones I kept here, I kept in my car, because I thought they would never check my car. I stuck it all in my car, or put some at my Dad's. For the first time I felt nervous about doing my art.

There was recently an appeal. I have to pay the $3000 fine first, kind of like a bond. They estimate a year before the appeal comes to trial. But right now all the conditions of probation continue. I'm still working 48 hours a week. At first, when the judge granted an appeal, I thought all my immediate problems were over. So I went out to celebrate and ended up going to a video arcade. I could never go there when I was under probation because of the kids. Then, about a week later, my probation officer called where I was working and told me, "I don't know what your lawyer told you, but until you pay the money, as long as you're on proba-

tion, all of the conditions are still in effect." That pissed me off again, so I had to go back to my community service and all that shit. I'm talking to the Comic Book Legal Defence fund now, hoping that they can come through for me so that I can go ahead and get off this probation for sure.

At first, because I was so worried about it from the lawyers, I was considering plea bargaining, so I wouldn't have to deal with going to court. That would have probably got me six months probation. But I'm glad I didn't do that because that would have been letting them win and giving up. And I knew that if I did it that way, that would be something that I would always be wishing I had done differently. If I had pleaded guilty to the crime then, they would have said I was doing obscene drawings. I didn't want them to say that.

---

*Mike Diana's drawings, as well as a story that lead up to his trial appeared in **Gauntlet #5**. Back issues are available. The original cartoon strip included with this article is Mikes' as well.*

DEVIANT '94

Bobby London And The Air Pirates Follies

S.C. Ringgenberg

In addition to his fame as the creator of the award-winning "Dirty Duck" comic strip in *National Lampoon* and *Playboy*, and his stellar work carrying on Segar's *Popeye* for King Features, Bobby London has been notorious since the early '70's as one of the legendary Air Pirates.

Who were the Air Pirates, you ask? They were a group of underground cartoonists led by "Ods Bodkins" creator Dan O'Neill that also included London, "Dopin' Dan" creator Ted Richards, "Trots and Bonnie's" Shary Flenniken, and sign painter turned cartoonist Gary Halgren. Their notoriety rested on the two issues of the *Air Pirates* underground comic that caused the entire group (with the exception of Flenniken) to be sued by Walt Disney Productions for copyright infringement. What prompted the suit were the lead stories in each issue, written and drawn by Dan O'Neill, that depicted Mickey and Minnie Mouse having sex, getting high and smuggling drugs.

But as Bobby London pointed out when recalling the case, "Mickey Mouse was pretty much Dan O'Neill's baby. The only things I were really interested in at that time was Dirty Duck and Shary Flenniken. And those were the two main reasons I stuck around with the group called the Air Pirates. Everything else has always been credited to O'Neill. It

was his brainchild and he took credit for it publicly at the time, and so it should be known as his thing. *Popeye* was always my thing, *Mickey Mouse* was Dan's thing." London does not deny that he was named in Disney's original suit. "I was involved, certainly, because I was involved in the publication of it, and my name was right there and I was part of it. However there was a rumor, an erroneous rumor, that *Dirty Duck* was part of that lawsuit and that wasn't true. *Dirty Duck* was never touched by that lawsuit."

Disney's response to the this perversion of Mickey Mouse's "image of innocent delight" (wording that stems from Disney's original suit) was quick and to the point. Within a short time of the publication of the second issue of *Air Pirates*, all the artists involved were served with a summons. The *Air Pirates* case subsequently

Annie Rat meets the Grateful Dead

dragged through the courts for years, becoming something of a *cause celebre* in the world of underground comics. The case has been depicted in the media by some of the principals, chiefly Dan O'Neill, as an example of underground cartoonists courageously fighting for their First Amendment rights against a large and powerful corporation and winning.

As Shary Flenniken recalled it in a 1980 interview: "What happened was really beautiful. The case was never won in court. There was what they called a summary judgement passed, which was like an out of court (settlement) between the Walt Disney lawyers and the judge. There was never a trial. It went to the state Supreme Court and was finally turned down by the federal Supreme Court, as far as I know, on appeal."

But did the Air Pirates really win their case against Disney? Bobby London remembers those events somewhat differently. He recalls that period in his life not through a rosy, nostalgic haze as a time of underground camaraderie and commitment to the principles of free speech, but as a time of great personal and professional stress. For Bobby London, his involvement with the Air Pirates was anything but a victory. As London recounted the events of twenty-odd years ago for *Gauntlet*: "It was the most frightening time of my life and I don't know where these people come off trying to make it look like it was a really wonderful time."

To better understand why Bobby London came to feel this way it's necessary to know how he became involved with O'Neill, et. al. In 1969, after short stints working as an underground cartoonist for underground papers such as New York City's *The Rat* and *The Chicago Seed*, London trekked to San Francisco, the underground cartoonists' Mecca at the time. As London wryly noted, "after I left, every paper would get taken over by Weathermen or SDS people. And I didn't get along with these people very well because they wanted me to draw a lot of communist propaganda. I was not a political person despite what Shary Flenniken said in her interview in *The Comics Journal*. I considered myself to be a cartoonist first and I had been resisting for the longest time to just be a pair of hands for the counterculture."

Upon arriving in the San Francisco area, London started working for *The Berkeley Tribe*, an underground paper which he described as "an offshoot of *The Berkeley Barb*." London first made the acquaintance of Ted Richards, a cartoonist newly arrived from Cincinnati, and subsequently met O'Neill and Flenniken (his future wife) through Richards at the 1970 Sky River Rock Festival. London's first substantial contact with O'Neill came when London hitched a ride home from the Sky River Festival with him. "I got a ride with O'Neill, and O'Neill stopped off at his place in Marin County and showed me his studio and told me that he wanted to put together a comic book company. And he talked about how great it was to do a syndicated cartoon strip but he wanted to put together an underground comic book company, and he was looking for a group of artists to help him."

At the time London wasn't really interested in working with O'Neill, having just broken up with his girlfriend and deciding that life on the West Coast wasn't for him. After returning to New York and making a vain attempt to patch up his relationship with his girlfriend, London did, in fact, return to the West Coast eventually settling in what he described as "a really terrible section of Oakland".

While living there and "just wondering what the hell was going to happen to me", Dan O'Neill reappeared in London's life, having somehow tracked him down, and urged London to join forces with him. London stubbornly refused for several days, then relented and moved in with the older cartoonist. "I was living a nice, quiet life in O'Neill's little crackerbox house off the Russian River. I was perfecting my drawing technique. And the best thing about that period was getting to watch a real, professional daily comic artist meet his deadline up close, which was a great opportunity.

"The idea sort of was that I would be (O'Neill's)assistant, whatever that meant. Actually, I did my own little "Dirty Duck" strips under his and we talked about this comic book company, and there wasn't much mention, or any mention at all, actually, of Walt Disney characters or anything like that. His idea was that we would assemble a group of artists, maybe four or five of us. At that time he had his eye on Gary Halgren, (Ted) Richards, (Shary) Flenniken and me. He wanted to produce one comic book a month. He said none of this namby-pamby underground stuff where you meet deadlines whenever you want. We're going to put out a monthly periodical. It seemed like something that was really too good to be true at this point. I was just all for it."

Despite his enthusiasm for the idea of an old-fashioned cartoonists' studio, London did have some reservations about working with O'Neill. "As we worked on the "Od Bodkins" deadlines, I just began to notice that he was using lots of Disney characters in his stuff. When he began to suggest that we use the Disney characters in an ongoing serial in the back of the book, I said, 'No way.' I do not want to do that. I am not using other people's characters. I do not want to engage in any copyright infringements, or trademark violations or anything like that. The idea of doing, lampooning establishment characters in some kind of *Mad* magazine way just seemed ridiculous to me because I had created my own characters and I wanted to pursue that and that alone." However, after London voiced his objections to O'Neill's concept, London remembers O'Neill trying to reassure him by saying, "'Look, my lawyers did some research and they found out that the copyrights on the earliest thirties Disney comic strip characters are in public domain. The copyrights have expired. If we use these characters and we don't use any names they may try and take us to court. They may do some kind of thing in the papers, but they won't have a leg to stand on and nobody will get hurt.'"

Despite his reservations, at the time London felt inclined to believe O'Neill, noting, "Look, the guy was a syndicated cartoonist and so when he said he had lawyers, I'm twenty years old, I believe he had lawyers, you know. And I didn't say yes and I didn't say no, but he had really hooked me with the idea of doing a monthly comic book. That was what I really wanted to do."

In 1971, after being dispatched to Seattle by O'Neill to bring Ted Richards and Shary Flenniken back to the Bay area so they could all begin working on O'Neill's comic book company, London wound up being united with Flenniken and settled down with her, sharing a house with her and several other women. During a brief breakup with Flenniken, London lived alone in the house, concentrating on developing his cartooning skills. "That's where I drew the first twelve or fifteen *Dirty Duck* pages. It was incredible. I was just learning and developing in leaps and bounds. It was a very inspired time for me." Those first *Dirty Duck* pages eventually wound up being included in the first issue of the *Air Pirates*.

After completing them, London went back down to Berkeley with Ted Richards, but without Shary Flenniken. Several weeks later, Flenniken arrived in San Francisco, and "We set up this shop in the industrial district of San Francisco and started to work." The Air Pirates' original studio was small, and personal tensions ran high. "It was like five people in

two rooms. It was very, very weird. Ted and Shary did not get along. Dan and Ted barely got along. Gary (Halgren) was his quiet self and I was just like, just trying to write and draw for everybody. I just burnt myself out to a crisp within a few months."

Even at the beginning of the Air Pirates saga, London sensed trouble on the horizon. "We were getting the first issue together. I'm sitting at the drawing board, and O'Neill passes this board with a drawing on it to me, and there it is, you know. It's two panels with Mickey Mouse in them. He had told me there would be no trademark violation, and so that's why the title of that story was called, "The Mouse," because he was placating me at that time. He didn't want me to leave. And, so I just sort of took a deep breath and went along with it, and I don't know what he told Ted. I don't know what he told Shary at the time, but I'm not sure that it was the same thing that he told me because this whole deal about pubic domain was just in my head and Dan had put it there. I didn't really speak to the others about it and they thought I was crazy for doing this. And so a real row developed and there was a split in the group and somehow the first two issues came out."

By this time, London's reservations about O'Neill's use of the Disney characters had resurfaced, "I remember where I reached one point where it was generally agreed that we were going to hear from Walt Disney Productions and what were we going to do? And I had suggested that we just drop the Disney thing, keep cranking out the books, but just use our own characters, which was the idea that I thought we were going to do to begin with. And that was soundly hooted down. At that point I began to lose interest in the group."

What happened next are events that were permanently burned into

Bobby London's brain. "Dan disappeared about three or four days before the process server turned up." What caused O'Neill to take flight, London speculates were a number of factors, "Some kind of fight ensued. It looked like (O'Neill) was having a nervous breakdown, but actually, I think it was a combination of things. Part of it was that he began to really guilt-trip over what he had told me and he just got in a fist fight with Ted, jumped on his motorcycle and took off into the night. And about three days later the process server comes to the door." As soon as the papers were served, London remembers being, "absolutely petrified." However, with O'Neill absent, other priorities reasserted themselves. "The first thing I had to do was keep working because we had moved to a larger studio that was owned by Francis Ford Coppola. It was some sort of firehouse that had been turned into a warehouse for American Zoetrope. It was something like four hundred dollars a month. We had absolutely no money, and it was decided that Bobby was going to start cranking out comic books that were going to pay the rent. And they pre-sold, without my permission, really, there was a pre-sold *Dirty Duck* comic book so that the Air Pirates could get their thousand dollars and not be thrown out into the street. And it was up to me to crank out a thirty-two page book in about two weeks."

Despite numerous distractions, and the enormous pressure of the Disney lawsuit, London managed to complete the promised *Dirty Duck* comic book, though he notes with some bitterness, "It nearly killed me. It sent me to the hospital. Shary Flenniken jokes around in her *Comics Journal* interview about how I was so stoned I was lettering too small. The actual fact was that I was so distracted by all the fights between her and Ted,

and Dan taking off, and having to get this thing out so we all would not get thrown into the street that I just zoomed through all this stuff and just did these Herriman-looking pages and finished the deadline, and within a couple of weeks after that I was in Franklin General Hospital being treated for anemia. I had a 106 degree fever and the doctor told my father that if my temperature had gone up maybe one or two more degrees I probably would have died, because I was totally undernourished.

I was living on Oreos and pork buns that were provided by Ron Turner and Last Gasp for three months. I think the only thing that happened between the *Dirty Duck* book fiasco and my collapse was the press conference for the Air Pirates."

Dirty Duck a Registered Trademark ™ *U.S. Pat. Off. by Bobby London*

Following his recovery, London wed Shary Flenniken in San Francisco, and the couple were contacted by *National Lampoon* editors and invited to audition for the magazine. London and Flenniken's strips were both accepted, and the pair relocated to the Seattle area and settled into a comfortable routine of producing *Dirty Duck* and *Trots and Bonnie*, their respective Lampoon strips.

Meanwhile, the Air Pirates case continued to drag through the courts. Then in 1974, in London's words, "something very bizarre happened. Dan O'Neill's lawyers sent me an out of court settlement with the Walt Disney Productions people and he had told Gary Halgren that it would be perfectly legitimate for him to sign it, and in fact he probably should. And I was about to sign it when Shary gives me this whole lecture about the First Amendment, my loyalty to Dan O'Neill, Lenny Bruce, Dick Gregory and how could I sign this thing. She basically talked me out of it." Within four months, however, the entire situation had wreaked its toll on London and Flenniken's personal life, and the couple split up. London perceives the breakup of his marriage to Flenniken as just one aspect of the fallout from the *Air Pirates* case.

In the period following the breakup of his marriage, London travelled to San Francisco, lived briefly in Washington D.C. and Provincetown, Mass, before moving into Manhattan. Although he went through "a very hard period" one winter during which he was living in a drafty flat and getting served with divorce papers, by the following spring things were looking up for the young cartoonist. He began getting illustration work from publications like The *New York Times, The Village Voice* and *Esquire*, and at one point, "Harvey Kurtzman was grooming me to be a gag panel cartoonist for *Esquire*." Following Kurtzman's departure as *Esquire*'s art director, London gravitated to *Playboy* around 1976, at first just writing scripts for cartoonist Ralph Reese, but soon producing color *Dirty Duck* strips for *Playboy*'s Funny Pages.

London was now working for *Playboy*, one of the most prestigious American markets for any cartoonist. Things were looking up for Bobby London after a string of personal and professional setbacks. "I had gotten to the point where I had broken up with Shary and moved to New York and finally got used to living on my own and was starting to get some semblance of a life on my own. That's when Dan O'Neill decided to break

the federal injunction on his Disney drawings one more time."

What happened was that Dan O'Neill, chafing under the weight of the original Disney suit, decided to form the Mouse Liberation Front. As Shary Flenniken described it, "What Dan O'Neill did was start this massive publicity campaign at these conventions. He got these other artists, fine artists, and people who'd worked for Disney to do their version of any art they wanted to, with a mouse in it as a theme. Dan took this work around to conventions and showed it. And they sold merchandise with 'MLF — The Mouse Liberation Front' on it. He had Mouse Liberation Front belt buckles and rings and little boxes of malted milk balls called 'Mouse Droppings.'"

The effect of O'Neill's actions on London's life was disastrous, both personally and professionally. "I was trying to settle out of court with Disney on my own, once I was away from the Air Pirates. And when Dan had drawn those first Mouse Liberation

Front drawings, I was in the middle of negotiating out of court with Walt Disney and finally settling this thing for me. But once the Mouse Liberation Front surfaced, they pulled out of negotiations with me because they thought that I was part of it. When Dan heard, as part of trying to settle out of court with Disney, I was explaining to Disney how the whole thing came to be, he went berserk and started calling me up at all hours of the morning and saying not nice things to me at this point. All hell seemed to break loose. I was ready to get married for a second time. I was actually making money, and all of a sudden, this happened and just scared everybody away from me, and of course, the settlement with Disney just fell through."

One of the most unfortunate side-effects of the situation was that London's reputation was damaged. "This whole Mouse Liberation radicalized people in the underground comics. All of a sudden I became a bad guy because Dan, at the time, was trying to paint me as being some kind of a Judas."

London's involvement with the Air Pirates ended in 1978, the same year London notes, "I went to (Italy) get the Yellow Kid Award" as the best writer/artist of the year, in recognition of his work on *Dirty Duck*. Ultimately London says he "considered it over when it was over when my lawyers here in New York finally got a separation from Dan O'Neill's lawyers from me."

Upon London's return from Europe, he received news of the final chapter in the long and twisted Air Pirates saga when, according to London "Disney just plain threatened to throw Dan in the clink for contempt of court and he finally signed a settlement with them. And it was officially over at which point he went around telling people that we won."

A phone call by O'Neill to London's home gave Bobby London's mother a chance to have a last word of sorts on the *Air Pirates* case. As London remembered it, "He called my house in Queens one time and he said to my mother, 'We won. Did you hear?' and my mother says, 'What did you win, the booby prize?' Good 'ol Mom. She was pretty upset about the whole situation."

There is, however, a final ironic coda to the whole affair. Several years after the *Air Pirates* case was settled, *Playboy* axed their entire funnies section as a cost-cutting move, leaving Bobby London high and dry, since drawing *Dirty Duck* for *Playboy* was his sole source of income at the time. While London cast around for some other way to make a living, "A friend of mine told me to try and get a job at the Disney merchandising art department here in New York. And after laughing wholeheartedly at this idea, I decided to give it a try." Ironically enough, London was hired. No one ever mentioned the *Air Pirates* while London worked there, though he recalls a rather awkward moment when, "one day the art director, who had become a very good friend of mine, came out and talked to the artists as he customarily would do at the end of the day, and he made some sort of joke about dirty Mickey Mouse comics and the place got really quiet. I didn't look up or move or anything, I just kept working, and it just passed. Apparently some people up there at Disney knew and they didn't mind because they got to know me and they got to like me. So, I kept the job. The only reason I left Walt Disney was because while I was there, I got a call from King Features asking me to try out for *Popeye*."

IN THE LINE
OF FIRE UPDATE

Richard G. Carter

[Editor's Note: The following article is an update to **Gauntlet's** awarding Anthony Griffin its first In the Line of Fire award, along with $500. Oddly enough, while copies of the article and press releases announcing the award were sent to all major news organizations and the black press, not **one** of these publications/columnists deemed the story worthy to print. Griffin, a true American hero — who according to Richard Carter cost himself as much as a half-a-million dollars supporting the KKK's First Amendment rights — can't snare as much as a blurb in the print media, yet whether ten or a hundred of O.J. Simpson's hairs should be taken for analysis garners half-a-day of network TV exposure. A sad commentary on the medias warped priorities, to be sure. In any event, what follows is a conclusion to the case, which also received scant media attention.]

Anthony Griffin has won his case.

The 40-year-old black activist lawyer, retained early in 1993 by the American Civil Liberties Union to represent the Grand Dragon of the Texas Realm of the Ku Klux Klan, has successfully protected the right of the Klan to keep its membership list secret.

And the predominantly white housing project in Vidor, Texas, where the State Commission on Human Rights investigated the Klan for its intimidation of black residents which led to the case, has been integrated. Said Griffin:

"The Texas Supreme Court entered an opinion where it basically said we recognize this is the Klan; we recognize all of the controversy that has gone on in Vidor, but the First Amendment still applies. And the Court rejected the argument by the State saying since it's the Klan and because of their history, the First Amendment does not apply.

"And it rejected outright the argument of equality — or someone being discriminatory in nature — represents a significant governmental interest and, therefore, membership lists should be produced.

"I think it's a wonderful affirmation of the First Amendment for the Texas Supreme Court to speak directly to the controversy and basically say that's what the First Amendment's all about. There's no better case to demonstrate the virtue of the doctrine than something as stark as the Klan — and what they represent.

"So I really do think it's a wonderful opinion and it also deals with exactly what's been argued around the country — and that is, correct speech, political speech or talk kindly of me. The Court said if we create those doctrines, we really do destroy the First Amendment. And that's why the opinion is important."

However, his defense of the KKK in Texas took an unusual turn, which still bothers Griffin.

"The contradictory or the ironic aspect of the case is that the NAACP national office filed an amicus brief — or friend of the court brief — on behalf of the State of Texas saying that the Klan membership list *should* be produced."

And why would they do that, he was asked.

"I don't know," he replied. "It doesn't make a whole lot of sense, particularly when the NAACP's brief takes the position that the case of the NAACP v Alabama is *distinguished*, but it doesn't apply to a group such as the Klan. And they actually *write* that."

The reference was to the fact that the premier case on the membership list issue occurred in 1958, when the State of Alabama sought to obtain the membership list of the NAACP.

"They (the NAACP) take the position that free speech should be in context and you should look at circumstances in the group. It was almost tantamount to an argument that we can protect our friends but we don't have to protect our enemies," Griffin said.

"The other ironic thing about it is that 11 of the states filed briefs in *support* of the State of Texas — saying 'take the Klan's membership list.' So if the State Supreme Court had ruled on behalf of Texas, think how it would affect organizations. There are folks waiting in the wings — states and government entities — to get *anybody's* membership lists. And I don't think this is isolated to the Klan."

Griffin said he hoped the National NAACP's action wasn't related to its decision to drop him as their Texas legal counsel when he agreed to represent Michael Lowe, the Texas Klan's 45-year-old Grand Dragon.

"I think it got personal," he said, "and I've always tried to keep it nonpersonal. I totally disagree with the organization's position in this case, but we've had no further discussions."

Griffin said the press informed Lowe of the decision.

"He called me and thanked me. He was ecstatic, to say the least. But we're not buddies. I kind of teased him and said, 'Michael, I guess that means Long Live the Klan.' And he laughed and said 'I guess that's what that means, huh.' So I guess it was a bittersweet pill. He's still probably marching and organizing."

Griffin gave out with an emphatic "no" when asked if he feels vindicated. "I take the position that I didn't *need* to be vindicated. It was not about *me*, and I've always tried to focus it *not* on me. I think the doctrine has been vindicated and reaffirmed.

"There are probably still some folks who feel I've done the wrong thing and all you can do is keep trying to educate them on the issue."

On the practical side of the ledger, Griffin, and 18-year-old veteran of litigation, civil rights and criminal defense law in the Galveston-area, says the Klan case cost him about a half-million dollars. He received his hourly attorney fees and expenses, but the time he spent, the business he lost and his unbilled business during the four months he wasn't able to do trial work, took a heavy financial toll.

He said that had he been hired by a private organization in the case instead of the ACLU, he would have made about $150,000 in fees alone. "But I did it on principle and feel real good about the way things worked out at this level. It relieves you to a great degree."

Finally, Griffin said "it was shocking" to learn he'd received *Gauntlet's* "In the Line of Fire Award" and its attendant $500. He said he heartily thanked Editor Barry Hoffman with a personal letter.

Richard G. Carter, a freelance writer and talk show host in Milwaukee, is a former columnist for the **New York Daily News**.

EROTIC ELEVEN UPDATE: JUSTICE DENIED

Bobby Lilly

January 6, 1994, I was on my way out the door heading to the Consumer Electronic Show (CES) in Las Vegas when the phone rang. It was Dominic Gentile, the lawyer for the Erotic Eleven. He had been able to work out a deal for the women. The prosecutor had agreed to drop all charges of felony lesbianism and pandering against the women in exchange for their guilty plea to a misdemeanor. While the women wanted to take their battle all the way, they couldn't handle the possibility of a conviction and having to face the six to twelve years in jail. And, unfortunately, with Seymour Butts, the videographer of the event turning his tapes over to the grand jury, the women knew the prosecutor had evidence that some of them had, in fact, engaged in sexual activity with each other in front of an audience. Nothing they hadn't done every time they stepped in front of a camera. Nothing they were ashamed of. But, while none of the women believed that they had done anything really wrong, they realized it would be difficult to convince a potentially very conservative jury of that. Although the prosecutor agreed not to ask for any jail time or any fines, he demanded that the women make a "voluntary" donation of $20,000 to local charities. It may have been blackmail; but, the women had no choice. No money — no deal was the prosecutor's position.

I grabbed the Freedom Fund checkbook on my way out the door but knew we had to collect BIG money in Vegas if this case was going to end any time soon. None of the women had that kind of available cash but, before the weekend was through, I was able to turn over $20,000 to the attorney with the help of the Erotic Eleven, their husbands, friends and members of the adult video industry at the CES. My thanks to everyone who supported the women that weekend in Vegas. Your generosity was overwhelming.

By the end of January court paperwork was finalized. The case was over. The women had pled guilty to a misdemeanor for "performing in an obscene, or immoral or indecent performance". Although there was no clear "Victory" in this case for us to celebrate, keeping these women out of jail was worth it. Everyone was relieved and looked forward to getting on with their lives.

Unfortunately, over the past year two of the eleven women had dropped out of sight. According to people who knew her, Naughty Angel, a newcomer to the adult video industry deliberately disappeared and cut all ties to the industry shortly after the original incident in July of 1993. Shalene who had kept in touch with us through November of 93 also couldn't be found. Hopefully, she will be in touch with the attorney soon so that matters can be straightened out. If not, both she and Naughty Angel will find they have federal fugitive warrants out for them.

That's one aspect of the case that makes me furious. For trying to help support freedom of expression both women have become fugitives. Naughty Angel's friends are sure she was so afraid her children would be taken from her that she decided to disappear. The fear of this mother at the possibility of losing her children forced her to become a fugitive. Any sex worker who is a mother shares that fear. I would guess Shalene's disappearance is probably more accidental than anything else. Over the past year, she has moved often and each time kept in contact with us. I'm sure that, if she even thought about it, she figured that it had been so long nothing was going to happen after all so just didn't bother to let anyone know when she moved. This kind of scenario makes sense to me, especially if she decided to leave the industry. In the past I had always been able to reach her through her beeper — but not the last time I tried. Her absentmindedness and/or desire to move out of the adult video business shouldn't qualify her for a fugitive warrant.

Nina Hartley, one of the Eleven (and my "wife") was scheduled to do a ten day publicity tour across Canada for Adults Only Video (AOV), a chain of video stores, only three weeks later. Imagine my shock when I got her call saying she was being detained by Canadian Customs because of her guilty plea. Can you imagine, her misdemeanor conviction was already in the Canadian Customs computer. Her conviction put her in a class of people Canada did not want working in their country. Never mind that she has worked there for seven years with no problems, followed all their rules, paid all her taxes to them or generated employment for others while in that country. She was ignominiously sent home. After conferring with AOV lawyers, Nina thought it would be okay for her to return as a ordinary citizen, go along on the tour and meet her fans as long as she wasn't being paid. So, she returned to Canada a day later. Unfortunately, Canadian immigration didn't see things the same way the lawyers did. A week later they picked her up in Winnipeg. She spent Monday night, Tuesday, Wednesday and Thursday morning in jail before a deportation hearing could be arranged. Nina tells me that it may be possible for her to apply for and get an okay to return to Canada. All she needs are the appropriate letters from the appropriate government officials but, any time in the next five years she wants to return, she will have to go through the same humiliating process over again and so will the other women. Up to now we do not know exactly how difficult or even impossible this task might be. If Nina is not allowed to work in Canada it will cost her thousands of dollars because of contracts she will be unable to fulfill. The other women are in the same boat. Unfortunately for Nina and the other women, the stigma of this conviction and its limitations on their lives is something they will have to live with the rest of their lives.

The pain I saw in Nina's eyes when she returned home from Canada and the catch in her voice broke my heart when she told me how she was sitting in the plane waiting for takeoff when it really hit her that she was essentially branded. The realization that she had a record and would carry it with her wherever she went from that point on hit her hard. She's essentially been a "good girl" all her life. She pays her taxes, votes, and has always tried to stay within legal limits as a performer who prides herself on her professional behavior. She admitted that it was painful for

her to accept the social stigma implicit in Canada's rejection of her.

I felt like I had failed her. My worst nightmare had come true when I heard that she was being held in jail. I've always known that part of the reason I fight so hard for freedom of expression is the fear I have for her and the possibility she would come under attack for her outspoken defense of sexuality but there was no way to protect her. I wasn't able to protect the woman I love or do anything to help the situation in which she found herself. I wanted to rush to the Canadian Consulate and demand they release her NOW; but, I knew it wouldn't work. I wanted to hit something, anyone. I couldn't stop thinking about her in jail. Dave was even angrier and more frustrated than I was. I don't know how he was able to keep himself from doing something drastic. I know how angry and upset I was.

Unfortunately, while the case is over the women's difficulties continue. The last bill from the lawyer was close to $30,000. I don't know what kinds of costs there will be for Nina or anyone else trying to return to Canada but, with lawyers involved, I know the dollars will add up quickly.

All together, since last year, we've raised over $50,000 to help pay legal expenses for the Erotic Eleven. The Freedom Fund is continuing its efforts to raise money to help. Unfortunately, the women can't begin to put this case behind them until ALL the bills are paid. Please help spread the word. Any donations should be made out to *THE FREEDOM FUND* and mailed to me at 2550 Shattuck Ave, #51, Berkeley, CA 94704.

---

*Bobby Lilly has tirelessly followed the case of the Erotic Eleven for **Gauntlet** for the past two years.*

CAR 69 WHERE ARE YOUUUUU??? (Is the Porn Industry the FBI's Favorite Scapegoat?)

Wally Anne Wharton

Despite snazzy Matt Helm-influenced sex educations, our well-Doctored, mini-skirted majority still fosters a relentless love-hate relationship with pornography. Studies show that our sex-drenched society would like to incorporate a little smut into its aerobicized lifestyle, but Society doesn't know how. "How can I deep throat and still remain politically correct?" Deep-throating a democrat. "Can I still maintain my family values while getting fucked in the ass?" Why not die trying?

Many people feel compelled to channel their underlying fascination with pornography by minimizing readily-available smegmatic imagery. In other words, they can't jerk off without feeling guilty about it. At plutocratic cocktail parties when word leaks out that I review X-rated movies under Larry Flynt's come-soaked corporate umbrella, people automatically assume a defensive air of condescending ennui. "X-rated movies are so boring . . . . is Nina de Ponca still around? Hyapatia Lee? Why aren't they all dead from AIDS? Do those cock enlargers really work?"

Before you can say "Doc Johnson" I'm delivering a lecture on the porn industry and answering the endless questions of the very ones who say they're bored by my cockular and clitoral coterie.

Yes, Virginia, I will concede that many X-rated videos are indeed boring. Sifting through the dregs can prove downright tedious. I have to fast-forward through a dozen ill-lit, anti-climactic efforts before I stumble upon that erotic tour-de-juggernaut. But this is often no fault of cast and crews: The real culprit is that vague, uncertain something called obscenity. Due to the fact that producers and manufacturers are often crippled by government fines and legal fees, most of the cheezier-looking vids are shot in one day on a budget that couldn't keep Michael Jackson in Max Factor Clown White for a week. I would like to see television alone work under the restrictions imposed on adult entertainment for a season. Without being able to exploit Amy Fisher and Heidi Fleiss, television would wither on the prime time vine.

Another popular but often-left-unvoiced reaction to porn:

"I could do that . . . that's easy. I could handle them both, no problem-o!"

Keep in mind that watching porn performers is like watching the Bolshoi Ballet: the pros make it look easy. Combine sexual acrobatics with the threat of STDs and getting arrested mid-stroke and you've got "wood" working under a helluva lot of pressure. Fortunately performers

one an Olympus.

Veteran studsman Buck Adams bends newcomer Chase Manhattan over the black leather seat and tilts her denied ass into my lens. That's what I call sheer pornographic know-how.

I'd been told I might have a hard time getting X-rated actors and business people to talk openly but Patrick Garbiras, president of Hollywood Video volunteers candid articulation on adult entertainment's on-going strained relationship with law enforcement. Garbiras is a successful manufacturer who's had considerable experience with local vice and the FBI. Somehow he manages both a cool head and a detached amusement.

Another interesting thing about Patrick: He doesn't flirt. He approaches scantily clad babes on the set with his hands in his pockets. Translation: this certified pornographer must be harboring a strong sense of self and genuine respect for women. What a weirdo!! (But getting spared the "Hi-honey-you're-cute" crap did make me wonder if I had my make-up on okay . . . .)

By sheer coincidence a black and white patrol car cruises the parking lot. The actors stop clowning. The officer in the passenger seat nods and manages a wan smile. We do the same.

"They're just checking up on us," Patrick muses. If he had a beard he'd be stroking it.

"Looked like he didn't really want to bust-up the shoot. I think he seemed even a little apologetic about

are seldom caught by police with their pants down unless they're attempting to have sex in plain view of the public. So are X-rated productions fairly safe from hassle in private homes or professional sound stages? Not necessarily.

Right now I'm standing outside Volgel Studios in Canoga Park waiting to be admitted onto the set of the latest Heidi Fleiss-based video entitled, "Heidi Gate (The Real Heidi Flesh Story)" a new film produced by Hollywood Video. Henry Pachard, sitting in for another director at the last minute, allows this nosy girl reporter to graze on the catered action and snoop around the very same bedroom and office sets I've seen in hundreds of X-rated productions. If this swivel chair could talk . . . .

It's six o'clock on a hot August night. I'm hanging around with nothing better to do than take pictures of the actors gathered around a Harley-Davidson. How do you break up a cold reading workshop? Toss some-it." There I go optimistically ascribing my own values to the opposition.

"Don't kid yourself." His eyes follow the car. "They'd love to be able to make a few arrests today. They take it very seriously,"

"So you've got to take it seriously as well."

(Actually I probably didn't say anything quite that apropos, but let's pretend I did anyway.)

The evening proceeds without incident but why were the cops compelled to check up on the shoot? What exactly were they hoping to find? I'd hate to think it's because it's more fun to arrest naked women than it is to arrest dangerous criminals.

In an attempt to minimize the chances for getting charged with prostitution, pandering and lewd behavior, the X-rated industry continually swallows its pride and tries to comply with The Censors who exist in Oz-like omnipotence. Pay no attention to that pervert in the raincoat. And no matter how consensual the sex, the Big Dykes on Toast cry "Rape."

Over-the-counter, glossy box covers cannot feature actresses wearing little girl dresses or pigtails, thus implying kiddie porn. No film can feature "High School" in its title, that being an indication of sex with minors. Older "High School" films have been renamed "college" or "co-ed" to insure the participants are at least eighteen. (I myself, was so much more mature at age eighteen than I was at seventeen and half.) Henri Pachard's 1985 "American Taboo" series would not be made today on the grounds that manufacturers would be reluctant to distribute a film with a backdrop of incest.

Censorship is not confined to conceptual execution. If you watch an X-rated video closely, you will see a subtle pattern unfolding before you like high-speed nude Tai-chi. Pornographers are now compelled to substitute plot, metaphor, structure and syntax with as much censor-approved screwing as possible.

Screenwriter Raven Touchstone (*Nothing to Hide 2/ Justine, Hothouse Rose 1&2, Roxy, The Loose End* series): *The sequential formula is usually a combination of the following: boy/girl, boy/boy/girl girl/girl/boy, girl/girl and another boy/girl, depending upon the preference of the director and/or producer. All scenes usually culminate in total sexual fulfillment, with very few scenes left "dangling." This is especially true of films shot by inexperienced directors and often the case when shooting "one-day wonders."*

Despite the fact that it severely expurgates itself, the industry faces ever-increasing risks of getting arrested during some aspect of the film making and distributing process.

Mistress Jacqueline, the World's Foremost Dominatrix: (*Bondage Fantasies, Enema Obedience, Seduced into Submission, Journey into Servitude, the Pleasures of Ultimate Humiliation, Amazons from Burbank*)

I really have to be careful with what I tape and distribute. I can't mix sex acts with S & M. I never draw blood, or stick anyone with needles. I also have to be very careful with my 900 number. After about a month in the (phone sex) business, I got a letter from the phone company informing me my message was too explicit, and I couldn't mention certain parts of the body on my tape. For instance, I can't say 'Lick my pussy.' I have to say 'Put your tongue where you want it to go.'

(Hmmm . . . maybe this censorship thing ain't too bad after all if it upgrades the erudition of porn.)

M.J. *Now it's the law that I have to print the price of each phone call half the size of my name. If some guy goes crazy* and calls the number constantly, and racks up a $500 bill or something, he can get amnesty, and I don't get paid for all the time he's wasted tying my phonelines. But you have to comply with everything if you want to stay in business.

I promised I would print Mistress Jacqueline's mailorder address and phone number (7095 Hollywood Blvd., Suite #350, Hollywood, CA 90028. 1-900-230-5555 - $1.99 per min. 18+).

Porn director F.J. Lincoln (*Love on the Run, Last Rumba in Paris, Puttin' Out, Kiss My Grits, Wicked, Barbara Dare's Roman Holiday, Wet Dreams 2001*):

We've got people in this business going to jail for making videos that 70 million Americans pay money to see. Rapists get off for raping. Murders get "aggravated assault" and get out in three months . . . . And we're going to jail for making movies about fucking and sucking? Are you crazy? Everybody in the world fucks or sucks something. If they don't they want to . . .

A couple of years ago I filmed this scenario. A burglar in a ski mask breaks into a woman's bedroom. She pulls a gun and forces him to fuck her at gunpoint because she's so horny. The manufacturers saw the first cut and said 'Lose the gun.' Now the scene has no meaning. We see some clown in a ski mask arbitrarily fucking some broad, and the viewer doesn't know why or how he got there. It's really hard to make films with a considerable amount of dramatic content when manufacturers are afraid they'll get arrested. And getting arrested costs them the most.

Patrick Garbiras, president of Hollywood Video and Free Speech Coalition Board (*Caught From Behind series 1-18, Boob, Butts and Bloopers 1 $ 2, Hollywood Heinies, Asian Appetites, The World of Modeling*) is a man "on the front line."

I do so much 'business' with the government that I sort of think of government as my partner — and a certain amount has to go to your partner, right? Last time they (the FBI) were here (Hollywood Video Headquarters), they hung around all day. One agent who specialized in armed robbery said he was wasting his time here. But I know that he's gotta do what he's assigned to do or lose his job. I served them coffee. If you're nice they remember. If you're not, they remember that too.

W.W. Must be hard to be nice when you think of the money it's going to cost you.

P.G. *It doesn't matter whether the tape is even illegal or not. You're guilty until proven innocent. Getting busted always costs something, that's for sure. So even though it's difficult to convict me, if I get slapped with a $300,000 lawsuit here, and another $200,000 lawsuit there, it could eventually put me out of business. That's the governments' long-term plan. To put manufacturers out of business through attrition. They have unlimited funds; we don't . . . . Making the charges stick depends on the county and state you're busted in and what their "community standards" are. We got busted in Las Vegas. But look at their community standards: there is legalized prostitution, adult videos in every video store, sex shops, strip shows. "Community standards" are less than strict, so I'll get off. But I still have to hire a lawyer. It's still costing me. I've got a guy on retainer there right now. Down in Memphis they'll bust you transporting videos, throw you in jail and wait until your court date before they determine if the tape is even illegal or not.*

W.W.: Don't you have a handbook of do's and don'ts to follow?

P.G: *Sure, but they change the rules without telling us. The rules change all the time so it's like there are no rules.*

W.W: Are they looking for specifics, like sex with animals?

P.G: *Anal scenes might be considered taboo, but basically it's up to a particular community's whim. The FBI tries to get me to ship to the Southern states where views (pertaining to obscenity) are different from those in California. It would be easy for the FBI to win a conviction in the Bible Belt, therefore there are twelve states I won't ship to. I won't even touch them. Some manufacturers take the risk. To me it's not worth it. Why sell someone a hundred dollars worth of product just to get slapped with a $400,000 attorney fee and possible jail time? I sell to safe distributors in safe areas. It's funny, they have sex shops in the Southern states, but if you can't send them any product, what good are they?*

Patrick Garbiras' late father-in-law, producer Hal Freeman helped set a precedent making it more difficult to be prosecuted for pandering. This ruling saves a lot of asses in the long run, but it hasn't stopped manufacturers from getting arrested and spending hundreds of thousands of dollars in fines and legal fees.

P.G.: *The government judges what's obscene and what isn't even though the First Amendment says they can't do that. However, the Supreme Court threw out his (Freemans') conviction for pandering which made it legal to shoot (X-rated videos) in California. That was one of the biggest cases in California because everybody wants to shoot here. They busted Charles Brickman, they busted Chuck Zane (Zane Entertainment). Everybody was trying to make a deal with the FBI, but Hal got convicted. In the end they couldn't get him. Even though people were having sex on film, they were essentially actors portraying people having sex, and were not setting out to gratify each other. Their job was to gratify the viewer. But it took its toll on him . . . . (Freeman passed away shortly after his vindication.) Our attorney, Stuart Goldfarb, handled everything brilliantly. When the FBI arrived, I immediately called Stuart who was in* court at the time. He rushed over here, and wouldn't let them get away with anything. They wanted a list of my distributors, and Stuart said no way, that's not on the warrant.

W.W.: Why does law enforcement have it in for the porn industry?

P.G.: *I think they get pressure from the fundamentalist religious sect. They're more powerful than we even know. Former FBI agents have said there are a certain number of religious zealots within the government itself who let organized religious lobbyists influence the government. We (the adult industry) don't have any group that lobbies our favor. We stand alone. We don't get support from mainstream entertainment or from any other groups — most people won't even admit they watch X-rated movies.* W.W. But people haven't voted away their rights to view pornography.

P.G: *Maybe it's only a matter of time. Tight-knit religious organizations are getting together and saying, "We don't like this, we don't like this!*

W.W: I was under the impression there is a division between Church and State.

P.G: *Ideally.*

W.W: Maybe fundamentalists groups need scapegoats so they can rest assured they're not going to be the ones burning in Hell.

P.G: *It's supposed to be us. I get letters in the mail from people saying I'm going to burn in Hell. They quote the Scriptures. But if they met me on the street, they'd see I was an ordinary person; I've got two kids, a wife, I'm a regular family man. Then they'd find out what I did for a living and they'd go running for the hills.* (rueful chuckle) *It still amazes me that mainstream movies like Robocop 2 can show children after they've been shot and lay dying. To me, that's obscene. Somebody once said that if a filmmaker depicts a breast getting cut off with a knife it's okay, if you show someone kissing that same breast, it's obscene.*

W.W: Yes, I've heard that one.

Could you get busted for your X-rated cartoon line?

P.G: *Probably not, but I suppose they could try. There are drug dealers and criminals running around and yet they want to bust me for something that is optional viewing. No one stands on the street corner pushing my tapes — "Psst! Hey, look at this, buddy! C'mon, take it, take it!" Doesn't make sense.*

W.W: On top of what they make off you in fines the government also taxes your income.

P.G: *True.*

W.W: Why do you stay in the business?

P.G: *I enjoy it. It's fun. I like the people involved. I like making movies. Best of all, this business enables me to provide for my family. My family's the most important part of my life. Thinking of them really helps me keep everything in perspective.*

As sympathetic as I am to the plight of the adult filmmaker I felt compelled in all fairness to sing out the view of the opposite side of the issue, to brave City Hall parking fees to give the vice a chance to revel in their doctrinaire-but-vague beliefs on censorship.

I spoke briefly with a Lt. Duncan of the Los Angeles Vice Division to address certain issues I'd touched upon with Patrick.

W.W: Are obscenity rules and regulations outlined clearly in a handbook that's available to all filmmakers?

LT. Duncan: *It's called the Penal Code. And an obscenity violation is called a 311.*

W.W: Recently I spoke with a manufacturer who says the rules change so fast he can't keep up with all the amendments.

LT. D: *Ignorance of the law is no defense.*

W.W: The manufacturer thinks that law enforcement is greatly influenced by the pressure from anti-porn fundamentalist religious groups.

LT. D: *That is absolutely untrue. We are not influenced by any one social or political faction. We base our arrests on the three C's:*

1) conspicuous — like if actors are performing sex acts on a public beach.

2) commercial — as in transporting obscene materials to areas where they're prohibited. And finally:

3) complained of — that's when neighbors complain of visible sex acts. We had a case like that on a deck in the Hollywood Hills. Even though they (the actors) were on private property, their actions were still in plain view of other people in the neighborhood, children included. We don't care who makes the complaint, whether it's a neighbor, a minister(!!!!!) or whoever, we have to answer the call.

Now don't get me wrong — I have a great respect for officers of the law. Their job takes courage and guts, they take way too much crap from too many jerks, and they have do it all in Polyester! But speaking with Lt. Duncan I got the feeling I was talking to a brick wall in blue.

Upon Patrick Garbiras' recommendation I tried to speak with Officer Jim Como. Patrick had said Jim was a really nice guy and he WAS over the phone but he kept postponing our session until I came to the conclusion that his commanding officer or his theatrical agent advised not him to meet the press after all. Too bad. I never got to find out if he was related to Perry.

Attorney Gilbert Levy is a prominent legal eagle fighting on the behalf of the anti-censorship cause. As he wrote in his articulate stand against NOEU, (National Obscenity Enforcement Unit) that appeared in a 1990 *Hot Times* magazine: " . . . . There is no longer any such thing as probation. One conviction for commercial distribution for obscenity can easily result in a Draconian prison sentence."

I contact Mr. Levy at his office in Seattle to see what progress, if any, has been made over the last few years, specifically citing the infamous Adam and Eve case.

Attorney Gilbert Levy: *Phil Harvey's case was an important victory against NOEU a few years ago. In P.H.E., Inc. us UPS. Dept. of Justice, Adam and Eve Distributors won a preliminary injunction against multiple state indictments against their company. The court said that Adam and Eve was confronting annihilation by attrition* (there's that word again!) *if not conviction and issued a preliminary injunction that said Adam and Eve can only be prosecuted once.*

W.W: Has the new Democratic administration alleviated some of the witch-hunt mentality?

G.L: *Things have lightened up some, but not enough. They* (the FBI and NOEU) *still try to bust manufacturers by "forum shopping"* (the act of setting up phony distribution companies that lure manufacturers into sending them product to areas where they're bound to be convicted). *What bothers me most is the fact that a manufacturer can't get a concrete definition of what's obscene and what isn't. A vice cop will usually say, "As far as I'm concerned, all X-rated tapes are obscene." That's the prevailing attitude that we're up against.*

Ultimately, with creative hands tied and manufacturers battling government-sanctioned extortions both Art and Viewer lose big-time. Until censorship is repealed or at least until obscenity is clearly defined, the netherworld of sex, thighs and video tape continues to lower its standards in order to ride out the one-dimensional deluge. That is, until the Revolution! Jerkers, unite!! Marxist Pornography? You heard it here first. On the other hand, if you don't feel like fast-forwarding your life away, you can always dust off Henry Miller.

Wally Anne Wharton contributes a regular column to "Hustler Erotic Video Guide" and has recently joined review ranks at "Adam Film World." La Wally will be visible in a BBC special entitled, "Ruby Wax's Hollywood" with Joe Mantagna. She also plays herself in Henri Pachard's new cinematic raisin d'etre, Eclipse.

BEFORE WE START SHOOTING THE FLIC LET ME INTRODUCE YOU TO YOUR DIRECTOR, PETE. PETE THIS IS ANDREA. ANDREA, PETE. AND THIS IS ... ER... SPECIAL AGENT CALE OF THE **FBI.**

WARDLE '94

TORONTO'S BBS BUSTS

Scott Nesbitt

In the early morning of October 21, 1993, members of the Metropolitan Toronto Police Force converged on eight Toronto-area buildings and prepared to bust a group of pornography distributors. However, there was a twist to the story. The buildings weren't warehouses filled with magazines, videos and still photographs. The people targeted weren't involved with organized crime or even an organized porn ring; chances are they didn't know each other. The police had converged on the sites of eight computer bulletin board systems (BBSs for short), which allow callers with a computer and modem to communicate with other computer users and even to copy and trade software files. Thousands of dollars worth of computer hardware and software was seized and the operators of the BBSs were charged with distributing obscene and degrading material.

According to the police, the raids focused on BBS operators who were distributing child porn and other graphics that displayed bestiality and what one officer involved in the case termed "extremely degrading acts." Some of the graphics, police claim, depicted children taking part in sex acts with adults. They found out about it by following up a complaint made by computer users.

Computers and porn. The two somehow don't seem to go together. But since the early days of personal computing, there have been adult and X-rated graphics on computers in one form or another. Back in the 70s, programmers and computer users would spend hours keying into their computers images of women in various stages of undress. Today, thanks to sophisticated and relatively inexpensive optical imaging and scanning technology, photographic-quality pictures (black-and-white or color) can be loaded into and displayed on just about any personal computer. All you have to do is get a picture from any magazine and run it through a device called a scanner. The scanner converts the original image into bits of digital information which a computer can than read and display. These scanned images can even be combined to create short animated "films" depicting sex acts in their many, varied forms.

Toronto's BBS busts have put what has been described as a "porn chill" on the city's bulletin board operators. Many are worried that some of the graphics they carry violate Canada's fuzzy obscenity laws. In essence, the arrests and seizures have chiseled away at Canadians' rights. But raiding BBSs isn't going to stop the influx of porn to Canada. Adult graphics can be purchased through shareware stores in Canada and the U.S. Most of the images found on BBSs come from Europe via international computer networks, such as InterNet. The origins of the graphics can't be traced and Canadian law doesn't apply to

Europeans. On such a network, a user can often find the heading "SEX". This could be porn, but it could also be legitimate research into sexuality, into the legislation of porn, etc. If it's erased, valuable research is lost.

Canada's obscenity laws are vague on what constitutes obscenity. According to the Canadian Criminal Code, to be considered obscene a graphic (or book, film, photo, or magazine) must display "a dominant characteristic (of) the undue exploitation of sex or of sex and any of the following subjects, namely crime, horror, cruelty and violence." Notice that there is no global definition nor is there any real differentiation made between porn and erotica. The police must look at the material and decide whether or not it's obscene. This opens the door to all kinds of abuse. The operator of an adult-oriented BBS said "One cop will say that's (a graphic) okay, then another says 'I don't like that, you're busted'." And you can be sure that most people, BBS operators included, don't have a copy of the criminal code lying around to consult in time of need.

In an opinion piece published in *The Computer Paper*, computer consultant and BBS operator Gordon Tulloch wrote: "If a special interest group takes exception to the materials on a BBS (whether regarding pornography, politics, anti-religious themes and so on) there is a good chance that a BBS system will be seized and held."

And all it takes is a single complaint to bring the forces of the law down on a BBS operator.

There are other problems facing both the police and the operators of bulletin boards. Most BBSs receive upwards of 30 megabytes of information per day in uploads (i.e. software put onto the BBS by users). It is impossible for an operator to vet that much information in a week, let alone a 24-hour period. However, it is possible for someone to mischievously upload graphics that the police would deem obscene and then complain to the authorities. The police would check the BBS and, upon finding the graphics, could shut down the entire operation.

Many BBSs host conferencing

groups (also called newsgroups), some of which deal with sex and sexual themes. Anything uploaded onto a BBS by a member of such a group could be in violation of Canada's obscenity laws. And the BBS operator wouldn't know about it. One solution to this problem that has been put forward is that bulletin boards be treated like telephone companies. As a telephone company can't be held responsible for illegal or obscene conversations that take place over phone lines, BBS operators question why they should be responsible for files that drift onto their systems. While this seems a reasonable settlement, it will be a long time before the police stop holding BBS operators responsible for anything and everything that's on their boards, even if the operators don't know about it.

The police themselves just can't keep up with the volume of files, adult and otherwise, passing through a BBS. "It's a whole new ballgame," admitted Constable Austin Ferguson of Project P, the Toronto Police's anti-porn squad. The unit, which consists of four officers, is literally overwhelmed by the amount of data it must sift through. Ferguson said: "We are certainly not about to go out and jump on (everyone) running a computer BBS. We just don't have the time or manpower."

While this may be true, the existence of the anti-porn squad and its actions have sent a chill through Toronto's BBS community. At the time of this writing (early December, 1993), repercussions were already being felt. Fearing police action, two of Canada's largest BBSs have purged their systems of all adult graphics. CSR Online of Mississauga, Ontario deleted all images that could be considered pornographic in November, 1993. CSR General Manager David Chaloner said "It came down to the vagueness of what Canada's pornography law is and how it applies to computers.

Internex, a large BBS with international connections, took its adult files off-line in October. Internex president Dave Mason said "the decision (to remove the graphics) was in direct response to the police department's aggressive campaign."

The Cellar, an adult-oriented Toronto BBS, virtually shut down after learning of the October 21 busts. Ray Ryan, The Cellar's operator, said "We're covering our ass".

Other Toronto-area BBSs are covering their respective asses as well. To them, self censorship in the form of erasing any and all potentially obscene files seems the better part of valor. For example, in December, 1993, the following message appeared on Toronto's The One Thousand BBS:

IMPORTANT NOTICE

During the last few months, there has been a lot of discussion related to Adult files. Many people have attempted to get clarification on just what constitutes an Adult file. Descriptions have been vague, at best, and now in light of the recent raids on several area BBS's who continued to carry Adult files, we have decided to shut down our Adult files area immediately.

Sorry folks, but it's just not worth the risk of losing our equipment during a police raid to continue carrying them. Should the law become clearer sometime in the future, we will reconsider carrying this material again.

These actions do seem cowardly, but from the operators' points of view it spells survival. A police raid would mean the confiscation of equipment and lengthy legal battles which most BBS operators could not afford. (See sidebar). However, some BBS operators are trying to find a way

around the law. Instead of purging many of these files, some BBS operators are doctoring them. What were once nude shots have become graphics of women in tiny bikinis, bikinis which can conceivably be removed by those with the proper software and expertise.

Some computer publications are also starting to cover themselves. Beginning in the December, 1993 issue, the masthead indicia of *The Computer Paper*, Canada's largest computer publication, there is a note stating "Specifically, ads referring to Adult Software or X-rated software will be refused." It's interesting to note, however, that such ads appeared in the publication before the October busts occurred.

But how will this affect BBS operators and users in the U.S.? Unless copy-cat legislation is introduced in the United States, BBS operators won't be affected by the changes in the Canadian obscenity law. The authorities in Canada will be unable to block Canadian computer users from accessing American BBSs or vice-versa. However, the changes in the law and the recent action taken by police in Canada could conceivably force BBS operators south of the 49th Parallel to restrict the access Canadian users have to adult files.

In the aftermath of the raids in Toronto, Canadian BBSs are now facing an onslaught of Big Brother-type scrutiny. While it's literally impossible for them to monitor every bulletin board in a city or, for that matter, in the entire country, Toronto police are intent on checking BBSs if a complaint is received.

"When you get a complaint of child pornography, you need to have the tools to conduct your investigation," said Project P's Detective Robert Matthews. The operator of any BBS carrying what the police deem to be obscene or degrading material, Matthews said, will be prosecuted.

In the end, it all seems a gross waste of time. There are too many holes through which adult and X-rated graphics can slip into Canada. No matter how many of these holes the authorities plug, someone will always burrow new ones. As a Toronto anti-censorship activist stated in a published interview: "It is an incredible distraction to think you can control an evil phenomenon by controlling the representation of it."

---

*[Editor's Note: From letters we've received the "Information Superhighway" is rife with examples of censorship. Seems the law cannot keep up with emerging advances in technology. If you are aware of censorship problems related to BBSs and would like to write an article for **Gauntlet**, please query with a SASE. We don't want anything overly technical. This article should serve as a guide — concise, to the point and something even those who aren't computer literate can understand.]*

In May 1993, eight bulletin boards in Winnipeg, Manitoba were busted by the police on allegations that those boards were distributing obscene material. In the raids, the houses of BBS operators where entered by police brandishing search warrants. If the BBS operators weren't at home when the police arrived, a locksmith was called in to open the doors.

In the eight raids, the police confiscated computer hardware, software, peripherals, manuals and anything else having to do with computers, including books and magazines. And it was all done without impunity. The police went to all the effort of getting the search warrants and seizing private property. But to this day no charges have been laid against the operators. None of the seized equipment has been returned to its rightful owners.

While this was the first of such seizures in western Canada, many believe it won't be the last. The Winnipeg busts appear to be designed to tell BBS operators that possession and distribution of adult and X-rated software will not be tolerated by the powers-that-be. There were even suggestions that the raids took place because of pressure put on the police by the courts and by Manitoba's strong anti-pornography groups.

In their usual fashion, the police have blown the entire situation out of proportion. Police officers involved in the busts were quoted as saying there are four hundred BBSs in Winnipeg; there are actually fewer than 100. Twenty-five percent of these, Winnipeg police said, carry pornography. Actually, the number is less than ten percent.

Unfortunately, the seized equipment won't be returned to its owners until the police decide to return it. Going through the courts to get the computers and other gear back is not a viable option but a luxury few if any operators can afford. One Winnipeg BBS operator stated that it would cost him at least $30,000(Cdn.) to fight the police.

In fact, the Winnipeg busts have sent a message to BBS operators everywhere. That message is "Keep your head down. Don't carry anything that will offend anyone." Unfortunately, by doing that the diversity and excitement of the universe of BBSs is being buried under a thick layer of paranoia and fear.

As you read these sentences, the latest stone in the vast wall of tyranny is being cemented into place.

FOR YOUR INFORMATION

The following is a list of shareware/software distributors that carry adult and X-rated graphics:

Profit Press
2956 N. Campbell Avenue
Tucson, AZ 85719

Digital Dreams
P.O. Box 47386
Chicago, IL 60647

Compuware
P.O. Box 430
Oakland, CA 07436

International CD-ROM House
18075 Ventura Boulevard
Encino, CA 91316

Marcom Computers Canada
4490 Chesswood Drive, #3
Downsview, ON, CANADA M3J-2B9

CBS GIF
607 Gerrard St. E.
Box 193
Toronto, ON CANANA M4M-1Y0

For shareware distributors in your area, check your local computer publications or in a recent issue of *Shareware Magazine*.

LIBERATION: FIGHT BACK!
THE UNDERGROUND NEWSPAPER RIDES AGAIN

Remember "underground newspapers," walk-outs, sit-ins, and other trappings of the protest-filled '60's and '70's? Over the past two decades, the fiery spirit that once engendered passionate reaction to society's great pageant seems to have been rerouted from affairs of state to matters of wardrobe and music.

What's more, a process of de-evolution has been at work that appears to have mutated the vast majority of high school students into a race of apathetic, acquiescent, uninvolved yuppies-in-training, more interested in their zits than their *raisons d'etre*. But there may be hope. At Franklin High, a school of some 1200-plus students in the little burg of Reisterstown, Maryland, an "underground newspaper" is prompting at least a few of the walking dead to wake up and smell the *lattes*.

Apparently it's also giving the resident caretakers at that particular mausoleum of learning a case of the jitters. After all, aren't the brain-dead supposed to . . . *stay dead*?

Started in response to a set of rules and regs instituted by the school's new administrators this past fall, LIBERATION: FIGHT BACK! not only questions authority, it calls it out for a showdown at high noon. Primarily targeting new principal Evelyn Cogswell and assistant principal Sylvia Brooks-Brown, the newspaper's 16-year-old "Phantom Editor" takes square aim — and occasional pot-shots — at the inequities in the

system. And he's loaded for bear.

"Back in November, Cogswell put forth this edict called, 'Statements on Discipline,'" explains the 11th grader, whose widely known/suspected is protected by students and supportive teachers alike. "They were outrageous . . . totally pointless."

Neither a part of the Baltimore County Public School code, nor contained in the Student Handbook, Franklin's "Statements on Discipline" decree detention and suspension for minor, even first, offenses; and nebulously address in-class behavior, the Phantom says. "Very vague, general language, like, 'insubordination' and 'disruptive behavior,' which could be interpreted any way." And often is, he adds. "I've seen people threatened with suspension for sneezing in class . . . [The teacher] thought they were doing it on purpose."

One week after the "Statements" hit the hallowed halls, LIBERATION: FIGHT BACK! made its first appearance. The cheaply-produced, one-page, two-column paper, photocopied and further distributed by any students who can lay claim to a copy machine, contains editorials, info-bites, a smattering of *non sequitur* clips and pix from other publications (from the *Weekly World News* to *Newsweek*); even letters to the editor and occasional guest-editorials.

It also contains what the Phantom calls "exposes," such as the recent account of an illegal locker search conducted by principal Cog-

swell and vice principal Otis Mitchell. "In the second issue (of LIBERATION), one of the columns was about your rights as a student, taken directly from the Student Handbook; and I put in there what the requirements for a locker search had to be," the Phantom recalls. "Apparently, they were going through this kid's locker and he wasn't even there . . . They took something out of it . . . and a couple of minutes later — I actually saw this guy — an armed police officer came into the school."

Not surprisingly, nothing about the incident ever appeared in the school newspaper; but, "Things get back to me," the Phantom says. "If something is going on, people tell me about it, because they know that it'll somehow get to the Phantom Editor and get into the paper."

Exposing violations of students' rights is one reason parent Barry Lee is a staunch supporter of the underground rag. "There are so many people mad, fed up and disgusted with that school," reports Lee, himself the father of two sons who have been on the receiving end of the new justice a few times too many.

One boy had a ring, purchased for him at a local antique shop by Lee, confiscated as a "weapon"; the other was suspended so often by Brooks-Brown that he actually failed 10th grade — even though vice principal Mitchell later stated that the boy's behavior did not warrant such action, according to Lee. (Brooks-Brown refused to return all phone calls for comment during preparation of this article.)

Lee, whose repeated tangles with school officials over students' rights led to a court order preventing him from setting foot on Franklin's grounds, has no problem with disciplining errant students. But, "The rules and regulations are unfair, they are improperly enforced," he claims. "The kids have no rights. How are you supposed to teach them respect for authority when the authority is totally abused?"

Officially, English teacher Jeff Tarlow disagrees. "The learning experience had been greatly weakened by a small community of kids, and this discipline code was aimed (at them) . . . (The code) has no impact on 95 percent of the student body," insists Tarlow, adding that it was unanimously passed by the teachers.

Why, then, are so many teachers — including Tarlow — supporting the underground paper, even offering to post it in classrooms? And why is Tarlow, who soon — and correctly — identified the Phantom by his writing style, *not* sharing that information with administrators and teachers who want to know? "I don't know," he responds, "it's not a big deal. To me, the paper is harmless."

Is it harmless? *Are* students rallying? Tom Dunn, 16, who says he risks disciplinary action each time he distributes the paper on campus, thinks not . . . yet. "The paper is gaining popularity . . . but the only thing is that some people aren't doing the things they need to be doing to try to stop the problems at our school."

Tarlow, too, sees *reaction*, but little *action*, as a result of LIBERATION. He dismisses LIBERATION as "a fun little thing . . . like *Mad* magazine . . . (The editor's) peer group thinks it's making this wonderful impact . . . To me, it's had rela-

tively little impact." Then why is the school librarian monitoring the Xerox machine to prevent students from churning out copies of LIBERATION?

Meanwhile, teachers continue questioning LIBERATION readers about the Phantom's identity and confiscating copies carried into classrooms; and the administration, in the time-honored tradition of ruling bodies that downplay the power of the opposition in an effort to weaken it, denies that the paper is a problem.

"I really haven't paid much attention," says principal Cogswell; who calls the paper "a creative way for (students) to express themselves." She also dismissed it as "harmless," on the grounds that the paper "doesn't contain anything libelous, or bad language".

Maybe somebody censored her copy: LIBERATION contains *both*; repeatedly likening Cogswell to Adolf Hitler, and peppering prose with the ever-popular f-word. So is Cogswell showing false bravado, trying to lull the Phantom into showing himself . . . or just not paying attention?

The administration-censored school newspaper is definitely feeling the competition, according to staff member — and LIBERATION supporter — Richard Berkowitz, 16. "Some people (on the staff) think it takes away from us . . . is just causing trouble," he says. They want the paper shut down, he says, and "tear each issue apart verbally."

True, LIBERATION hasn't touched off a mutiny yet; but, "It

makes people think," Berkowitz says, "makes them look at their surroundings . . . at what's going on."

And that, according to the Phantom Editor, is a good start. "If people don't have all the information, they can't make reasonable judgements," he maintains. "If you keep people in the dark, if they

don't have access to information, it's easier to control them.

"And high school *definitely* should not be a place where the people are controlled," the Phantom contends, "because if kids are presented this narrow little view of reality, as soon as they get out of high school, their reality is going to collapse around them, because they're actually going to have to make informed decisions and they're not going to be used to that . . . (they will have had) all their decisions made for them."

And so he keeps publishing, sometimes twice and three times a week. Isn't the Phantom afraid of being turned in? "Constantly. But,

hey, you've gotta take chances, you gotta get this stuff out . . . get people involved, informed. Because a lot of people just roll over, just don't care. And that's a sad thing," he concludes. "I'm just trying to get people more involved in standing up for themselves . . . I figure, if I'm going to have to do (high school), I should try to make it a better place while I'm here — *and* have as much fun as possible!"

Shades of the '60's, man. Power to the people and let the presses roll on.

For obvious reasons the writer of this story wishes to remain anonymous.

Dictionary of Cautionary Words and Phrases

Illegal alien: often used to refer to Mexicans and Latin Americans believed to be in the United States without visas; the preferred term is undocumented worker or undocumented resident.

Late in May, Mr. John Lorenz, chairman of the science department, had his life threatened by a student who also made a bomb threat during one of his classes. All bomb threats must be taken seriously under school code, and when Mr. Lorenz tried to call 911, our principal, Evelyn Cogswell, told him to just call the local police because she thought all the attention from 911 would be "bad for the school's image." He complied, but the local police told him that they didn't have a bomb squad and to call 911, which he did. The police arrived, took care of the situation, and everything settled down. Later, Mrs. Cogswell stripped Mr. Lorenz of his position as chairman because he called 911, and the next day she told him to make a top 10 list of the schools he'd like to be transferred to. She then transferred him to the school that was his last choice.

In mid-June, when I saw a petition started by Mr. Lorenz's daughter, a former graduate of our school, and heard about the circumstances under which he was fired, I immediately wrote an article about it and published it on Friday of the same week. Come Monday morning, the school was covered with posters reading "Keep John, Toss Evelyn," among other slogans, and there were no less than 6 petitions, all with over 100 signatures each. On Tuesday, a student's father went into the school to reprimand Mrs. Cogswell, who promptly called Dr. Stuart Berger, the superintendent of schools. The student's father, however, has pull with not only the county executive, but also the governor, and called THEM in on the matter. When questioned about the situation, Mrs. Cogswell was caught in a lie when she denied the bomb threat story which already was on record, and also denied that one of the Vice Principals, Dr. Sylvia Brooks-Brown had been accused of abusing students, which was also already on record.

Meanwhile, Mrs. Cogswell's usually passive reaction to the paper took a sharp turnaround, and she was described as "livid" over the newspaper by the parent. The word has it that she wants the editor of Liberation in her office and the underground paper shut down permanently. This is the first time her usual response of "Oh, I'm not concerned" has been absent, and she has been doing everything in her power to prove my identity so she can punish me.

The petitions grew in number, and Mr. Lorenz has been granted an audience before the Board of Education to present his case, and to examine the actions of Mrs. Cogswell. Mr. Lorenz will be bringing with him copies of the issue of LIBERATION that started the uproar. As for Mrs. Cogswell, her job is on the line because of the lies, and all will be decided over the summer.

There will be an update in the next issue of Gauntlet.

STEREOTYPING HOOKS 'PETER PAN'—A CLASSIC PLAY PROVOKES INDIAN IRE

Claude Lewis

America is beset by controversy. One storm is centered around widespread complaints of insensitivity to gender, age, race, ethnicity and religion.

Increasingly, such complaints are being taken seriously rather than casually dismissed. Indeed, educational institutions (both high school and college), police departments, professional sports franchises, restaurant chains, corporate boards and Hollywood — all have begun to re-examine their regard for people who have traditionally been overlooked.

Some believe it's not merely a matter of being overlooked. They also complain of being maligned by stereotypes that inflame passions and that promote long term anti-group feelings.

The latest example of the increased consciousness concerning a minority group involved several Native American students who expressed resentment about a play that many other Americans think of as a theater classic: *Peter Pan*.

In Southampton, L.I., Peter Pan was scheduled to go into production at a middle school until administrators decided its portrayal of Indians was offensive to members of the Shinnecock tribe, whose reservation borders the town. Native American children make up nearly 9 percent of the district's student body.

"We wouldn't do *Uncle Tom's Cabin* in a school," said Sherry Blakey-Smith, a Cree-Ojibwa Indian who directs the Southampton School District's federally financed Indian Education Program. "For Native Americans, *Peter Pan*'s scene with the Indians is very much like that. We don't have pickaninny warriors," Blakey-Smith argues. One song in the play, "Ugg-a-Wugg", calls on the children playing the role of Indians to sing about the "brave noble Redskin".

Many of the problems relate to the times. Changes in modern culture and attitudes have placed many plays, books and movies beyond the limits of good tastes and acceptability.

Many believe that such protests simply take place because some people are "oversensitive". But Hispanics, Jews, and more recently, Asians, all have expressed unhappiness at stereotyping.

Sound frivolous? Far from it. Professional sports teams, including the Cleveland Indians, Atlanta Braves, and Washington Redskins have come under fire by Native Americans who resent the images promoted by such teams. And papers such as the *Minneapolis Tribune* and *Portland Oregonian* have announced that they will not use the team nicknames in print.

Resentment by Native Americans goes deep and it is hardly regional. The Florida State Seminoles have suffered criticism for using images of Native Americans, though their mascot's uniform was designed by a tribal member.

In Northwest Wisconsin, controversy abounds at Rice Lake High School where sports teams known as the "Warriors" are under fire both because of the name and the fact the team's logo is an Indian wearing a warbonnet.

This has led the school board to consider changing both name and logo — even though one of the school's greatest football heroes, Darrell "the Horse" Russeau, was an Indian whose grandfather had played with Jim Thorpe.

According to Warren Leary Jr., the retired editor and publisher of the local paper, "political correctness" is at fault. He wrote in his weekly column that "I've never encountered an Irishman who objected to my alma mater (Notre Dame) being dubbed the Fighting Irish." He facetiously suggested the team be renamed the "Petunias".

Several books that were considered classics have been deemed harmful to the image and self-esteem of some Americans. Mark Twain's *Huckleberry Finn*, and more recently, Alice Walker's *The Color Purple*, have led to protests.

In this latest situation involving *Peter Pan*, the play's cancellation infuriated many people, including one sixth grader who had spent long hours rehearsing for his part in *Peter Pan*.

FOLLOWING OUTCRYS FROM THE NATIVE AMERICAN POPULATION, A HIGH-SCHOOL THEATRE PRODUCTION OF "PETER PAN" WAS REPLACED WITH "THE WIZARD OF OZ". BUT WHAT ABOUT THE FEELINGS OF...

...the HOMELESSLY DISPLACED...

...the COURAGEOUSLY UNDER-PRIVILEGED...

...the MENTALLY CHALLENGED...

...the CARDIACLY DISENFRANCHISED...

RUFF

"Everybody picks at what everybody else is doing — soon we're not going to be able to do anything," one boy fumed with a wisdom that exceeded his years.

His anger is understandable, but so, too, is the resentment of those who consider themselves victims. The school hopes to present another play, *The Wizard of Oz*, unless other groups finds it, too, is offensive.

"You never know who's going to be offended by something," says Anthony Rogers of Philadelphia, who has long protested against "stereotyping" of African Americans.

I agree. There's not much question as to whether images largely created outside a particular group have proved harmful. Maybe the problem is that too few Americans spoke up in the past, and everybody's now paying the price of that silence.

I favor an end to stereotypes which harm groups and individuals because it's clear that one person's "classic" can often be another person's calamity.

*Claude Lewis is a columnist for the **Philadelphia Inquirer**.*

POLITICALLY PANNED IN NEVER, NEVER LAND

Richard R. Becker

Several Shinnecock Indians will sleep better now, knowing that the play *Peter Pan* was banned in Southampton. After all, neither they nor their children will be subjected to offensive songs like "Ugh-a-Wugg," which makes references to "noble, brave Redskins."

Personally, I'm still not sure which word — noble or brave — the tribe finds offensive. Maybe Shinnecock Indians don't like the idea of Native Americans being portrayed as good guys.

And maybe, if we never mentioned Native Americans in any articles, works of literature, films or any other media . . . one day they would just cease to exist and their hurt feelings too. Then, the next time fifty students spend months rehearsing a play, it won't get scalped.

The hero is Samuel French, Ltd. who wouldn't allow the play to be altered and more "politically correct," just because a few so-called "adults" blew a light-hearted child's play out of proportion. (Disney take note.)

Yes, I know the term "Redskin" is offensive to most Native Americans. Just as Bible Thumper, Camel Jockey, Chink, Cracker, Dyke, Fag, Fatso, Flat Lander, Kid, Hillbilly, Hippie, Jew, Johnny Reb, Nazi, Nerd, Nigger, Old People, Spick, Wap, Wasp, Yankee and a million others are likely to offend someone.

Am I a bigot? Heartless? Failing to see it from the "offended" parties point-of-view? None of the above. All people, good or bad, site differences in others to express hatred, humor, and sometimes qualities they hope to have.

For example, I doubt teams like the Atlanta Braves, Washington Redskins, and Kansas City Chiefs are looking for the 'Drunk Indian' stereotype. I don't believe The New York "Yankees" are trying to conjure up images of Union Soldiers shooting Southerners and burning farms.

It's exactly the same. "Yankee" is a negative name created to place negative stereotypes on Americans (even big black ones) and is still used as such all over the world (even for little slant-eyed ones).

And when the name-calling really is meant to instill hatred (which the above references are not), I say good. At least we know who doesn't like us.

The alternative: force bigots to keep their mouths shut and let them silently hate us even more. Ten to one odds: one of those "pale face" kids will grow up hating Native Americans because "Tonto" banned his school play.

Still, don't just blame Shinnecocks or Native Americans for our current state of affairs. They are relatively late-comers to the "Politically Correct" band wagon. (You readers in Germany know the term better as "Politically Unobjectionable," coined by Hitler.)

In America, the movement started in May 18, 1989 in the United States Senate when New York Senator Alfonse D'Amato ripped up a work of art called "Piss Christ." This one action inspired Senator Jesse Helms and other cronies to start carving away the First Amendment.

Today, we're all contributing. We're proud to do it. We even like it.

In Los Angeles, state authorities padlocked a strip joint because the Disabled Access Division of the Department of Building and Safety, determined that a shower stall meant for nude dancers was inaccessible to performers in wheelchairs. No, the club did not have any.

The Associated Press reported a Malcolm X mural was destroyed at a San Francisco University because it contained anti-Semitic symbols. The mural featured Stars of David with "African Blood" written above and below. Artist Senay Dannis said he wanted to reflect Malcolm X's anti-Zionism and said he didn't have to explain his actions to "white people." Good for him.

I do, though, consider this an ironic twist in events. Jews helped promote Black Rights in the 1960s. And "white people" were the first race to abolish Black Slavery, which — get this — was originally invented by Muslim caliphs. Sorry Malcolm, Arabs were also the last to give it up.

As Australian, Robert Hughes, puts it in his book, *Culture of Complaint, the Fraying of America*, "Complaint gives you power — even when it's only the power of emotional bribery, of creating previously unnoticed levels of social guilt. Plead not guilty and it's off with your head."

He also says, "If they (Americans) are fraying now, it is because the politics has, for the last twenty years, weakened and in some areas broken the traditional American genius for consensus, for getting along by making up practical compromises to meet real social needs."

To me, it's rather haunting to think someone in another country would say this about the home of the free. (We should probably ban that little Aussie bastard.) What's even more haunting is: he's right. Did censoring *Peter Pan* put food on the tables of less fortunate Native Americans? No, but at least they can starve to death with their self-esteem intact.

In Ray Bradbury's classic, *Fahrenheit 451*, he describes how it starts: " . . . minorities, each ripping a page or paragraph from a book, until one day the books were empty and the minds were shut and the libraries were closed."

Read the news, everyone is a minority. American-born Germans can censor *Shindler's List*, because it brings back memories of burning Jews. Once slave-owning families in the deep South can shred the film *Gettysburg* because it breeds resentment. Let's even burn Stephen King's book *The Stand*. After all, Las Vegas doesn't want to be home to the devil. And, don't stop there.

The predecessor to George Orwell's *1984* was called *We*, written by Russian-born Yevgeny Zamyatin. An excerpt from the first page, translates, "If they will not understand that we are bringing them a mathematically infallible happiness, we shall be obliged to force them to be happy." The message in the book was from the fictional OneState to any people who still live in the primitive state of freedom.

Aldus Huxley said that one day we were working to thrust ourselves into a welfare-tyranny of the Utopia under the need of efficiency and stability. And Charles Bradlaugh said,

"Better a thousand abuses of free speech than the denial of free speech. The abuse dies in a day, but the denial stays the life of the people, and entombs the hope of the race."

What? Sorry Charlie, but the Shinnecock Indians and the rest of America disagrees. We're going to erase everything we don't want to hear and we might as well start with you.

And, when the Shinnecock Indians want to say how the "white man" did this and the "white man" did that, tough luck. It offends me. More than that, history in any form is offensive. It creates tension between all races and all people at one time or another and even cites who won and who lost.

In truth, some Native Americans I talked to don't want it that way. What these Native Americans thought, including *my Native American aunt*, was that the banning *Peter Pan* is absurd. Sharon Chayra, a public relations director for an ambulance company and Native American, agreed, adding, "People who scream discrimination or racism are usually groups that want attention and don't have any better way to get it."

And, while Cathy Collins, a successful business owner and Native American, explained to me in depth why Native Americans feel the way they do, she also said, "No one should have the right to dictate what someone can or cannot say." During our conversation, she also said that peo-

ple should try to understand each other instead of running into the court room.

Don't get me wrong. The Shinnecock Indians had every right to be offended and say so. (As Voltaire once said, "I disapprove of what you say, but will defend to the death your right to say it.") Heck, I even like Native Americans. But, instead of turning the situation into some sort

NEWS ITEM: ON LONG ISLAND, PETER PAN BECOMES THE LATEST TO FALL BEFORE THE "P.C. MENACE"

of Hate Fest '94 to ban a play forever, the Shinnecock Indians could have used this opportunity to educate Southampton about true tribal customs.

Ironically, Southampton school children later performed *The Wizard of Oz* after a multi-cultural board approval. All things considered, I'm surprised. The only play that would put witches in worse light is Arthur Miller's about the Salem Witch Trials.

Laugh if you want, but Wicca is a real and recognized religion.

Just goes to show you: censors don't care if they hurt other people's feelings. They only care about themselves.

Richard R. Becker is a freelance writer and regular **Gauntlet** *contributor.*

REQUIRED READING FOR REVOLUTIONARIES

Russ Kick

Lost Rights: The Destruction of American Liberty
James Bovard
St. Martin's, 1994

It seems like something terrible is happening in America. We are constantly hearing reports of police seizing property without due process just because they think the owners might possess drugs. Of the IRS terrorizing citizens in special IRS courts where the defendant is guilty until proven innocent. Of corporations suing citizens who protest environmental destruction. And then there are the big events, such as the Waco massacre, that show unjustifiable abuse of power. Wouldn't it be nice if someone did a detailed study of these abuses and many others? Wouldn't it be nice if someone put the scattered pieces of the puzzle into a coherent whole that shows that we truly are living in a borderline police state? And wouldn't it be great if this person wrote about all this with cynical wit fueled by mistrust of authority? Well someone has.

Journalist James Bovard has assembled an extremely damaging document that needs to read by everyone in America, because every one of us is affected. Bovard covers so much ground and shows so many civil liberties going up in smoke that my mind reels. In discussing the laws that destroy rights in the name of the War on (Some) Drugs, the author says, "Today, because some people grow marijuana, government officials must effectively have unlimited power to trespass on almost all private land . . . . Because some teenagers hide tiny bags of drugs in their underwear, government officials must be allowed to closely inspect schoolchildren's crotches. The government vigorously prosecutes dancers for indecent exposure for getting naked in front of willing viewers — but it is supposedly okay for school officials to forcibly strip a person."

The chapter "Spiking Speech, Bankrupting Newspapers, and Jamming Broadcasts" covers censorship. When trying to get material declared obscene, and therefore illegal, " . . . prosecutors go out and commandeer the most revolting material, put twelve people in a government courtroom, show it to them while declaiming how horrible it is, and then seek to use that small group to restrict what everyone else in the community can see." Censorship is also occurring through libel suits, using the RICO Act to utterly destroy small time pornographers, and not allowing alcohol to be sold simply because of its name (i.e., PowerMaster malt liquor and Black Death Vodka).

Among the many other subjects dealt with are seizure laws, declaring old privately-owned homes to be historic sites and depriving their owners of their rights, harassing people who modify their property (by creating duck ponds) if it is considered "wetlands", the FDA's endless red tape for new drugs ("The FDA sometimes manipulates test results, or forces drug companies to use weaker doses of a drug in tests, and then pronounces the drug ineffective."), the Post Office's monopoly on letters, ridiculous child labor laws, the subjugation of students by public schools, the Americans with Disabilities Act ("one of the worst written, most morally pretentious laws of the modern era"), the assault on the right to bear arms, the IRS's war on self-employed people — the list goes on and on. I've really only scratched the surface of what this book has to offer.

Lost Rights is one of the most important books to come out in a long time. No one can afford to be without it.

Our Vanishing Privacy: And What You Can Do to Protect Yours
Robert Ellis Smith
Loompanics Unlimited, 1993

Smith is the publisher of the *Privacy Journal*, perhaps the most respected privacy publication. In this book he takes us on a rollercoaster ride through 1984-Land. "Are Your Papers in Order?" looks at the government's demands that you always have identification on you. Another chapter looks at how marketers invade our lives: "Kids and adults who ordered the Cap'n Crunch Dick Tracy Wrist Watch Radio through a Quaker Oats offer in cereal boxes were sent an intrusive questionnaire about these three political issues [drug testing, school prayer, and gun control], plus street addresses, income, what credit cards the family uses, the names, ages, and preferences of smokers in the family, and who has what diseases in the family."

Other chapters deal with the intrusiveness of Caller-ID, the ease with which your medical records can be gotten by interested parties, the Social Security Number as national identification number, polygraph, urine, and blood tests, how the press invades privacy, taxes on periodicals (which amount to "a state-issued license to publish"), and the "let's do it till we get caught" attitude of the three major credit bureaus.

The book ends with a crash course on the laws that protect our privacy and on the twenty principles of information privacy. In all, *Our Vanishing Privacy* shows a wide array of ways in which our privacy is being invaded. Unfortunately, it doesn't live up to its subtitle, only presenting ways to protect your Social Security Number and to get around caller-ID.

Banned in the U.S.A.: A Reference Guide to Book Censorship in Schools and Public Libraries
Herbert N. Forestel
Greenwood Publishing Company; 1994

Schools and libraries being forced to remove controversial books has become a familiar event. Guardians of purity step in to yank any book that doesn't give children a candy-coated, sissyfied view of the real world. The author does a great job chronicling this phenomena in a number of ways.

Chapter 1 presents some major bookbanning incidents from 1973 to 1992. In West Virginia, a school board member, who also happened to be a preacher's wife, charged that textbooks under consideration for use were "filthy, disgusting trash, unpatriotic, and unduly favoring blacks." The school board adopted all but eleven of the books and all hell broke loose. Of the county's 45,000 school kids, 9000 were kept home by their parents, and practically the whole county went on strike. "A *Charleston Gazette* article revealed: 'A few extremists among the churchmen who wanted 'godless' textbooks removed from the schools became so fanatical they discussed bombing carloads of children whose parents were driving them to school in defiance of a boycott called by the book protesters." In fact, one school was dynamited and another was firebombed, school buses were shot at, and homes of children who attended school were stoned. By the next school year, new bland books were approved, and some schools even went back to textbooks they used in the 1940s.

Chapter 2 examines all of the Supreme Court cases relevant to the freedom of schools to use books. Chapter 3 contains the author's discussions with several of the most banned authors, including Judy Blume. The final chapter lists the 50 most banned books of the 1990s, with a short history of the battles surrounding each one.

Raising Hell: An Encyclopedia of Devil Worship and Satanic Crime
Michael Newton
Avon; 1993

A most unusual reference book containing hundreds of entries covering crimes enacted in Satan's name. Entries cover individuals, Satanic groups, and phenomena said to be related to Satanic crime — animal killing, corpse stealing, child abuse, Dungeons and Dragons, heavy metal, etc. In the introduction, the author says he's trying to walk the middle ground between Christians who see Satanism as the force behind everything bad and "apologists" who claim that Satanic violence is an urban legend.

The entries make for fascinating reading, but many of them don't tie the crimes to Satanism very well. For example, one entry tells of two Chilean tribesman who sacrificed a man to appease water gods, not Satan. Another bothersome element crops up when the author discusses Anton LaVey, founder of the Church of Satan, whose *Satanic Bible* has been quoted as a source of inspiration by a number of murderers. "If homicidal misfits take him literally, LaVey — like Pilate before him — is prepared to wash his hands of all responsibility." This sounds suspiciously like the "don't blame the person who committed the act, blame the book or music that *made* him do it" mentality that is responsible for lawsuits against Ozzy Osborne and Judas Priest and the creation of the victims of pornography legislation that would let rape victims sue porn makers for the crimes of some twisted bastard.

Satanic Panic: The Creation of a Contemporary Legend
Jeffrey S. Victor
Open Court; 1993

Dictionary of Precautionary Words and Phrases

Wheelchair: Preferred term is "uses a wheelchair." Do not use wheelchair-bound or confined to a wheelchair.

This book states flatly that the stories of a plague of activity by Satan worshipers who sexually abuse and torture children, sacrifice people, kill animals, deal drugs, and create pornography are groundless. "None of these claims are supported by reliable evidence," according to the author. In this lengthy book he examines the evolution of the satanic cult legend, the social dynamics of a rumor-panic, how Satanism scares start and spread in communities, "survivor" stories (the quotes are the author's), Satanism's alleged threat to children and the real evidence, juvenile delinquents and pseudo-Satanism, the search for Satanism in schools, books, music, and games, the alleged link between multiple personality disorder and Satanic abuse, the real crises that families are facing, the search for scapegoats, the people who are leading the crusade against Satanism, the roles of the government, courts, and the media, and the underlying dynamics of the satanic panic.

Several appendices present contact information for people and groups combating the Satanism scare, guidelines for dealing with Satanic rumors in a community, and synopses of Satanic scares and abuse trials across the country during the past several years.

This book presents much evidence damning the notion of an epidemic of Satanic crime and violence sweeping the country. Personally, my jury is still out on the subject till I find out more. However, as always, I feel sure the truth lies somewhere between the hysterical alarmists and the flat deniers.

Russ Kick is Gauntlet's non-fiction book reviewer. Books for review can be sent to him at Gauntlet's mailing address.

STREET SMARTS

Anthony Alcaraz

The Select
F. Paul Wilson
Morrow $22.00

Fatal Cure
Robin Cook
Putnam $22.95

Natural Causes
Michael Palmer
Bantam $21.95

Early-1994 saw the release of no less than three major medical thrillers. Why the fascination? Possibly because once one has entered a hospital one is totally at the mercy of others. Decision-making, especially during emergencies, is completely out of the patient's hands. Laying there waiting for that elusive diagnosis one conjures up the worst, while hoping for the best. Such a setting is rife with opportunities to play on our fears of hospitals and the unknown world of medicine.

And now more than ever before, with debate on President Clinton's health care reform package dominating the news, the time is ripe for medical thrillers to climb up the bestsellers lists. It was widely reported, for example, that copies of Robin Cook's *Fatal Cure*, were purchased by a congressman and given to his colleagues due to its timeliness; *Fatal Cure* deals with a HMO with its eye on the bottom line, seemingly oblivious to patient care.

But what if these Knights in shining armor, bound by the Hippocratic Oath, are involved in diabolical schemes for profit whatever the cost in human terms? Such is the premise of these three medical thrillers.

The link between these three books is *conspiracy*. It's also the main weakness of the genre. Doctors and hospital bureaucrats, at one time dedicated to healing, become jaded and self-serving and somehow find others like themselves willing to follow their lead regardless of the consequences for the patient. It's a wonder these conspiracies haven't unraveled long before a naive young doctor, resident or medical student uncovers the sordid truth.

F. Paul Wilson's *The Select* (*** out of a possible **** stars), about a medical school for the cream of the crop, is the best of the three, even though this is the author's first medical thriller. Wilson, unlike his counterparts, is a *writer* who just happens to be a physician. He has a slew of horror and suspense novels to his credit, some of the best written and most compelling of the genre. He initially was set to release *The Select* under a pseudonym. A $900,000 contract "convinced" him to release the book under his own name.

As always with Wilson, the story is compelling, the characters believable, the dialog first-rate. *The Select* also features the most memorable scene of the three books; a surreal burn ward in which one of the main characters awakens to observe his own imminent demise, yet is powerless to communicate his plight. It's vintage Wilson, and gives hope that as he becomes more comfortable with this genre he will transcend its confines, break rules (as he often does with his horror) and create masterful fiction.

Michael Palmer's *Natural Causes* (** 1/2 out of ****) introduces a slew of interesting characters in a story of women who literally bleed to death while giving birth. As a whodunit, Palmer's book is the best; the author not tipping his hand until just the right moment. But, as the massive conspiracy unravels, Palmer loses control and the books loses its credibility. Palmer also tries too be too clever for his own good, with one villain too many just when the reader — so hopes the author — has let his guard down. It just doesn't work.

Robin Cook, the dean of the medical thriller, has written some terse, tense novels with strong characters and masterful plotting. *Fatal Cure* (* out of ****), unfortunately, is not one of them. *Fatal Cure* fails in every sense of the word. Its two heroes (a married couple just beginning their medical career in an idyllic community) are unsympathetic whiners. The dialog is forced and trite. Evil doctors and bureaucrats are flat stereotypes. The book, moreover, fails as suspense; the reader should spot the murderer two-thirds through the book, as if one were watching Columbo. Unlike the rumpled detective, Cook doesn't *intentionally* tip his hand so soon. The perp's just too obvious to miss. As with *The Select* and *Natural Causes*, there are a host of villains here, all conspiring to thwart the isolated and shunned protagonists, as patient after patient kicks the bucket with no one else seeing anything alarming or nefarious.

Treat to yourself to *The Select* for a glimpse into the future of the next medical thriller megastar. (Better yet, check out Wilson's backlist for some of the best written, expertly plotted and captivating characters to appear in print.)

If this genre's your cup of tea, Palmer's *Natural Causes* is worth the read. As for Cook, just like athletes, writers can fall flat on their faces and recover. Cook's track record overall is good and one rotten outing doesn't mean he won't come back strong in 1995.

Heat
Stuart Woods
Harper Collins $23.00

In *Heat*, the prolific (two books per year) Stuart Woods grabs the reader from page one and refuses to let go till the very end. A self-proclaimed minimalist, Woods is interested in plot and characterization and decries the overwriting of so many books today. The versatile writer has shunned series and sequels because he doesn't want to be pigeonholed. "I don't want to write the same book and use the same character over and over again," he told *Gauntlet* as to why he eschews series. He'd much rather surprise his many readers than make them feel comfortable. "I don't want people to know what to expect from me. The one thing I want my readers to expect when they see my name on the book is to think it will be exciting and new."

Woods has done so in *Heat*, a non-stop thriller revolving around a former-DEA agent framed and serving what is for all intents and purposes a death sentence at a federal penitentiary. His former employees give him a chance for a pardon, if he can infiltrate a right wing religious cult in Idaho, with a fortified compound that is reminiscent of the Branch Davidians in Waco.

Asked if he got his idea from the government's confrontation with the followers of David Koresh, Woods told *Gauntlet* he'd sent in his proposal along with six chapters a few weeks before Waco broke. "In fact, I had to make some changes in what I planned to do. I intended to have a siege situation much like in Waco, but I felt I had to change that to keep from seeming to capitalize too much on what happened there." And surprisingly, Woods didn't do extensive research on cults prior to penning his novel, just followed accounts of cult activity in the newspapers. "There have been plenty of cult things that have come up over the years. There always seemed to be a lot of gullible people who were willing to follow anybody who would tell them what to do, and I just wrote it from that viewpoint." Yet the cult Woods creates and the devoted following its leader attains is as believable as any real-life story of existing cults.

Where Woods excels is creating memorable protagonists and secondary characters. Jesse Warden (Jesse Barron after he infiltrates the cult) is not your typical hero. Survival is his top priority and he bends (and breaks) the law more than once to to ensure an equal playing field. To Barron, the DEA at times seems more his enemy than the cult; fearing a double-cross Barron is covering all his bases. A realistic portrayal for one who has been burned by his former-employers once and has come to expect duplicity.

A complex, compelling character, we feel his pain and frustration, as he is manipulated by the DEA on one hand and the fanatical cult leader on the other.

It's a rollicking ride one wishes would last longer (you won't find Woods penning 600+-page epics when he can tell his story is a sparse 300-pages).

As a storyteller, Woods has few equals. *Heat* takes it place among the best of Woods' novels. Calling it a page-turner — which it is — doesn't do the book justice. Simply put, *Heat* is a damn fine piece of writing.

Anthony Alcaraz is **Gauntlet's** *regular fiction book reviewer.*

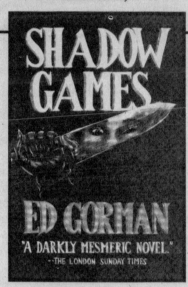